THE
RED KING'S
REBELLION

THE
RED KING'S
REBELLION

*Racial Politics
in New England
1675–1678*

Russell Bourne

Atheneum

NEW YORK 1990

Atheneum
Macmillan Publishing Company
866 Third Avenue, New York, NY 10022
Collier Macmillan Canada, Inc.

Library of Congress Cataloging-in-Publication Data

Bourne, Russell.
The Red King's rebellion : racial politics in New England, 1675–1678 / by Russell Bourne.
    p.   cm.
Includes bibliographical references.
ISBN 0-689-12000-1
    1. King Philip's War, 1675–1676.   2. Wampanoag Indians—Wars.   3. Mashpee Indians—Wars.   4. Indians of North America—New England—Wars—1600–1750.   5. Indians of North America—New England—Government relations—To 1789.   6. New England—History—Colonial period, ca. 1600–1775.   I. Title.
E83.67.B74   1990
973'.2'4—dc20   89-17581
                                                                CIP

Macmillan books are available at special discounts for bulk purchases for sales promotions, premiums, fund-raising, or educational use. For details, contact:

Special Sales Director
Macmillan Publishing Company
866 Third Avenue
New York, NY 10022

10 9 8 7 6 5 4 3 2 1

Printed in the United States of America

to Mimi

Contents

Illustrations

Oil portrait of Major Thomas Savage, attributed to Thomas Smith. Courtesy of the Museum of Fine Arts, Boston.

Indian Assault on Ayres' Inn, August 4, 1675. Originally published in G. M. Bodge's *Soldiers in King Philip's War,* 1906. Courtesy of the Haffenreffer Museum of Anthropology at Brown University.

Grandfontaine's 1671 map of Pentagouet and northern New England. Courtesy of the Public Archives of Canada, National Map Collection, and the Bibliothèque Nationale, Département des Cartes et Plans, Paris.

William Hubbard's map of King Philip's War sites. Courtesy of the John Carter Brown Library at Brown University.

Map of New England, 1675. Reprinted with permission of Charles Scribner's Sons, an imprint of Macmillan Publishing Company, from *Atlas of American History,* edited by James Truslow Adams and R. V. Coleman. Copyright 1943 by Charles Scribner's Sons, renewed 1977. Inset engraving by A. B. Durand after a drawing by James Eastburn of "King Philip's Seat," courtesy of the Haffenreffer Museum of Anthropology at Brown University.

Preface

Ten years ago in the *New Yorker* Paul Brodeur wrote an unsettling piece on the Mashpee Indians of Cape Cod. The story caught my eye initially because of Shearjashub Bourne, who—for all the comedy of his name— seemed to have carried out filially and imaginatively the work of his father (an ancestor of mine, as it happens), Richard Bourne. By 1675 Richard Bourne had created such a solid community of Christians, or "Praying Indians," among the Mashpees that those Indians were spared the ravages of the inexactly named seventeenth-century war in which so many other native New England peoples became involved.

In the manner of the journalist, Brodeur explored the vexing irony that the Mashpees, who had been an established group of Algonquians since long before the Pilgrims' landing, and who had been defended in colonial times by Shearjashub Bourne and other advocates, were unable to prove in the 1970s their legal existence. And because of that absurd difficulty, they could not get either federal assistance or a favorable judgment in any land claims. Both intriguing and infuriating, Brodeur's account closed on the hopeful note that the Mashpees (historically a part of the Wampanoag Federation which once spanned the territory from the Rhode Island border to the tip of Cape Cod and the islands) had been so stimulated by the legalistic debate about their own existence that they came to believe more strongly in themselves and in their imperishability.

The deeper-lying reason why the *New Yorker* story ended up in my "Book Project?" file was that, with all its grizzly flashbacks to battles of yore, the Wampanoags' story was not a tale of extermination or genocide. They and the Pilgrims had sought to help each other, it appeared, and had succeeded through years of mutual assistance in building a biracial society not generally reported in the history books. It's the more recent white citizens who have put the final squeeze on their red neighbors; it seems—those white citizens and their colonial forebears—not the most ancient white settlers.

Fascinated, I soon realized the perils of ignorance in this touchy area and sought out the assistance of Smith College Professor Neal Salisbury, who graciously agreed to start me down the trail toward that unknown, unevenly acceptive biracial society of New England three centuries ago. With Neal's help, I managed to capture a view of the times and of the contexts into which the Wampanoags and many other native American peoples fell—the era that is most often summed up, and dismissed (oh, just another war!), as "King Philip's War."

For nearly fifty years, the simple 1620 treaty signed by Massasoit, a sachem representing, it was believed, the entire Wampanoag Federation, and Plymouth's Governor John Carver worked splendidly. By the treaty, both parties pledged that they would not "doe hurte" unto the other, a pledge that was maintained throughout extremely provocative and risky times. Then in the 1660s came the cultural disturbances that led to King Philip's War—the war that totally ruined the peaceful accommodations of two generations of native and English diplomats.

Like a litany of accusation, the charge is leveled periodically at English-descended New Englanders that the English colonists were nothing but religion-crazed exterminators whose single purpose was to extirpate the natives and seize the land for themselves. Worse than the contemporary Spanish or French colonists, the English pursued a racial policy whose deliberate purpose was not enslavement but annihilation. Along with others, I quailed before this blast. But now, suddenly, I had evidence of a fact to the contrary—the successful treaty. With Neal Salisbury's guidance, I moved farther into the subject, and immediately discovered that it was a very special domain, full of competing professionals. These historians and other social scientists seemed to agree on only one thing: all previous generations of historians were off base. Whether bloody-minded Puritan chroniclers or Victorian nationalists, all the preceding writers on the subject of King Philip's War were grotesque distortionists.

Take, for example, the late-nineteenth-century author John Fiske, author of *The Beginnings of New England:* he had tried to demonstrate that the conflict between the two cultures (that is, "King Philip's War") was inevitable because of the superiority of the one race and the inferiority of the other; the weaker would naturally be eliminated. And of course, in his view, the Indian was morally and intellectually less keen, less committed to victory. In his words, ". . . the Indian knew little of that Gothic fury of self-abandonment which [possesses the Puritan and] rushes straight ahead and snatches victory from the jaws of death." Because of Fiske's dated, Darwinian understanding of the red-white relationship in war and peace, more recent historians have been having a delightful time making sport of him and his ilk.

This battle among the generations of historians was clearly too high-stakes a game for me, an editor of historical books but no historian. Therefore I decided, with Neal Salisbury's concurrence, that my venture into this contested sector would be nothing like an academic thesis but more of a personal narrative . . . more of a journey in search of the spirits of Richard and Shearjashub Bourne than an attempt to come up with a new historical theory. I would seek to find out what had happened to the biracial harmony that was blasted apart by King Philip's War—not as a scholar with a hypothesis to propound but as a visitor among the peoples.

The decision to become a rover among New England's affected communities—that is, among such aged and notable towns as Bristol, Rhode Island (near which site Massasoit's capital had been located), and Pemaquid, Maine (where the British crown finally established a military base that succeeded in extinguishing the last flames of King Philip's War)—appealed to me greatly. And, in Neal Salisbury's view, I might find with the aid of historical societies in these quite different regions bits and pieces of local memory that would add up to something of a contribution. That has been my objective, more in quest of the peculiar social harmony that was destroyed than in search of arms or the men or the motives of war.

Yet I could not be blind to some commonalities among the communities—to the fact, most obvious of all, that across all New England the settler and native societies were blundering through a *political* experience. For a number of reasons (which I can and do name but cannot categorize definitely), the great diplomats of the first two generations of red-white contact were succeeded by a new generation of less accommodating, more bitter personages, of whom Metacom, or Philip, was one and Major Josiah Winslow was another. The political solutions that had been worked out by such geniuses as Roger Williams in Rhode Island and Passaconaway in Massachusetts and New Hampshire gave way to feuds, flare-ups, and brutal repressions. It's for this reason that I came to see the entire scene in terms of a political implosion, a collapse of creative political solutions.

Ultimately, credit for whatever light is shed on the embattled scene by *The Red King's Rebellion* belongs not to me as wanderer but to those among whom I wandered. I do therefore direct the reader's attention to the Acknowledgments section in which I name the local historical societies and professional diggers and probers who helped me come to an understanding of the political nature of this confrontation. To those researchers, once again, my thanks . . . and my wish that their work of preservation and analysis may lead to a broader appreciation of peace as the prevailing norm, of war as the failure and never the triumph.

I

The Perceived Prince

Philip of Pokanoket

After leaving Boston for home in 1663, the English traveler and chronicler John Josselyn wrote with great excitement of his glimpse of a certain young native leader: "Prince Philip . . . had a coat on and buckskins set thick with these beads [of wampum] in pleasant wild works and a broad belt of the same." Then, in another burst of amazement: "His accoutrements were valued at twenty pounds."

Philip was apparently a sinewy and dazzling figure, of the sort to incite envy or speculation. How did he come by his riches? What were his strengths and what might be made of him? As he strode the streets of Massachusetts Bay's capital with his entourage, making heads turn, he was in his twenty-third year, proud of his lineage, confident of his destiny. A son of the recently deceased Massasoit—the great sachem who had befriended the Pilgrims and helped them through the first miserable years of settlement—he might one day inherit the leadership himself.

But for now he could play the prince. In disapproving tones, the historian Samuel Eliot Morison reports that Philip ran up bills in Boston. But is that not to be expected of royalty?

This was the same native leader who but a dozen years later would be named as the chief architect of a massive uprising, the rebellion against English authority known as King Philip's War. What a strange contradiction: first the pampered prince, then the remorseless foe of the very society that had accorded him honor and privilege. And that contradiction is linked to another: since 1620 New England's religion-centered settlers had enjoyed a full half-century of peace with the natives, a troubled peace stapled together by contrived agreements, a peace that was apparently no peace at all. The war in King Philip's name to which it led (1675–1677) would not only annihilate the natives of southern New England as an effective power, but would also deprive Puritan New England of its independence and almost of its life.

Red and white, what could have turned the two societies of New England, both of which had contributed to the creation of a mixed and mutually beneficial economic system, into opposed camps bent on each other's destruction? And how did Philip, that ostentatious prince, become the alleged organizer of this racial rebellion/suicide? With the scratchy compulsiveness of a dog who cannot find a particularly important bone, historians have continued to dig at causes and results: the virtual extermination of a pivotal group of native Americans. Yet, despite a heap of theories, no satisfactory rationale for this mysterious war has been found. In the words of the Smithsonian's Wilcomb Washburn: "One finds today irreconcilable differences among historians concerning Philip's motives and deeds."

Successive generations of American sages have sought to explain King Philip's War to readers of their own times. First the struggle was portrayed as a classic and necessary victory for the nation yet-to-be-born. Then repressed truths gradually surfaced, such as that the rebellion had nearly succeeded: more than half of New England's towns were attacked; with refugees crowding Boston and the few safe coastal towns, the English were on the point of being driven into the sea, the Puritan theocracy discredited as weak and inept.

Though the basic material to be mined for these discoveries is severely limited, the writers have struggled to work over that material again and again and to find a *root cause* that will correspond to contemporary beliefs about humankind.

A look at how Philip is represented by various schools of authors at the time of his next appearance in Boston may reveal the respective biases. That visit to the Puritan capital occurred under more serious circumstances, in 1671, eight years after Philip had been seen by the amazed Josselyn and four years before the outbreak of the war. By 1671 Philip had been raised by his older brother's strange death to the position of leadership of his people, the Pokanokets. Their domain (a small portion of the lands within the Wampanoag Federation) comprised but eight villages on the twelve-mile-long peninsula that thrust out into Narragansett Bay from Plymouth-owned territory in the neighborhood of Swansea, Massachusetts. As sachem, Philip, now thirty-one, was expected to take charge during the crisis caused by his brother's death: he should somehow relieve the increasing tensions between the Pokanokets and the Pilgrims or accept personal blame and punishment for anything that might harm his people. All eyes were on him, so say the oldest sources.

Leaving aside for a while the actual participants in the war who left diaries or memoirs, the first commentator on Philip and his disastrous rebellion was the Reverend William Hubbard, a Puritan clergyman whose popular *History of the Indian Wars in New England* came off the press in 1677, the last year of the war. The most notable feature of this caustic and bitter document is its self-justifying militarism. Hubbard described Massachusetts Bay as "the Israel of God" on the march in the New World; whatever the colony did was determined by God, carried out in his name by his triumphant warriors. There is but one side in his narrative, the cause of armored righteousness. As for Philip, he deserves only to be called "this treacherous and perfidious Caitiff." At various places in Hubbard's text, he speaks of the native Americans as "cannibals" and "wild beasts." He never recognizes that peace or negotiation might have been a valid option for the people about whom he writes; he rarely admits that certain native people may have suffered injustices at the hands of the English setters; and he only occasionally gives credit to those Christianized Indians who chose to fight alongside the English.

This series of prejudiced ramblings, in its original form and subsequent editions, may be thanked for setting early colonial minds on one undeviating track: the English, by their battlefield valor, were the proper possessors of the land. Emphasizing the "miseries and hardships" that our "renowned ancestors" had endured in order to win us salvation from the heathen, Hubbard's text was repackaged and sold to the eager Americans of the Revolutionary era. With its inspiring message of hate for the enemies, an edition appeared in 1775, within less than a month of Bunker Hill.

For this edition, Paul Revere prepared a particularly repulsive, pygmylike image of King Philip, making the point that enemies deserve nothing but contempt. By the time of the Civil War, this rather primitive philosophy had become accepted as national policy: war was the divinely ordained way to deal with rebels. Furthermore, in rationalizing the destruction of one group of Americans by another, the editors of the 1865 edition of Hubbard's *History* looked to "natural" (that is, scientific) causes. They urged their contemporaries to understand that the native Americans, by their less advanced condition, were doomed. For

> it is a natural consequence, that any People living by the Side of another more prosperous than themselves become Envious. Incapable of equalling their Neighbors, their Envy in time becomes Hatred, and this begets Violence and War. That was the condition of the North and South before the present Rebellion.

Echoing that Darwinian sentiment, George Ellis and John Morris, in their *King Philip's War* (1906), stated without sorrow that "the historic fact must be accepted that between peoples the fittest only survive, and that as between races ethics rarely exist." To put a scientific cast on human affairs was, apparently, not to increase one's understanding of the natives.

The nationalistic historians of the nineteenth century were, if possible, crueler in their perceptions of the native Americans than the God-fearing Puritan chroniclers. Another quite typical work from this era is John Fiske's *Beginnings of New England, or the Puritan Theocracy in Its Relation to Civil and Religious Liberty* (1900). When writing of Philip at that crucial historical moment of his Boston appearance in 1671, Fiske refers to him as a "crafty savage" who spent his time plotting a regional rebellion with nearby chiefs and planning time-stalling deceptions against the English. Fiske allowed a certain romanticism to this brigand, but regarded him as essentially obsolete. Fiske says nothing about the fact that Philip, trapped by Plymouth into a revised treaty within which he could not live, had appealed to authorities in Boston for an amelioration. Or that those authorities listened attentively to his case when he appeared before them. This author would never tolerate a view of Philip as a constructive politician on the interracial boundary. On the contrary, Fiske portrays Philip as a troublesome Robin Hood, wickedly hoodwinking the Pilgrims, contritely confessing to the naughtiness of his heart, and falsely agreeing to the surrender of certain weapons, simply because that would cause further strain. In these pages, the prince appears sly but silly: "With ominous scowls and grunts some seventy muskets were given up." The "humility" with which Philip expressed obedience to Plymouth in 1671—he would pay five wolves' heads a year by way of tribute—was obviously nothing but a cover-up.

A portrait of Fiske's time shows Philip in a Byronic pose— big, brooding eyes; long, sensitive nose; a tilted little crown. The resentments are obviously seething within his chest (visible via his opened shirt). The expiration of such a quaint potentate obviously could not be avoided.

In our own half-century, the nobility of national destiny and the dismissal of the natives have been quite turned around. This has been a time of revision and review. Much sympathy is now given to the native Americans, their values and their purposes. As far removed from Hubbard's and Fiske's philosophies as possible, modern authors tend to lay all war blame on the neurotical, aggressive Puritans. *The Invasion of America* (1975) by Francis Jennings is a key work on this revisionistic side of the library shelf.

Jennings suggests that a central part of the Old Testament for the Puritans was the admonition in Genesis to the Israelites that they should "subdue the earth and have dominion over everything that moves on earth." His theory is that the Puritans and their cohorts the Pilgrims carefully planned and executed

two massive aggressions against New England's resident Algonquians. The first, the Pequot War of 1636–1637, was a stage-
setter for the second, King Philip's War. And both were
outright land grabs, illegal and unjustifiable usurpations of native territories by English would-be estate owners.

The Pilgrims' trick, the device that would bring about the
wipe-out of Philip's Pokanokets in the view of Jennings, was
their establishment of the town of Swansea in 1667. Because
this new settlement was so close to the Pokanoket village of
Sowams (Massasoit's old capital, present-day Warren, Rhode
Island), it was only to be expected that English settlers' cattle
would wander into the Pokanokets' fields, that complaints
would be raised to the courts that could only be decided in the
settlers' favor, and that native resentment would lead to a war
they would lose. In that war the superior Puritan military machine would seize not only the Pokanokets' territories but also
the lands of heretical Rhode Islanders. And if any other native
peoples happened to get involved . . .

Dark, psychohistorical examinations of the Puritan mental-
ity accompany these revisionistic interpretations. John Winthrop, governor of Massachusetts Bay, is called nothing but a
"real estate speculator"; Massachusetts' subsequent witchcraft
trials are seen as part of this same perception of the devil in
unorthodox peoples. Richard Slotkin goes so far as to characterize the Puritans as seeking "regeneration through violence."
In their *Puritans, Indians, and Manifest Destiny* (1977), authors
Charles Segal and David Stineback emphasize that the Pilgrims (after the death of their friend Massasoit) believed that
"no dealings with the Indians could be aboveboard." And
they justified this immorality by pointing to the no-holds-barred
way the ancient Jews had fought the Canaanites for the Promised Land.

As for Philip the Prince, in the revisionists' view he was, of course, blameless. The innocent victim of Puritan skulduggeries, he might resemble Thomas Hart Benton's portrait of him—the natural figure in the landscape, tortured and exploited by the ruthlessness of oncoming civilization. For when the revisionists compare Puritans and Algonquians, they find the former perverse and the latter in perfect harmony with nature: the natives washed themselves more than the English, needed no prisons or magistrates because there was no crime among them, and fought in a truly less "savage" way (indulging in neither tortures nor rapes, both of which were common features of European soldiery).

The revisionists, following the lead of Francis Jennings, take particular pains to excoriate Puritan missionaries for their intrusion into the Algonquians' traditional ways of life, their arrogant and dishonest and hypocritical assault on native beliefs. John Eliot, the most notable of the missionaries, is revealed as a front man employed to bilk English donors of contributions for fake proselytizing work in New England, which money would actually be used for the Puritans' own purposes (such as putting up the first brick building at Harvard). And the initial sparks between the Pokanokets and the Pilgrims flared, according to the revisionists, when Philip and his brother declined to become conforming Christians and to play the land-sales game by the rules of Plymouth. The Pokanoket princes had sold certain valuable acreage to the settlers of Rhode Island, ignoring the Pilgrims' territorial delineations. Obviously they would have to be crushed.

In more recent times, a more objective, less blame-throwing breed of analysts has appeared in the battle-torn realm of American Studies. They're mostly anthropologists or archaeologists or ecologists, scientists not with axes to grind but with tools to unearth and contemplate. Both these social scientists and their immediate predecessors were accurately described by Alan and Mary Simpson in their excellent 1975 introduction to the diary of Benjamin Church (one of the most credible participant-chroniclers of King Philip's War):

> Anthropologists and archaeologists have steadily advanced our capacity to understand the Indian's culture in its own terms and the dynamics of the interaction between his culture and ours. The re-thinking and re-writing of black history in the past decade has stimulated a desire to re-think and re-write red history. Ignorance of Christianity and scepticism about its missionaries [had] made it tempting to see nothing but racism in a Puritan mission.

The new scholars find excuse for a given group's antisocial actions in the fact that the group was then undergoing great stress—fundamental socioeconomic or ecological perturbations. Even the aggressive Puritans are to be forgiven, for they had come out of one revolution in England (agriculturalism vs. commercialism) only to enter upon another here (trader economy vs. land economy). Hence their paranoia.

Yet today's deep-level probers, for all their tolerance, conclude with regret that historians rarely tell the full story, that their writings are skewed by the biases inherent in European writings. They themselves, offering up hard evidence from dwelling and burial sites, urge the overturn of many old-faithful historical concepts (such as that native and English religions tended to grow weaker as bicultural contacts intensified). They feel that, in many cases, the true story lies not in the library but beneath our feet.

One of the most engaging of the new scholars is the anthro-

pologist William S. Simmons, who has specialized in the folklore of the Algonquians. His *Spirit of the New England Tribes:
Indian History and Folklore, 1620–1984* is a tremendously exciting blend of memories, myth, and modern deductions from
ancient materials. For him, a significant piece of the King Philip
puzzle is the actual role of the sachem in native societies: how
central was he to the peace or war question and did he actually
exercise *any* military authority? Simmons emphasizes that these
leaders did not rule but functioned in consensus with the people's council, taking command in a European sense only in time
of war. Further, the small-scale extent of the sachem's authority
must be understood; in most cases the sachemdom

> could be divided into [still smaller] sachemdoms. On Martha's
> Vineyard, for example, in the early historic period, four sachems
> presided over distinct territories, each of which included smaller
> subdivisions ruled by minor sachems. . . . The Narragansett, often
> thought to include all Indian groups on the western side of Nar-
> ragansett Bay, actually comprised only one sachemdom among
> many along the Rhode Island coast.

Philip must therefore be seen not as the hugely influential,
scary figure in the portrait by the colonial propagandists, nor as
the romantic "chief" in the portrait by the nineteenth-century
nationalists, nor as the hapless victim of Puritan machinations
in the portrait by the revisionists. Rather he must be perceived
as a subtle negotiator between his and neighboring people, in
the manner of other sachems whose historic functions are
known. Some of these, like Massasoit of the Wampanoags and
Canonicus of the Narragansetts, seem to have earned the title
"great sachem" for their success in pulling together "confeder-
ations" of partially related peoples. But none of these native
leaders, in the field or in the council house, could be called a

Caesar or a Spartacus, and certainly not a Judas Maccabaeus. For the sachems rarely included within their inherited secular authority any *religious* authority.

As explained by Simmons:

By virtue of their control over spirits, the *powwows* advised their sachems. . . . The inspired role of shaman and the hereditary role of sachem did not overlap generally in one individual, and the few persons who combined those roles were thought to be extremely powerful. Tispaquin, the "Black Sachem" of Assowampset (now Middleboro, Massachusetts) who supported [Philip], was said by the Wampanoag to be "such a great *Pauwau*, that no bullet could enter him."

If today's anthropologists and archaeologists were asked to characterize Philip, they would have difficulty representing him in the flesh, as a physical personality. But they might offer up a certain marvelous, authentic portrait of a roughly contemporaneous sachem—Ninigret II, sachem of the Niantics. This totally believable but rather disturbing painting was executed in 1681, scholars believe, just four years after King Philip's War. It honors a native leader slightly younger than Philip who, along with his father, chose the English side rather than alliance with Philip. Thus the Niantics of Block Island Sound endured the intercultural disturbances of the seventeenth century.

Young Ninigret II, draped in a trade-goods blanket and rigged up in a European-cloth breech clout, wears as decoration an elaborate wampum headdress and a heavy silver gorget hung from a wampum tie around his neck. For all his grandeur—the staff in his hand, the dagger at his belt—there is a curious tentativeness about this representational sachem. Is his expression one of regret or of fear? Without half trying, we can see here intimations of Philip on that day in 1663, but two decades before the portrait was painted, when he appeared before the authorities in Boston.

Whether by portrait or by other artifacts, the process of discerning Philip and the war he may or may not have inspired is a tricky business of comparing impressions. The theorizing of historians in past generations may indeed make the process unnecessarily difficult, just as the modern scientists claim. This effort brings to mind a remark about colonial America by J. Hector St. John de Crèvecoeur, French author of *Letters from an American Farmer* (1782). He wrote that here "all is local with man, his virtues and his vices, his tastes, and even his prejudices." So perhaps if we were to visit some of the points of contact between red and white societies and some of the communities where the war began to smolder, Philip and his bicultural times would be brought more vividly to life. Perhaps the mystery would even be solved of how the long-lasting peace had been broken and the people blown away. For it was down along the shores of these rivers, upon these hillsides, that the actual people lived, not in historical conceptions or in excavations.

The face of New England in the 1670s was like a figure by Picasso, wracked by change and disruption. First and foremost: its native peoples had been so destroyed by European diseases that in southern New England but twenty thousand remained of the Algonquian-speaking peoples who had once numbered three or four times that number, "the flower and the strength" having been killed by European microbes against which the natives had no defense. By contrast, there were some fifty thousand English colonists, growing in number and in power.

Howard Russell, in his admirable *Indian New England Before the Mayflower*, estimated that there were perhaps 325 native villages scattered across New England before the waves of disease depopulated the land. Even in the early 1630s, when the radical separatist Roger Williams was exploring out from Plymouth, he stated that in traveling twenty miles a wanderer might come to twenty villages. It's with this presettlement native density in mind—not the later, depleted condition—that Russell drafted some astonishing maps of native villages and connections.

Not included on Russell's maps are the Pilgrim and Puritan and unorthodox settlers' communities that were so swiftly developed, from the very tip of Cape Cod to the Housatonic River and from southern Connecticut to mid-coast Maine. But New England, even in the earliest time of settlement already looked like a highway engineers' dream, with a network of trails knitting together the villages, a pattern of local connectors and long-distance routes. One observer three centuries later judged that these still detectable, carefully designed trails, which ever followed the most efficient ways over the ridges and toward the river fords, were "the greatest asset bequeathed by the redmen to the first Europeans." Some of the important trails—like the one from central Connecticut to the Providence area—had been so heavily pounded by moccasined feet that they ran twenty-four inches below the surface of the surrounding woodland.

The settlers soon became aware of these beckoning highways. What is now the Boston Post Road was called the Pequot Path; the route between Boston and Hartford became known as the Old Connecticut Path; and from Albany to Springfield ran the Bay Path, which, after a jog, continued on to Boston. The west-east path to the north of that route earned the awful name of the Mohawk Trail, for it was along this route over the Berkshires that the much-feared Mohawks, allied to New York's

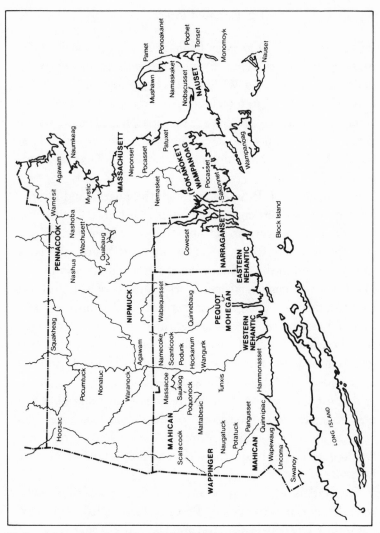

Native peoples of southern New England lived in approximately these locations early in the seventeenth century. Note homeland of Philip's Pokanokets.

Native peoples of northern New England tended to be divided between the western and eastern Ab[e]naki, the latter falling under French influence.

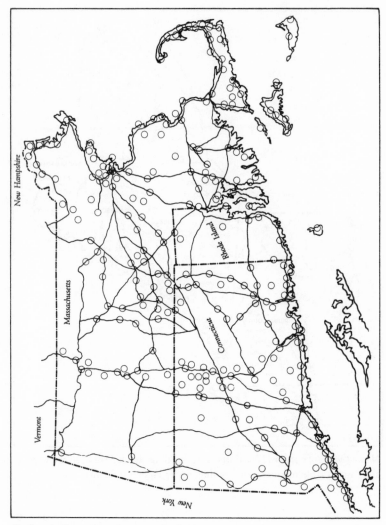

Trails and villages of southern New England's natives are sketched on this map. Philip escaped pursuers on a trail northwest from the head of Narragansett Bay.

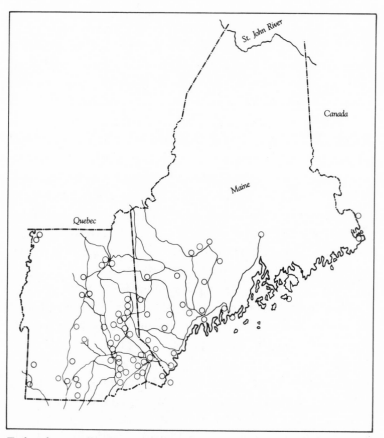

Trails and native villages in New Hampshire and western Maine were almost as dense as in the south; northeastern natives traveled mostly by canoe.

hostile Iroquois, came charging down into the Algonquian villages of the upper Connecticut River valley. Their depredations were so severe that, by the time of European discovery and settlement, the valley seemed very thinly populated.

Along New England's eastern coast, where contact with Europeans had been longest (going well back into the 1500s) and plague impact heaviest, there was an even greater silence. The Europeans found cleared fields, abandoned villages, demoralized and weakened natives willing to make any kind of treaty with the settlers that would give them peace and protection. The ghostly landscapes, white skulls, and bleaching bones beside abandoned cornfields were called "a sad spectacle to behould" by trepidatious English settlers.

When the Pilgrims moved from their first landing place at Provincetown to the stream-nurtured site of Plymouth (a location previously spotted by, and recommended by, John Smith), they were amazed at the readiness of the place, a home for the taking. Only from Samoset—the neighborly sachem who had caught a ride down the coast on a merchant vessel from his Ab[e]naki village at Pemaquid in Maine—did the Pilgrims learn what had happened here. The native name for this already prepared townsite was Patuxet (meaning Little Bay or Little Falls); so empty, so occupiable because of the massive plague that had struck in 1617: smallpox, most likely introduced by European fishermen on the New England coast. Few of the Pilgrims wasted sympathy on the disaster; they thanked their God for having laid out the tillable fields, for having cleared the broad stretches of open forest, for having made "a way for them" in the wilderness.

Though the Pilgrims numbered a spare hundred in 1620, the Puritans' numbers soared over a thousand soon after 1628, their first year of landing. Governor John Winthrop, who had arrived on Boston's North Shore in 1630, immediately took note of the docility of the natives and the open condition of the land, ready for anyone who would claim it and improve it. He wrote that the plagues must have been divinely ordained; "God [hath] thereby cleared our title to this place." Not for a moment, according to contemporary commentators, did the English express appreciation or wonder at the natives' modes of clearing the land and managing their agriculture.

In fact the English settlers had come into the midst of a people whose technology—without a wheel, without a loom, without domesticated animals—was quite adequate for the task of bringing forth the necessary food and making a comfortable living. But that was just the beginning of what the English did not care to understand about this social landscape, these ghost-haunted people who greeted them with such careful friendship.

A symbol of native-settler cooperation at this early time is the little herring that Squanto did or did not use to show the Pilgrims how to fertilize their corn hills. Squanto, who had left his home village of Patuxet in 1614 courtesy of an unscrupulous slaver and who had returned in 1620 to find the Pilgrims in occupation, is generally credited in most traditional histories with having instructed the plebian and thus land-ignorant Pilgrims about "how to dress & tend" the soil, hoeing it into sizable hillocks, and enriching the sandy soil by fish or humus. But the revisionist historians find this gentle tale of interracial tutelage hard to take, along with Squanto's altruistic loyalty to the Pilgrims; they deny that the herring could have existed. In more recent years, however, Russell and other ethnohistorians have been able to put the herring back into its traditional corn hill.

What's at issue here is the dawning, difficult understanding that these two societies needed each other, respected each other (even as we may not respect them, from our supposedly superior cultural position), gave each other strength and profit when the century was young. There was no wipe-out plan on either side—though of course there were fears and suspicions. There were also strange conceptions and weird expectations: some of New England's Algonquians wondered if the fundamental reason for the English settlers' appearance among them was that they had destroyed all their wood at home and had come to the New World to find fuel for their fires; the Puritan divines listened to the Algonquian language and, in putting it down on paper, found clues that these people were really one of Israel's long lost tribes, now ready for reuniting with the rest of God's people.

There was indeed much to hope for in this conjunction of land and humanity. Even before the English settlers' arrival, New England's natives had expressed eagerness for a beneficial association. In 1605, during his coastal explorations in Maine, Samuel de Champlain was told by a sachem named Bashaba of the Penobscots that the Europeans should come and dwell in their land so that the natives "might in future more than ever before engage in hunting beavers, and give us [Europeans] a part of them in return for our providing them with things which they wanted." Bashaba, a sophisticated, optimistic leader, foresaw a period of improved and more secure life once the native production of furs was increased to match the need of European markets.

Other ancient stories, other echoes of the time when the peoples still worked the land peaceably, whether singly or together, can be heard in various localities. In the northwestern corner of Connecticut, there are hills, still bare, that were regularly burned by the native Algonquians so that the hunters could spot deer (according to contemporary accounts) miles away. Along the shores of the Housatonic River you can see fields ripe with corn, as if the Algonquian farmers still lived there (as, in fact, some of their surviving heirs do). In the early 1600s natives from this productive region toted corn on their backs to help the Boston Puritans through their first winter.

But the landscape also rings with other memories. You can still find the Squannacook Swamps near Rehoboth, Massachusetts, where Philip and his Pokanokets used to hunt, as well as the great "mirey swamp" where he met his end. In fact, the word "swamp" was rarely heard in England before headlines in London's broadsides screamed the news of Philip's rebellion and his escape into and away from a swamp. Then, suddenly, it became the new word of the era. Like the herring, it remains now as a symbol, but a symbol of difference rather than harmony.

For, to the native and the settling peoples, swamps meant quite different things. Swamps to the natives represented an essential wild area, "the abode of owls" and other revered animals, the removed places where family members could be sheltered in times of war. To the settlers they represented the hiding place of the devil, the unreclaimable and useless land where wolves waited . . . that which was not subject to improvement and profit making.

For the Puritans, the concept of a people in harmony with nature implied a people in league with the dark forces—a point emphasized by the revisionists. Having found salvation for themselves in denial of worldly pleasures and in hard work, the Puritans were appalled at the "indolent" ways of the natives. Their twin motives in leaving England were to escape the religious persecutions of King Charles I's ministers and to find for themselves, as sons and daughters of middle-class families, the wealth that had been denied them by economic change at home. They would transform this land into their new Canaan, their profitable New England.

Professor Neal Salisbury, the Smith College historian who (as mentioned in the Preface) has helped provide a balanced view of the philosophies of seventeenth-century New England, points out that for the profoundly conservative Puritans, *change was sin*. Other writers (e.g., Philip F. Gura) have extended the thought, saying that "sin" was used by the Puritans to keep deviants (including Indians) in their place; those who challenged the status quo in any way were branded as sinners against God, doomed to the fires of hell. Edmund Morgan points out another Puritan eccentricity: while most Protestants of the day, including Roger Williams, believed that they would inherit in this world "nothing but paine and sorrow, yea poverty and persecution," the Puritans believed that "outward blessings would be procured from God as a result of their covenant."

In the Puritans' Calvinistic cosmos, the church community on the land, possessing an individual covenant with God, was at the center of all matters. Things civic were identical with things spiritual, for they both were of the community. Although a missionary intention may be found in Puritanism and although John Winthrop had styled his commonwealth as a "Modell of Christian Charitie," there was still the suspicion that (in Cotton Mather's words) the devil had "absolute empire" over all heathens, including the Indians. So outreach was perilous.

Perhaps conversion of some outsiders was possible, but if so, the Puritans demanded that any converts would have to live strictly in keeping with civil standards, forsaking traditional ways. This prejudice slowed down missionary efforts in New England to a crawl. The cautiously built communities of "Praying Indians"—in which the traditional rounded native dwellings were replaced by lined-up, straight-sided houses in the English manner—became a distinguishing mark of the landscape. These were far removed from North America's Roman Catholic communities of mass converts to the south and north, where sympathetic priests made swift and undisturbing impact on the native cultures. However slow they were to get started, by 1675 there were fourteen "Praying Towns" throughout New England with more than a thousand practicing adult inhabitants—another bit of evidence that these two societies could get along with each other, though often at the pain of the one and the advantage of the other.

The most impressive change taking place on the New England land in the mid-1600s was the increasing power of the burgeoning Puritan communities and the new and related vigor of the native peoples, rebounding from the ravages of disease of the previous decades. The old balance between needy settlers and plague-blasted natives had been replaced by a "golden age" of mutual prosperity (which the ostentatious Prince Philip had represented quite handsomely). Yet that splendid era, shortlived as it was, was also a time of corruption. Many of the trusty old agreements, such as the ancient treaty between the Pilgrims and Massasoit's people, had been set aside for more pragmatic relationships. In Plymouth itself, the original communal ideal had been rejected; now prosperity was sought in trade and individual strivings. "Why wouldest thou have thy particular portion?" Deacon Robert Cushman had demanded in a sermon soon after the Pilgrims landed. He had urged them forever to eschew the "particulars" of *mine* and *thine* for the opportunity to live as one, as in heaven. But his voice was lost in the press of economic necessities and the lure of advancement for the sharper-witted.

Similarly, in Massachusetts Bay, the Puritans flung themselves into speculations. Whereas they had left England in part
because there one had to "pluck his means, as it were, out of his
neighbor's throat," now life in new Canaan had become hotly
competitive and socially divisive. The Bay General Court, ruling body of the colony, had decreed in 1635 that "no dwelling
shall be built above half a mile from the meeting house in any
new plantation." This decree is emphasized by John Stilgoe,
author of the tremendously influential book *Common Landscape
of America* (1985), as central to the whole Puritan plan. His
point is that these people (as well as the Pilgrims) had vowed to
live in walled-in communities of self-generating holiness, dramatically opposed to the native Americans' impermanent and
flexible residential patterns. Because of the dynamic, explosive
nature of Puritanism, the restrictive edict of 1635 did not last
long; oft-flouted, it was canceled in 1640. Nonetheless, at the
center of each Puritan town there remained the meetinghouse,
a sacred focus that commanded the attention of all citizens.
That basic concept would not be corroded.

Also, restrictions against voting by non-church members remained firmly in place. Unorthodox citizens could neither hold
office nor receive any other public recognition, but they had to
pay taxes to support the church and they were fined for non-
attendance. It might be said that as the century matured and
commerce prospered, Puritan society suffered from a corruption
of intensity. The myth that God favored this New England
society alone seemed proven as even Cromwell's Puritans in
England gave way to the restoration of the monarchs; self-
righteousness became the order of the day at the same time that
some observers saw a certain weakening of the society's vigor
and wisdom. Much as they admired the Puritans, historians of
the nineteenth century had to recognize that these people had

made enemies of the world. In their early history of King Philip's War, George Ellis and John Morris wrote that "The Puritan was not of a character, either individually or collectively, with whom men of any other race could be expected to maintain harmonious relations."

Likable or not, true to their old covenants or not, the Puritans and their Pilgrim neighbors (between whom cross-denominational marriages began to occur in the mid-1600s) succeeded materially. They provided the leading edge of what has been called the "nascent capitalism of New England" in the seventeenth century. Yet for many Americans, this turning away by their forefathers, away from utopian innocence and toward commercial profit, has been hard to deal with. Had the Puritans not once proclaimed that their theocracy would be "as a Citty upon a Hill"? Had they not recognized that posterity and the "eies of all people" would measure them by the well-being of their Christian experiment? Today's generally tolerant scholars, particularly the ecologists, would answer that question by saying that the wilderness forced the Puritans to change, compelling them in economic and cultural directions quite unimaginable back in the distant parsonages of England.

Many revisionist historians insist, however, that these people were greedy land-grabbers from the beginning—bent on conquest from the moment they stepped off the boat. These writers seem to react with a sense of shock to the idea that profit-tinged motivations intruded early upon the American scene. That misconception has a long history. Back when John Locke was so brilliantly writing about world affairs, in the eighteenth century, he aphorized that originally "all the world was America"—meaning that the name *America* then still stood for innocence. It was apparently very difficult to recognize that New England had been a functioning part of the traders' international world ever since the 1630s. Commercial life in this part of America had then gone on to become a fundamental aspect of existence. The issue for Philip and his people was not whether to be included in the evolutions of seventeenth-century commercialism, but what to do if their status as trading partners was ever undermined by a lack of demand for their basic products.

To become trading partners in northern New England, the Algonquian residents of those beaver-rich woodlands needed to alter their traditional lifeways very little. But the southern Algonquians, having determined that the best course for them was to turn to the production of wampum, made radical shifts in how they lived and how the labor of men and women was directed. Wampum called the tune; or, in the words of recent writers, the natives were caught up in "the Wampum Revolution." The gleaming beads of white and purple-black seashells—whose potential value the Pilgrims had learned from the Dutch—were regarded as signs of prestige by the native elite and, later, as an official medium of exchange by the colonial governments. The shells were ground to size and drilled and strung by peoples who lived along Narragansett Bay and Long Island Sound, particularly the Narragansetts and the Montauks. The twenty pounds' worth of finery that Philip wore when he first appeared in Boston demonstrated how the Pokanokets were also a part of this lucrative exchange: wampum for furs, then for trading goods.

Increasingly, the lives of the natives revolved more and more around the trading post—a seemingly natural development within such a commercial society. And the concomitants of that change seemed initially beneficial: the arising of a confident and wealthy class of native American leaders; the flowering of certain art forms; the improvement of everyday life by means of iron hoes, warm blankets, and copper kettles. For such a beneficiary of this golden age as Philip, it is quite remarkable what he commanded and what he could negotiate on the basis of his wealth; he was surely the equal of any Englishman.

There were, of course, negative aspects within this world of the traders and the fur and wampum producers: dishonest traders; the insidiousness of alcohol; and the inequalities of the English justice system. Furthermore, the native was pushed constantly out of his value systems and into the English modes—not so much for the sake of the missionaries as to be a fuller participant in the vitally important exchanges. Isaac de Rasieres, the Dutch trader and ambassador who had introduced the Pilgrims to *wampumpeag* ("white strings of money") in 1627, noticed how the natives even then were obliged to walk in the strictest interpretation of Plymouth's regulations. The Pilgrims, he wrote, have "stringent laws and ordinances upon the subject of fornication and adultery, which laws they maintain and enforce very strictly indeed, even among the tribes which live amongst them." Morality was but one feature of the natives' lives subject to review.

Whereas the southern New England Algonquians had been known for shifting their village sites and their houses with the season, moving from the hunting territories of the interior to the good fishing grounds on the coast and back as the year progressed, now they tended to stay by their "wampum factories." The men laboriously gathered the shellfish and the women artfully made the belts and headbands and stoles of the strung and woven wampum. Time was also found for farming—some communities having cornfields as large as two hundred acres. But corn had long ago lost its power in the traders' marketplace. Now the price offered for beaver pelts in London, and the translation of that into wampum, and the value of a fathom of wampum at the trading post were all that mattered.

Then suddenly the whole situation changed, and New England would never be the same again. Roger Williams, who had earned a reputation as an honest man among the Narragansetts in whose territory he finally settled, was tested to the limits of his patience to explain to the natives this new turn of events. To their protests that they were being cheated by the downward-spiraling price of wampum, he could only answer that, yes, one fathom (six feet) of the beads had been worth nine or ten shillings a few years ago, but now it was worth about five shillings. "The difference comes from the lower value of beaver furs in England," he kept saying. "But although I . . . explained this to the Indians, they [still] felt cheated."

To many writers of today it was economic reversal (a shift in the value of beavers, caused in part by a mid-century style shift in London)—and not devils or national destiny or perverted Puritans—that caused the social disruption that brought on the war. As described by William Cronon, author of *Changes in the Land: Indians, Colonists, and the Ecology of New England:*

> Demand for wampum fell, and Indians on the south coast suddenly found themselves isolated from markets on which they had come to rely. Indians for whom pelts had been their main access to trade had comparable experiences when their fur supplies gave out. These changes contributed to the conflicts leading up to King Philip's War.

The golden age of the fur-and-wampum prince was over. Now the natives' only resource, their only source of wealth and power, was land. And that was a limited, exhaustible commodity.

*   *   *

Concerning the land and its occupation, the early perception of the Puritans was that New England had once been divided into various Indian "nations," each with a kinglike sachem and a court organized to carry out his bidding. And these kingdoms tended to be arranged in the region's river valleys, bounded by the rivers' tributaries or other natural features. In the front-matter of William Hubbard's narrative, there is a remarkable woodcut map of this imagined land, this medieval tapestry of castellated towns and native territories. The artist shows where the "Pequid Country" stops and the Narragansetts begin, with the Nipmucks slightly to the north. He also shows King Philip's royal seat at "Monnt:hope" (which the Pokanokets named Monthaup, and is now known as Mount Hope), south of the settler town of "Seaconk."

Although Hubbard's map is strange-looking and hard to follow because of its east-west orientation, that bias says much about how New England seemed to those who had sailed into its Atlantic harbors from the east, with the Merrimack River to starboard and the Connecticut River on the westernmost borderline of their knowledge. Then, after the viewer does get squared away with this perspective, the map becomes both a delightful piece of folk art and a graphic presentation of how the war looked to English participants of the seventeenth century. They viewed the region from the coast in.

Today's scholars suggest, on the other hand, that the proper view of New England—the native Americans' view—is from the interior out. Anthropologist Harald Prins of Bowdoin College discerns a tremendous mobility among the native peoples; it was this ability to move swiftly across the interior distances, these flexible relationships between unrestrained peoples, that gave the Algonquians their unique mastery of the land. Professor Prins sees, for example, an overarching relationship between the Sokokis of coastal Maine and the Squakheags of the northern Connecticut River valley. Delimited by neither river bounds nor traditional hunting territories, the Algonquians moved as fluently and commandingly on land as the English moved on the sea.

That native command of the entire region seems confirmed by another remarkable and contemporary map, this one commissioned by the French from native sources in 1671. In contrast to Hubbard's perspective, this map looks south, from a point somewhere above Bangor, Maine. The Merrimack River is glimpsed in the right-hand corner. Interior New England here appears to be wide open to anyone who would travel by trail or river: within easy reach are Quebec, Portsmouth (Piscataqua), and Mount Desert. For such journeys, the southern Algonquians carved sizable dugouts out of beech or pine trees; the northern Algonquians were designers of the justly famous birch-bark canoes. As for the runners across this well-understood landscape, it was said that some of them could cover eighty miles from sun to sun. This was scarcely the static scene presented by Hubbard's medievally inclined artist.

In addition to their different approach to water-borne transportation, the northern and southern Algonquians of New England were separated by other significant differences. Of Maine's Abnaki peoples, the northeasternmost were the Tarratines, or Micmacs, on whom European ways had made minimal impact. They did not practice agriculture nor did they live in rounded *wetus,* made of bent-over sapling frames, as did their southern cousins; for them the wigwam, with hides stretched around tall poles in conical form, was the standard dwelling. For them, as the seventeeth century advanced, the French rather than the English became recognized as friends and supporters.

Immediately to the west of New England's Algonquians lived the Mohawks, known for their constant incursions. Eventually the Mohawks—whose raids along the St. Lawrence provoked the French into warring against them—became allies of the imperial English forces in Albany, as did the other members of the Iroquois Confederation. That alliance with King Charles II's royal governor became all the firmer after the expulsion of the Dutch from the territory in 1661. Yet this was an alliance that gave no ease whatsoever to New England's Puritans, who continued to distrust Mohawks and royal forces with an equal passion.

To understand the geopolitical insecurities of New England's settlers in the face of both Algonquian and foreign threats, it is helpful to look at a map of the time showing the confusion of overlapping claims and vague mandates. Philip and other native leaders were well aware of these contentions among the English claimants, their variegated laws concerning the land, and their conflicting authorities. The exiled Roger Williams, sensitive to both the niceties of the Algonquian language and the possibilities of trading with and bringing the Gospel to these people, had first found refuge within the territories of Philip's father, Massasoit. But because that territory belonged to Plymouth (in the English view) and because the Pilgrims were at that point "loth to displease [Massachusetts] Bay," the Pilgrims asked if Williams would please keep moving in exile "to the other side of the water." Across the Taunton River Williams dutifully went, having shrewdly prepared his way long before.

Massasoit was vexed at Williams's departure for Narragansett country—perhaps because the fluent trader-clergyman was a friend, perhaps because Williams represented another increment of power for the Pokanokets when he was in their midst.

But Canonicus, the chief sachem of the Narragansetts, was delighted to have this exile from Puritan lands on his side of the border. He scorned Massasoit's complaint and trusted that the building of a cooperative colony by Roger Williams near him would buffer his lands all the more securely from the aggressions of both Plymouth and Massachusetts Bay.

It mattered little to the rival sachems what theological dispute had compelled Roger Williams to come among them. But interestingly enough this notable Puritan divine—known for both his personal charm and his political-religious liberalism—had been cast out of his pulpit in Salem, Massachusetts, in 1635 by the General Court not for doctrinal disagreements, as is commonly believed; rather it was specifically because he declared the authorities in Boston had no charter right to be taking lands away from the natives, and because the civil magistrates, in his view, had no power over matters of conscience. With radical ideals of that variety issuing from his lips and pen, he was banished, forced to depend on his own resources—which were immense. But even after Roger Williams had founded his colony for "persons distressed of conscience" at Providence in 1636 and made "covenantes of peaceable neighborhood with all the Sachems round about us" to secure the land, he and Canonicus had to maintain a decades-long struggle to protect their borders from incursions by the surrounding Puritan colonies. Both sides of Narragansett Bay felt the pressure: the Pilgrims pushed for the eastern coasts, urging settlers into the lands of the Pokanokets and their allies the Pocassets and Sakonnets; the Bay's attempts to interfere with the dispute-clouded settlement of the Warwick area below Providence went on through the Cromwellian years. It was not until the restoration of the Stuarts, when Roger Williams made an emergency voyage to London in 1663, that "Rhode Island and the Providence Plantations" seemed securely situated on the political map of New England—a security cast into jeopardy by the war in King Philip's name that broke out a dozen years later.

The Narragansetts had always been somewhat apart from the rest of the New England Algonquians. Their wealth in terms of wampum, their power in terms of fighting men (nearly four thousand), and their impressive leadership all commanded respect. One contemporary traveler, William Wood, called them the "mint masters of New England." In the 1630s—when the "golden age" of prosperity was blessing both the Narragansetts and their neighbors to the west, the Pequots—it appeared that both of them had sufficient might to counter and even to rival the English colonies that were building so boldly from east to west. The most impressive aspect of the Narragansetts' society was its apparent immunity from European diseases, which of course bespoke the power of their shamans and powwows. Even when the era of wampum and furs had passed, and when diseases finally made their deadly inroads into the society's health and numbers, the religious leaders were able to keep the people faithful to traditional values. Yet the apartness and integrity of the Narragansetts and the Pequots would prove to be the provocative cause of their respective dooms.

In a northeasterly direction, New England's overlapping claims and the native relations were even less orderly. The English settlers north of the Merrimack River existed in towns established on grants given either to the Mason family (New Hampshire) or to the heirs of Sir Fernando Gorges (Maine). The natives, some of whom were prospering nicely in the fur-trading business, tended to be more and more victimized by unscrupulous traders in the territories farther removed from the moral strictures of Massachusetts Bay.

That is, the people near the Merrimack and called by the

name Wamesit (or Pawtucket) seemed to have established fairly harmonious relations with the Puritans, as had the Massachusetts—those few of them who had survived the smallpox. Slightly to the north, the Pennacooks, too, under the leadership of the sage Passaconaway, generally received fair attention in the Puritan courts and found they could live quietly within English bounds. But among the Kennebecs and Penobscots and other western Abnakis, there were early evidences of English dishonesty and injustice; hostility seethed, awaiting the sparks of King Philip's War to burst into flame. And, adding to the feeling of insecurity on this frontier were the raids of the easternmost Abnakis, the Tarratines, who had a history of storming down the coast north of Boston—a Viking-like tactic they had practiced even before English settlement began.

In 1643, just a few years after Philip's birth, the Puritans made a serious attempt to pull this tangle of confusions, these semi-patented colonies and insecure colonies, together into one political system. Their basic attitude in this effort was that all New England was theirs. Originally it was theirs through the royal claims resulting from explorer John Cabot's discoveries in the preceding century; subsequently it was theirs as a result of decrees from Cromwell's parliament. Therefore there was no need to take the Indian "nations" into account when forming a regional government—those people had no vested rights.

Wilcomb Washburn, head of American Studies at the Smithsonian, explains that "the Puritans chose to interpret the word [occupy] in terms of a settled agricultural people and to deny Indians ownership of areas over which they merely hunted or fished." The Puritan divine John Cotton had put the matter even more succinctly: "In a vacant soyle, hee that taketh possession of it, and bestoweth culture and husbandry on it, his Right it is." Because so many areas of New England had been "providentally" cleared of occupants by diseases or by raids, it seemed perfectly justifiable to move in and improve and organize the land.

Thus the United Colonies of New England came into being, without native representation. This political body, convening in Boston, consisted of representatives from Massachusetts Bay, Plymouth, Connecticut (meaning the families who had followed pastor Thomas Hooker to the site of Hartford on the Connecticut River in 1636), and New Haven, which then included Milford, Guilford, and Stamford. All of these colonies had sufficiently pure Puritan philosophies to be regarded as legitimate. Left out were Rhode Island (a.k.a. "Rogues' Island"), where dissidents like and unlike Roger Williams continued to gather, and the proto-colonies in New Hampshire and Maine. The Bay's governor, John Winthrop, told all who thought this an excessively exclusive political body that the Down Easters could not be included "because they run a different course from us, both in their ministry and their civil administration."

Many historians view the United Colonies not only as the official body that had to cope with King Philip's War but also as the precursor of the Articles of Confederation of 1781 as well as of all subsequent American unions. That view is eloquently advanced by Samuel Eliot Morison. As for the United Colonies' purposes and effectiveness, Morison wrote that

> the professed objects were to settle boundary and other disputes among the four member colonies . . . [and to provide] mutual protection against aggressions by French, Dutch, or Indians. Each colony appointed two commissioners who met annually, handled

Indian affairs, and had power to declare war by a vote of three to one. They managed to settle several intercolonial disputes, and in 1675–76 helped to concert military measures in King Philip's War.

And because of this primitive, representative form of government—so crude but so freighted with promise for the nation that would one day come into being—it is virtually impossible for most Americans to read the accounts of the war that follow in anything but a "we vs. they" manner. That tendency is furthered by the fact the Puritans' early accounts make such glorious reading. They're written by the eye-witness chroniclers and the propagandists who, like Hubbard, combined the purposefulness of the Old Testament with the poetic prose of Oliver Cromwell and John Milton. They're hard to rationalize against.

But the war which these bards sang and which the United Colonies coordinated was a disaster. There would be no bloodier war in American history, in terms of proportionate populations: of a total population of eighty thousand, nearly nine thousand were killed; of those, one-third were English settlers, two-thirds native Americans. Thousands of additional settlers became wards of the state, refugees on public relief, while thousands of additional native Americans were enslaved or prevented from reuniting with their people. Of New England's ninety towns, fifty-two were attacked, with twenty-five pillaged and seventeen razed. More than half of New England's native population was lost (many by starvation); the physical and psychic strength of Puritanism was mortally wounded. The once independent New England colonies, their inability to govern their own affairs having been revealed, were tucked firmly under the wing of the British empire, not to be freed until the revolution of the next century.

How could this have happened? How could God so have deserted his people of the new Israel? One answer, favored by the revisionists, is that the Puritans determined at an early point that they were militarily invincible; like Cromwell, they would be accompanied into battle by heavenly hosts, led by a "pillar of fire." So they brought the war on themselves in order to prove themselves, and in response to perceived threats and inner fears. A somewhat similar interpretation, by Neal Salisbury, is that they allowed themselves to be spooked into a war that begat its own brutality: "By convincing themselves that their lives were at stake, the English [of the United Colonies] found the motivation and justification for a policy of terror." In that reign of terror, all suffered.

Another ultimate question is, Who should be blamed? The Puritans, who were fond of assigning blame, first looked to themselves and their own habits for the failures of the war. Indeed, their whole attitude toward the war was that it was an essentially inward, spiritual experience (which may be one of the reasons they fought it so poorly). When the tide of war went against them, they sought within themselves the "provoking evils" that had angered their God. The colonial scholar Edmund Morgan sounds moderately amused when he reports that the Bay's General Court, in repentence, passed a series of laws against the following errors: long hair, excess in apparel, disorderly children, idleness, oppression, tippling, and the Quakers. But it was tremendously serious business.

It is worth looking at the records of the Bay Colony at this critical, worrisome period. They read as follows:

Whereas the most wise and holy God, for severall years past, hath not only warned us by his word, but chastized us with his rods, inflicting upon us many generall (though lesser) judgments, but we have neither heard the word nor rod as wee ought, so as to be effectually humbled for our sinns to repent of them, reforme, and amend our wayes; hence it is the righteous God hath heightened our calamity, and given commission to the barbarous heathen to rise up against us, and to become a smart rod and severe scourge to us, in burning and depopulating severall plantations, murdering many of our people of all sorts, and seeming as it were to cast us off, and putting us to shame, and not going forth with our armies, heerby speaking aloud to us to search and try our wayes, and turne again unto the Lord our God, from whom wee have departed with a great backsliding.

What makes that extensive apologia so fascinating is that there is in all that pietistic prose not one word about how the Puritans might possibly have done something ugly to the natives and might now revise that attitude. The near loss of the war drove them not toward greater acceptance and tolerance but in the direction of harsher religious and civil strictness. Could they not see that their disinclination to include the Algonquians in any meaningful political structure was at the heart of this God-inflicted war?

How tragic that these adept people were so inept in bringing about a political resolution. They made passing attempts at treaties and covenants from time to time, but once the war began, they could or would not end it. Nonetheless, fundamentally important dramas of reconciliation went on among the peoples. For example, a vignette stands forth from the first volume of *New England Begins,* the remarkable study of Yankee society in the seventeenth century prepared by the Boston Museum of Fine Arts in 1982. The item under discussion is a basket originally given by a Narragansett woman to Dinah Fenner at the latter's garrison house at Cranston in 1675, when the war was staggering toward a hateful, mutually ruinous halt, and now in the possession of the Rhode Island Historical Society in Providence.

The episode of the giving of the basket by a starving Narragansett to a war-battered settler was described in the original text as follows:

> The squaw went into the garrison; Mrs. Fenner gave her some milk to drink; she went out by the side of a river, pulled the inner bark from a wikup tree [basswood], sat down under the tree, drew the shreds out of her basket, mingled them with the bark, wrought this little basket, took it to the garrison and presented it to Mrs. Fenner.

Of such exchanges peace might be made. These in-contact people are the exceptional heroes and heroines behind the tumult of King Philip's War. However dim the perception of Philip himself may have become as a result of time's shiftings, these are the people who make his ghastly war a worthy chapter in the evolution of human affairs.

2

The Battle That Shaped New England's Mind

The Pequot War of 1637

Even before adventurous Roger Williams went journeying out from Plymouth among the natives with trade and possible enlightenment in mind, a wealthy merchant named John Oldham had made a number of revealing excursions along the coast and upon the inner waterways of New England. Oldham's single-minded purpose—to secure the most advantageous trade arrangements with the most important Algonquians—involved a complexity of negotiations. It happened, to New England's grief, that he approached the challenge with more vigor than subtlety, and helped bring on the first serious military conflict between the English settlers and the native Americans.

"A man of parts, but high-spirited and extremely passionate," were the words the Pilgrims used to describe the bluff merchant when he appeared in their midst in 1623. As an outsider, Oldham was prohibited from dealing with the natives and was expected to conform to the colony's religious precepts.

But as described in George Willison's *Saints and Strangers,* a man of Oldham's spirit could not long be restrained by the Pilgrim's restrictive arrangements with the Algonquians or by their regulations regarding worship and behavior. When the churchly Reverend John Lyford landed in Plymouth and took exception to the separatist beliefs of the Pilgrim fathers, Oldham joined in the clergyman's little plot to discredit the Plymouth leadership and take over the colony. Then he had the bad grace to pull a knife on Myles Standish. So it came about that he, Lyford, and their respective servants were hustled out of town, the charges against them being both civic and theological.

After many another maneuver, Oldham moved north to what would become Exeter, New Hampshire; there he undertook profitable trading with the Algonquians of the Merrimack region. His connections with Sir Fernando Gorges, purported owner of the territory that is now Maine, seemed to assist his success. Subsequently he returned south and became a citizen of the Massachusetts Bay Colony, trading among the Narragansetts, with whom he established close relations. He also journeyed far enough over Massachusetts Bay's western hills to explore the hemp- and mineral-rich valley the natives called Quinatucquet—"At the Long Tidal River." He confirmed that in this region of Connecticut (as the English renamed it) the Dutch were vying for fur mastery with the Pequots, who effectively owned it; at stake was an annual harvest of ten thousand beaver pelts. The swift winning of this region by the Puritans would give them the first taste of victory against the natives, stimulating the land lust that was one of the causes of King Philip's War.

By 1634 John Oldham had become a recognized power in the Bay Colony. That year he organized a variegated group of English settlers from Watertown, would-be frontiersmen, whom he led cross-country to the native village of Pyquag on the Connecticut (present-day Wethersfield, just south of Hartford). There the settlers bought land from an impoverished, fast-on-his-feet River Indian sachem named Sequassen. His undisguised intention was to secure protection from the Pequots, who asserted their monopolistic mastery of the region by exacting tribute from its weakened sachems. There was a string to Sequassen's hospitality: the English settlers were obliged by the purchase of his land to allow him to build a dwelling right in their town; he would become a member of their diverse community. An advanced idea, one might think.

In that same year of 1634, Oldham the power dealer was also involved in helping to hammer out a precedent-breaking agreement between the Pequots and Massachusetts Bay. The negotiations had been the Pequots' idea in the first place, as they had apparently seen that the Puritans were the emerging power in all New England; better a fur-trade alliance with them than with the Dutch (who had treated them murderously), even if that alliance meant a sharing of their trade monopoly. But by the terms of the treaty as laid down by Oldham and the Puritans, the Pequots (whom Oldham called "very false people") were asked to pay a gigantic annual revenue to Boston and to open their lands to settlement. The Pequot ambassadors, though charged with effecting an alliance, must have known that these terms, when reported to the people's council after the trip home, would be rejected as insultingly harsh.

Simultaneously, Oldham's tactics on another front were earning him a harmful defeat: a split developed between him and his former friends the Narragansetts. This divorce may have occurred because of Oldham's expression of unseemly anger when, after a terrible drought, the Narragansetts were unable to deliver the promised one thousand bushels of corn he'd ordered that year for his trading. Or it may have come about because of the Narragansetts' resentment at Oldham's decision to make a treaty with the rival Pequots, or even because they blamed him and other European traders for the smallpox outbreak in 1633. Whatever the reason, Oldham found himself persona non grata among the people who had supplied him with one of his vital trading commodities.

Yet two Narragansetts were still friendly enough to continue to serve as Oldham's boatmen. They were essential to him in the summer of 1636 when he began to load his vessel for an all-important sail along the southern New England coast and up the Connecticut River. This voyage, on which his two young sons joined him, would be the formal commencement of the harmonious commercial relations which had been proposed two years before between the Bay Colony and the Pequots (though the treaty had still not been ratified by the people's council or payment made). As he led his two children on board, and as the Narragansett crewmen heaved trading goods onto the deck of his shallow-draft pinnace, the bull-headed Oldham seemed determined to carry out this mission. For, as he saw the development of his fortune and the destiny of New England, they were both centered on the Connecticut River valley.

There was reason to be cautiously optimistic about how English interests were advancing in the region. Though the Pequots' former allies, the Dutch, were still trying to stir things up in the valley, having sent a force of seventy soldiers from Albany to remove a trading post that the Pilgrims had aggressively positioned above the Dutch fort at Hartford, the Pilgrims had been undeterred by the military display and, staring down contemptuously from their walls, had sent the foreigners packing. Then early in 1636 two groups of Bay settlers, ignoring Pequot claims and dealing only with the River Indians, had located themselves at important valley sites: one positioned opposite the Dutch at Hartford and led by the strong-minded preacher Thomas Hooker; and the other at Springfield, Massachusetts, led by the more liberally inclined William Pynchon. Finally, in this same important year of 1636, an English group led by Protestant noblemen distressed by Charles I's religious policies had combined to establish a fort at the mouth of the Connecticut River, in the very face of Dutch attempts to acquire the same site. Under the governorship of John Winthrop, Jr., and commanded by army engineer Lion Gardiner, this strategically located fort—called Saybrook after two of the English lords— seemed to symbolize the new security of the valley, now in competent English hands. Control of the valley would remain securely in those hands until it was almost lost in King Philip's War.

But as Oldham contemplated his situation, there were obviously some wild cards in the deck. First of them was a lecherous Virginia freebooter named John Stone, whose murder, committed allegedly by Pequots back in 1633, was occasionally brought up by the Puritans as an issue demanding justice. Indeed, the surrender of his murderers by the Pequots to Bay authorities was one of the demands in the unconfirmed treaty of 1634. Another continuing difficulty was Oldham's own relations with the natives—were the Narragansetts, through whose waters he would now be sailing, seriously grieved at him? And a third difficulty was the character of a diplomatic meeting that had just been convened at Fort Saybrook. Included along with Oldham were John Winthrop, Jr., and Lion Gardiner; from the Algonquians' camps came Sassious, leader of the Western Niantics, subjects of the Pequots, plus a number of Pequot leaders. Set before them all was the gift of wampum (two full bushels of it), which the Pequots had originally offered to the Bay Colony in an attempt to clinch the 1634 agreement. The wampum was now being returned, pointedly, by Bay officials, who were in-tensifying their demands for surrender of Stone's murderers. Now they insisted on the full and immediate payment of the previously mentioned four hundred fathoms of wampum, which historian Francis Jennings values at $50,000, nearly half the Bay's annual levies. The demands were such as might be deliv-ered to a dangerous trade rival, not to a potential ally.

Gardiner and other English representatives at the meeting knew how tense the situation was, for the return of an offered gift of such size was tantamount to a declaration of war, and the Bay's impatience left the Pequots little room to maneuver. But then Sassious, the Western Niantic sachem, eased the confron-tation somewhat by consigning his whole territory to Governor Winthrop, undoubtedly with the Pequots' knowledge and per-mission. This generous act should be listed prominently among other attempts by the natives in the history of New England to maintain the peace. Nonetheless, the Saybrook meeting ended unsatisfactorily, with the Bay's demands unaddressed.

Yet another wild card on the Connecticut scene was an important Algonquian known to Oldham only by reputation. This was Uncas, eventual sachem of the Mohegans—the man who would emerge from the Pequot War as the most powerful native American in New England. "Outstanding of physique and of overwhelming ambition," in the words of a later writer, Uncas had married the daughter of Wopigwooit (Tatobam), a widely respected Pequot sachem murdered by the Dutch in their earlier attempts to gain and maintain control of trading in the valley. As Wopigwooit's son-in-law, Uncas had considered himself in line for leadership of all the Pequots. When, instead,

Wopigwooit's son Sassacus inherited the sachemdom, a rivalry commenced that was one of the personal-political factors behind the economically induced Pequot War. Repeatedly Uncas made attempts to grab the Pequots' leadership; repeatedly he was rebuffed, exiled, yet tolerated by the affected Algonquians in a way that would have baffled the bloody-minded politicians of a European court.

Uncas had other proud credentials; the son of a Pequot sachem named Owenoco, he considered his lineage royal. But, because of his banishment from both Pequot and Mohegan territories, he found himself in the mid-1630s on the edge of affairs, possessing "but little land and few men." It is thought that he was then living among relatives in the Hartford area, making alliances with various of the Pequot-alienated River tribes and watching with care as Dutch control of the Connecticut River valley gave way to English.

He learned that the leader of the productive, Plymouth-built trading post at the junction of the Farmington and Connecticut rivers above Hartford (present-day Windsor) was an enterprising individual named Jonathan Brewster. Although Brewster was now reporting to Massachusetts Bay rather than to Plymouth (because such a great number of settlers from the former colony had flocked to the site), Brewster continued to exercise strong and sensitive command. Soon Uncas became a close confidant of this son of a Pilgrim father. After the Pequot War, when Uncas's star was in the ascendant, he helped ensure that young Brewster was given the first grant of land in former Pequot country. It was into Brewster's ears that Uncas now poured out tales of Pequot unrest, which tales Brewster duly passed on to the nervous administrators at Fort Saybrook. Thus did the settlers come to believe that Connecticut's mightiest warriors were about to arise, and that the English must stand resolute in their demands. So whatever the noble Sassious had done to ease the tensions was undone by Uncas's connivings.

But John Oldham enjoyed good trading success and beneficial encounters as he sailed into and along the Connecticut River. Much satisfied with the business and the restoration of working relations, he safely crossed the sandbar at the mouth of the river and turned east, across Block Island Sound, toward home. Though the wind favored his passage, it blew gustily, with uncomfortable strength. Oldham therefore decided to ease off and take shelter in the tranquil coves of Block Island. Some twelve miles out to sea from the Rhode Island shore, this cliff-ringed, five-mile-long island, with its fragrant moors and fresh-water ponds, has long seemed a God-deposited bit of solid land in the midst of the confused waters. To sailors bound east or west along southern New England's weather-wracked, tide-swept coast, it has often made the difference between safe homecoming and disaster at sea. And although Oldham knew that the island's inhabitants had been pulled this way and that between loyalties to Narragansett and Pequot overlords, they now seemed securely committed to the Narragansetts. He must have assumed that the Block Islanders who paddled out to hail his heavily freighted pinnace would cause no harm.

The next part of the story is given to us by a trader named John Gallop, who had been heading west along the Sound, toward New Amsterdam. Battered by the rising headwinds of that day, he too had sought shelter at Block Island. But, spying natives paddling away from a vessel he recognized as Oldham's, and noting that the vessel was being ineptly handled and swept away from the harbor, he decided to investigate. As he neared, he saw no sign of Oldham himself; instead, the ship's rail was lined with natives. He concluded that piracy was afoot and determined to ram and board.

Resistance from the Block Islanders on board Oldham's vessel was fierce but ineffective in the face of Gallop's superior firearms and seamanship. When most of the natives had been shot or lost overboard, Gallop grappled and boarded the pinnace. There he found the hacked-up, still warm body of Oldham, the mighty merchant's severed head rolling nearby, his terrified sons huddled below decks. In larger terms, what Gallop had discovered was the casus belli. The dismemberment of a leading Bay trader was offensive enough to give the edgy Puritans the excuse they needed to turn a bit of local piracy (if that's what it was) into justification for an attack against their trade rivals. The war that had been simmering for two years would be brought on by that attack. The fact that the war was eventually won by the Puritans was regarded as a sign that all New England could be won by the sword . . . though not all historians agree that this contest, so seemingly isolated and confined, may rightly be called the prelude to the wide-spreading King Philip's War. Let us see.

Roger Williams from his exile at Providence was among those who, despite the popular outrage at Oldham's murder and the cry for a bloody revenge, attempted to narrow and contain the conflict. His first action was to clarify the point that, although the piratical Block Islanders were at that time supposedly under suzerainty of the Narragansetts, the dominant co-sachems Canonicus and Miantonomo (Canonicus's nephew) had nothing to do with Oldham's death. This theory seemed confirmed as correct when Miantonomo on his own initiative dispatched a task force of warriors to punish the Block Islanders and to make sure that Oldham's two sons were brought safely home to Boston. The only loose end in this neat resolution—which might, in a calmer social setting, have taken care of the entire unfortunate episode—was that one of the captured pirates somehow managed to escape his Narragansett captors and flee to Pequot country.

From the Boston perspective, Williams's peacemaking efforts and the innocence of his friends the Narragansett sachems were quite beside the point. Someone had to pay; the authority of the Bay had to be demonstrated. If the Narragansetts could not be blamed for Oldham's death and the disruption of trade, that obviously meant that the Pequots would be blamed (for in the view of Neal Salisbury and other commentators, the Bay was seeking any excuse for its humiliation of the Pequots). These were the people, after all, who had murdered John Stone and never atoned for his death, coming up with story after story to explain the incident. These were also the people who were jeopardizing the settlement of the valley, their threats and pressures keeping both the English newcomers and the native inhabitants at risk. And here they were sheltering one of John Oldham's murderers!

In August 1636, Massachusetts Bay authorities met in Boston to decide what to do about the crisis Oldham's death had created. Governor Henry Vane—an ingratiating twenty-four-year-old Englishman who was supposed to represent something of a new wind in the colony's governance—had already sent a special delegation to corroborate that Miantonomo and the Narragansetts were blameless. The wrath of the Bay was then directed toward the Pequots, almost exclusively; that is, the crisis was converted into a power play against those Algonquians who had presumed to control trade and land in the valley. Military orders were swiftly issued. First a sizable task force would storm Block Island and kill all males, capturing the women and children for later sale as slaves. Then the force would proceed to Pequot Harbor (the mouth of the Thames River), where the Pequots would be commanded at pain of death to surrender the murderers of Stone and Oldham. One thousand fathoms of wampum would be collected, and a number of Pequot children would be seized as hostages until all demands were met. If the Puritans had the might and skill to pull off this military strike despite the greater numbers and the fighting reputation of the Pequots, they would then succeed in reducing their native rival to a subsidiary role.

The mood in Boston was more furious than rational—the righteous vowing to slay the infidels. Appropriately, the commander selected for the expedition was former governor John Endicott, a fanatical Puritan known for the fierceness of his zeal. Once with naked sword he had attacked the British flag and hacked out the cross of St. George, not because it was British but because it was a cross. An illustration of that event by twentieth-century artist N. C. Wyeth shows the fire in the radical's eye, the militancy of his brand of Christianity. Staffed by four officers (one of whom, John Underhill, would prove to be the best chronicler of the assault), the force was to be manned by ninety volunteers. Because the Bay's treasury was at a dangerously low ebb, the men would not be paid directly but would be compensated by whatever spoils they might find along the way. As would be the case with King Philip's War in the next generation, there was a strong theme of potential personal profit behind the religious militarism of these bold Puritans.

But ironically, the expedition proved to be a financial failure; the men and officers had to be content with their ruination of the countryside and the killing of fourteen civilians and warriors. On Block Island, where the natives had greeted the force with salvos of arrows, then vanished into concealing swamps, only a few mats and baskets could be snatched by those who had hoped to find wampum. The two native villages—which had at first looked rather grand in comparison with those on the main-land but which were found to be empty and valueless—were laid waste by the disappointed raiders, the extensive cornfields destroyed.

When the expedition's personnel-laden pinnaces sailed on to Connecticut and anchored before Lion Gardiner's fort at Say-brook, this seasoned officer was appalled at the expedition's foolhardiness. He saw the Bay's assault on the Pequots as noth-ing more than an ignorant outsider's attempt to destroy what little stability he and his meager contingent had been able to achieve in the region. "You come hither to raise these wasps about my ears, and then you will take wing and flee away," he protested to Endicott. He had already been given a taste of the Pequots' mood: their messengers had requested that a trading mission be sent to Pequot Harbor from Fort Saybrook; but when the trading mission arrived, only a behind-the-hand warning from sachem Sassacus's wife prevented a deadly ambush from taking place. But when Gardiner understood that his cautious objections would not prevail against the zeal of Endicott, he decided to cooperate. Perhaps his men could be of critical as-sistance . . . and perhaps they could seize some badly needed corn for the imperiled garrison.

Sailing into the Pequot River at today's New London with their augmented force, the Puritan warriors were at first greeted by the traditional welcoming call of "What cheer, Netop?" (*Netop* being trader lingo for "friend"). But grim Puritan visages made it clear that trade was not intended. And as Endicott's pinnaces moved upriver, shoreside shouts changed to: "Are you angry with us, Englishmen? Have you come to kill us?"

Wading ashore, the Puritan warriors found themselves in the midst of swarming Pequots, men to the fore, women in the background. Marching to a defensible position atop a hill, the heavily armored volunteers formed in ranks as Endicott continued negotiations begun on the beach. He presented the Bay's ultimatum and awaited an answer from the elderly Pequot who had taken the spokesman's role. When that elder statesman went off to obtain the demanded response, the kneeling and standing Puritan soldiers nervously faced three hundred or more encircling braves, many of them unarmed. A few of the Pequots could speak trader-English and questioned soldiers they recognized from Fort Saybrook about the intention of this incursion.

The negotiations dragged on, the Pequots taking advantage of the delays to hide their possessions and to conceal their children. At length Endicott realized that the promised arrival of a ranking sachem who could respond to the ultimatum was simply another stall, and that the convening of a native court (called to hear the case of the Block Islander accused of being Oldham's murderer) was also a fiction. He had no choice now but to attack—though first he released the messengers who had arrived under a flag of truce, allowing them to return to their people. Then the command was given. In the ensuing exchange of arrows and bullets, before the natives scattered into the woods, one man was hit. A Pequot.

All watched in horror as Cutchamakin, a Massachusett who had come with the English expedition as interpreter, dashed suddenly forward and scalped the slain warrior before his companions could remove him from the field. This action, Lion Gardiner said in his description of the battle, was the deed of blood that made it impossible for the Pequots thereafter to turn aside from war. Yet the kind of war they may have had in mind was nothing like the European-style slaughter that would soon envelop them.

For all their brash intentions, Endicott and his volunteers accomplished little more than a terrorizing of the countryside, destroying the two villages that stood on either side of the Thames River. The officers, having been educated in European wars that the best way to quell savages (the Irish, for example) was to ruin their food supply, next ordered that the Pequots' ripening cornfields be leveled. But, with that, there was not much to be proud of: the Pequots had avoided battle and had surrendered to none of the demands. Nonetheless Boston, in the way of most hometowns, welcomed back the expedition's weary men as victorious heroes.

As for Lion Gardiner, on the way home his men did succeed in finding some ripened corn for their garrison. Gardiner also learned, when a band of Pequots attempted to prevent the taking of the corn, that a small, well-drilled group of musketeers could hold off a far larger number of natives. The trick, he noted, was to retrieve what arrows the natives had shot from where they'd fallen in the field, one by one, while maintaining covering fire. Eventually the arrowless natives had no choice but to retire.

The subsequent war, in the telling, became glorious. And the modern reader, relying on the fast-paced narratives left behind by Gardiner, Underhill, and other Puritans, is hurried on, never encouraged to ask anything but what happens next and how our boys are doing. The story—the Puritans' story—becomes all, as events take the place of reasoned judgment. Fortunately, today's researchers are succeeding in balancing that seductive scenario with bits and pieces of the Pequots' own story. Through rigorous fieldwork and with the support of Pequot descendants (most notably the Mashantucket Pequot Tribal Council), strands of archaeological evidence and oral tradition are being woven together. The native voice is being heard, with all its distinctiveness and authority.

For example, until very recently, one read that the Pequots, whose name means "the destroyers" or "man slayers," were an outcast, marauding tribe. They and the related Mohegans had originally dwelled, it was said, near the Hudson River. Then, sometime around 1590, they had been attacked by the Iroquois-allied Mohawks and, defeated, swept eastward across what would become Massachusetts and Connecticut to their final home on the Thames and nearby rivers. The split between the Pequots and the Mohegans developed later, according to this version, mostly induced by Uncas's actions. But that's not the whole story, it now appears. Excavations at Pequot sites under the direction of the University of Connecticut's Kevin McBride have established that in their daily lives the Pequots used an altogether different kind of ceramic vessel than that of the Mohegans. And the artifacts show that the Pequots had occupied their own villages for many centuries *before* the European-contact era or before joining the Mohegans. They had always been their own people, it appears.

Another part of the white-repeated myth of the Pequots was that, upon their invasion of eastern Connecticut, these people had fought their way through the Niantics and destructively divided them. Then the Eastern Niantics became allied with the Narragansetts and the Western with the Pequots. But more recent linguistic evidence indicates that the two groups of Niantics had always spoken quite different versions of the Algonquian tongue; they had been separate for many years, with

the long-established Pequots between them. The distinction
between the two Niantic groups would affect both the Pequot
and King Philip's wars.

Often the fresh information of the scholars working with
tribal historians has deep-cutting connotations. On the matter
of leadership for the war that followed Endicott's incursion, it
is possible now to learn much more about the Pequots' command. Thanks to the work of archaeologists and anthropologists, the sachem Sassacus, who led the Pequots in the war,
appears altogether different from the all-powerful ruler of a
"fierce, cruel, and warlike People" as portrayed by chronicler
Hubbard and his followers. For the work of the scientists has
concentrated on the special kind of rulership found among this
people and the independent responsibilities of male and female
leaders during the mid-seventeenth century.

From the physical organization of the discovered Pequot
villages—and, even more dramatically, from the three sizable
fortified centers that have been located (one of which was Fort
Mystic, a key position of the war)—analysts have concluded
that an effective and respected hierarchy must have existed to
organize the people so decisively. There were, apparently, several levels of sachems, twenty-six sachems at the time of the
war. Some had achieved that rank upon becoming leaders of
their respective villages; others claimed it by lineage. Some
were very powerful, others not. Sassacus must be seen, therefore, as but one among many in the command structure; as with
Philip a generation later, his functions were limited. And although the division of Pequot society into commoners and
nobility sounds as hierarchical as European society, with position determined by blood, other flexible factors counted here as
well. The size and the desires of the clan, the number of warriors a man had been able to collect under his command, and

the record of his meritorious deeds all contributed to his rank and command authority.

Among women, too, there were those "of esteeme," the records tell us. Their ownership of wigwams and other property, as well as their kinship in the lines of sachems, endowed them with considerable power. Indeed, Kevin McBride has concluded that the marriage pattern suggests matriliny. Although Sassacus, first son of the Dutch-slain Wopigwooit, succeeded to his father's title directly, at the end of the war there was a scramble for leadership among the ambitious survivors; they strove to take as wives the women of the slain sachems and thus to enhance their own claims. Uncas, already married to Sassacus's sister, now married one of Wopigwooit's wives, according to Roger Williams. Another would-be sachem, the Pequot who helped guide the English forces to his people's first major defeat, married Sassacus's mother. Thus did a new rulership of Pequots establish itself for the future, by the female connections.

It appears from the evidence (the twenty-six villages and the ratio of men to women) that just before the war there were between three thousand and four thousand Pequots living within a radius of twenty miles from the mouth of the Thames River. But the modern historians who scorn fixed boundaries as adequate definitions for native populations describe "Pequot Territory"—that is, the area in which lived most of the Pequots and the people closely related or in fealty to them—as extending far up the Thames and Mystic and Connecticut river valleys. Within that large territory's population, some eight or nine hundred men were trained as warriors, ready to rally to the Pequot cause.

From these recent researches, it becomes clear that the Pequots, far from being the monolithic savages portrayed in the Puritan narratives, were a complex and creative people, well established and profoundly aware of their position in the New England power struggle. Although their war with the Dutch to control the Connecticut River valley had not gone well in the early 1630s, and although their combat with the Narragansetts seemed never-ending, the Pequot warriors and their commanders held the central part of New England in a firm grip. Lion Gardiner said that they fought better than the Spaniards he had encountered in the Low Countries. In order to demonstrate to skeptics in Boston the power and effectiveness of Pequot bowmen, Gardiner sent along for their examination the legbone of a slaughtered soldier; the arrow had been driven straight through the bone. And the sturdiest "targets" (shields) of the English were dented and bashed by the natives' metal-tipped arrows.

Gardiner also recognized that the Pequots' canniness in the field was an important part of their excellence as warriors. As the summer of 1636 turned to autumn and the Pequots sought to avenge Endicott's attack on their river port by laying siege to Fort Saybrook, their favored tactic was to lie in wait in ambush, concealed merely by marsh grass if that was the only cover available. Some unsuspecting trader or a settler gathering hay would surely come forth. And the tactic worked again and again, no matter how on-guard the English might be: dozens of the coastal region's men, women, and children fell prey to the unseen hunters that fall. All traffic along the Connecticut River came under the threat of this constant, subtle, wearying mode of attack.

Or a skirmish would suddenly break out. Reporting one such dust-up in which he was personally involved, Gardiner wrote:

> Then the Indians shot two [of my men] that were in the reeds, and sought to get between us and home, but durst not come before us, but kept us in a half-moon, we retreating and exchanging many a shot, so that Thomas Hurlbut was shot almost through the thigh,

John Spencer in the back, into his kidneys, myself in the thigh, and two more were shot dead. But in our retreat I kept Hurlbut and Spencer still before us, we defending ourselves with our naked swords or else they would have taken us all alive.

Behind the Pequots' command structure and military capability lay a sophisticated understanding of the world around them and of the strategic situation in which they found themselves. Even before the war had burst upon them, they had had the foresight to plant extra cornfields in removed locations on Fisher's Island, Plum Island, and elsewhere.

Pequot diplomats had tried and not quite succeeded in bringing Massachusetts Bay into a commercial alliance. Now the native diplomats attempted an even more brilliant stroke: to repair the breach with the Narragansetts and form a common front against the English. New England's two mightiest people would then be set against the Puritans, who stood alone and alienated from their own king's armies. The combined Algonquians would far outnumber the English forces.

The Pequot ambassadors must have recognized the great difficulties of overcoming decades of hostility with the Narragansetts. But they hoped to accomplish their purpose by stressing three themes: that the English had always been treacherous, having insisted on terms for the 1634 treaty that were obviously unrealistic and punitive; that the English were making even more outrageous demands on native populations (now one thousand fathoms of wampum!); and that the English hunger for land and trade would soon drive the original inhabitants from their rightful territories. This was clearly the time when joint action must be taken, before it was too late.

Rumors of these diplomatic efforts reached the ears of Bay authorities through the never-ceasing intelligences of Roger Williams. He reported that the Pequots, having terminated

their battles with the Narragansetts, were on the point of forming a grand alliance with them. Swiftly the Bay authorities sent
messages back to Williams (whom only the year before they had
cast out of their midst), beseeching him to do whatever he
could against the Pequots' plan, for the sake of all New England. He must somehow dissuade the Narragansetts from joining the enemy. The Bay authorities' apprehension was doubled
by the fact that this war—brought on not so much by the
murders of Stone and Oldham as by the recklessness of Endicott's expedition—was being lost at that time in the marshes of
Connecticut. For the already strong Pequots to be joined by the
massed Narragansetts would surely spell disaster.

Called upon to save the day by neutralizing the Narragansetts, Roger Williams responded with characteristic acumen.
Indeed he may be correct in judging that his fast action at the
end of September was the key contribution to ultimate victory
in the war. As he recounted the events in a later letter to
Connecticut's chief soldier, John Mason:

> Upon letter received from Governor and Council in Boston, re-
> questing me to use my utmost and speediest endeavors to break and
> hinder the league labored for by the Pequots against the Mohegans
> [Uncas's pro-English forces], and the Pequots against the English
> . . . the Lord helped me immediately to put my life in my hand,
> and, scarce acquainting my wife, to ship myself, all alone in a poor
> canoe, and to cut through a stormy wind, with great seas, every
> minute in hazard of life, to the sachem's house [Canonicus's capital
> village on Narragansett Bay's western shore]. Three days and nights
> my business forced me to lodge and mix with the bloody Pequot
> ambassadors whose hands and arms, methought, wreaked with the
> blood of my countrymen, murdered and massacred by them on the
> Connecticut River, and from whom I could not but nightly look for
> their bloody knives at my throat also.

Given Williams's canoeing skill, as well as his fluency and his status as a man of truth among the Narragansetts, the melodramatic story merits belief. It is also worth looking at as a turning point in American history, not merely because of the preacher-trader's physical heroism but also because of his success in negotiating the best solution for a desperately dangerous situation. He was seeking to hold his and the Narragansetts' trading world together in the name of ongoing peace. If this meant stopping the enraged Pequots, that was the first and necessary step.

The next step toward peace would have to be taken by the Bay's council. And Governor Henry Vane—who had agreed to the Endicott mission only upon the council's pressure and after his own investigation of the circumstances—seemed of a mood to take that step. He was most reluctant to be dragged into a widened war, if only because of the horrific expense. With marked displeasure he heard a petition of the council on December 13, 1636, saying that Massachusetts Bay should formally declare war against the Pequots.

Unfortunately for his well-reasoned, pacifistic position, the young governor was a known partisan of the troublesome Anne Hutchinson. Her very name had already become synonymous with antinomianism—the heretical belief that Christians did not need to heed the moral laws of the civil and church authorities. The situation of that independent-minded mother of four (pregnant with her fifth child) was presented with vivid prejudice by historian John Fiske:

> In a strong and complex society the teachings of Mrs. Hutchinson would have awakened but a languid speculative interest, or perhaps would have passed by unheeded. In the simple society of Massachusetts in 1636, physically weak and as yet struggling for very

existence, the practical effect of [her] teachings may well have been deemed politically dangerous. When things came to such a pass that the forces of the colony were mustered for an Indian campaign and the men of Boston were ready to shirk the service because they suspected their chaplain to be "under a covenant of works" [an adherent of the doctrine that good works—in addition to faith— are necessary for salvation; one of Hutchinson's accusations], it was naturally thought to be high time to put Mrs. Hutchinson down.

Puritans also noted with great displeasure that, in some of the discussion groups led by Anne Hutchinson, men were being instructed by women—a threat to God's order of things.

The Reverend John Cotton, the clergyman whom the emigrating Hutchinson family had followed from England to the New World, at first did what he could to defend his radical female friend. But when her brother-in-law, the antinomian-tainted preacher John Wheelwright, delivered a sermon that was adjudged seditious, Cotton began withdrawing his support from this disruptive element. It became a classic face-off between the perceived needs of the state and individual freedoms.

The state won. In an election following Wheelwright's sermon, Anne Hutchinson's most highly placed backer, Governor Vane, was removed from office, replaced by the solidly orthodox and generally bellicose John Winthrop, Sr. Vane, defeated, hastened back to England—but not before making the additional gaffe of suggesting that he might appeal the antinomians' cause to his father's friend, the king. With this young upstart of an ex-governor out of the way, there was now no doubt that the war would be pursued with fire and sword.

While affairs in Boston expressed themselves in religious and political terms, on the Connecticut frontier they were unmistakably racial. The settlers at Pyquag (Wethersfield) had made certain agreements, it will be remembered, with the impoverished River Indian sachem who had sold land to them and their leader, John Oldham. That sachem, Sequassen, had proceeded to build his house on the plot reserved for him, content in the thought that he was safe here, among the English, from any Pequot raiders. But, perhaps because these settlers from Watertown were a mixed lot (not an organized church, as in most other Connecticut towns), they were disrespectful of any treaty and contemptuous of any native in their midst.

Insults led to petty quarrels, then to a real altercation. Sequassen was summarily driven out of town—both a breaking of the agreement and a blow to his prestige. Seeking revenge, he turned to his former antagonists, the Pequots. Responding in force, a war party of Pequots attacked Wethersfield, slaying six men and three women, killing also twenty cows and a horse, and capturing two girls. Even the Bay's new governor, John Winthrop, in reviewing the aggrieved sachem's treatment, had to call the fierce and bloody Pequot attack "a just war." But it was not yet a war, really; it would become one only if the Puritans insisted on making it one.

The outbreak at Wethersfield occurred in April 1637, only a few weeks after the costly siege at Fort Saybrook had been relieved by two small forces of private citizens sent from Hartford and Boston in response to Gardiner's anguished pleas. Briefly, with the siege raised, the ambushes and tortures eased, and the Bay's declaration of war not yet put into effect, it looked for a moment as if a sensible parley with the Pequots might succeed in bringing the quarrel to a halt. But no one seemed to have sufficient political determination to make that happen. With the bleak news from Wethersfield on everyone's lips, and with both sides accusing the other of killing women and children (considered a taunt of cowardice), the meeting before the walls of Fort Saybrook ended in another angry exchange of gunfire.

By this month of April 1637, Massachusetts Bay was sufficiently pulled together politically to carry out the council's order and muster a sizable army of 160 men for a full-scale war. Lashed by criticism from Connecticut that the Endicott expedition had done nothing but start a conflict and run away, the Bay Colony's Puritans determined to complete what they had begun. But Hartford was not about to let the conquest of Connecticut lands be carried out by another colony; on May 1, Hartford, too, called for the gathering of an official colonial army of 90 men.

Given their fragile conditions, it might seem that Boston and Hartford were audacious and imprudent to organize armies against the masterful Pequots. The General Court at Hartford represented but a few hundred people who had barely put the roofs over their new cabins; the men and women who had followed Thomas Hooker had been in the valley for less than a year. With the exception of a few trained soldiers like John Mason—who, along with Gardiner, had served in England's battles in the Low Countries and was now, at thirty-seven, a strapping-tall, seasoned campaigner—the men in Hartford's army were but middle-class farmers, militiamen determined to get home as soon as possible. And the Bay Colony, for all its bluster and Puritanical ferocity and desire for booty, had learned from Endicott and Gardiner the formidable nature of the enemy. Governor Winthrop sought what help he could get from Plymouth, saying that the Pilgrims should recognize that all Indians were now a "common Enimie." But Plymouth balked at joining in the war, pleading impoverishment. So what secret weapon did the Puritans possess that made them think they could win?

Beside the oft-given answers of superior weaponry and a "moral imperative," another possible explanation may lie in a dynamic battle plan which Roger Williams had been given by the Pequot-hating Narragansetts. Even before the ousting of Governor Vane, Williams had given this plan to the Bay council; it was based on the Narragansetts' keen understanding of the countryside and of the Pequot forts' dispositions. Modern analysts believe that it was with this plan in mind that, on May 20, Governor Winthrop committed his troops to action.

First a small strike force under Daniel Patrick would proceed through friendly Narragansett country to destroy Pequot cornfields and supply lines; then Patrick's 40 men would prepare to swing west and strike the enemy at the fortified village now known as Fort Mystic. A larger force of 160 men would follow on Patrick's heels to carry the burden of the developing war.

Even as the Bay force was heading south, the Connecticut collection of militiamen was moving downriver, commanded by John Mason. With them came nearly one hundred Mohegans and River Indians under the leadership of Uncas, as eager to demonstrate his fighting support of the English cause as he was determined to secure his claim as sachem. So afire were the Mohegans to strike at the Pequots that, when Mason's river shallops grounded out in the shallows, the impatient natives charged ahead by land. On their way to the rally point at Fort Saybrook they ambushed and annihilated a band of Pequot warriors.

Nonetheless, Lion Gardiner was suspicious of these native allies. Could they be trusted in battle? To demonstrate their dependability, Uncas and his men accepted the challenge of tackling a dangerous group of Pequots at Bass River. After demolishing the encampment and killing four Pequots, Uncas returned with one captive. The issue of loyalty apparently settled, the English leaders not only permitted the Mohegans to torture the captive, but they joined in the entertainment, tearing the man limb from limb in the European manner.

In the company of the Bay Colony's John Underhill (who had arrived at Fort Saybrook earlier to help relieve the siege), Gardiner and Mason then reviewed the Narragansetts' battle plan for a knockout blow against the Pequots' most sensitive fortification. The plan called for the attackers to swing in from the east. This meant that Connecticut's forces would have to disobey their orders to strike the enemy directly at Pequot Harbor; they would have to sail past the Thames into Narragansett Bay where they would join with Patrick and hit the Pequots from their blind side. Though not all Connecticut officers agreed on the wisdom of the east-to-west strike, the army's chaplain, who had "spent the night in prayer," confirmed in the morning that God favored the roundabout maneuver—of which Mason had become a hearty backer. Thus were they committed.

Setting sail and catching the westerly wind, Mason's shallops surged swiftly eastward, arriving near Point Judith "in brilliant moonlight" on May 20, 1637. Captain Daniel Patrick from Massachusetts Bay rendezvoused with the Connecticut force soon thereafter. But immediately a controversy between the two colonies' leaders sprang up. For some reason, Patrick determined not to join Mason and Underhill in their swift strike against the Pequot position; he would go around to Pequot Harbor instead. This left seventy-seven Englishmen to march against the enemy, plus Uncas's ancillaries.

Miantonomo and Canonicus, the Narragansett sachems, into

whose territories the attacking force had come, approved without reservation the assault on their traditional enemies. But Miantonomo expressed reservations about the paltry number of English soldiers, given the great size of the Pequot army and the strength of the Pequot fortifications. Having made the point, he added his two hundred men to Mason's and Underhill's total. Less cooperative were the Eastern Niantics, possessors of the land immediately to the west, between the Narragansetts and the Pequots. Puritan narrators wrote that the Niantics' sachem, Ninigret I, refused to let the Englishmen camp in his village for the night. Another more likely version is that the English officers distrusted this avowed neutral and put his village under guard so as to prevent anyone from slipping out and warning the Pequots of the surprise attack. The next morning (May 24) Mason and Underhill marched farther west, finally reaching the eastern bank of the Mystic River. Now only two miles remained between them and Fort Mystic.

Gradually the accompanying Narragansetts drifted away from the English-led force, intimidated by the nearness of the massed Pequot warriors. They also held the Pequots' field commander Sassacus in special respect, saying that "he was [like] a God [and that] nobody could kill him." Uncas, however, remained constant to the cause, as did two renegade Pequots who gave Mason precise instructions about the strength and design of Fort Mystic, which stood nearby, atop a hill that loomed against the horizon. Though this was not where Sassacus would be found— he remained at Weinshauks, a fort some two miles farther west—Mason's resolve was to strike fast and hard, at the most easily reached objective. Both the weariness of his militiamen and the ever-increasing danger of alerting the entire Pequot army forced this decision upon him.

A fundamental part of the battle plan had been that the

English should attack by surprise at night, when their armor would not reflect the gleam of the sun. So Mason and Underhill halted before the fort, waiting for darkness to cover them. Throughout that long night sentinels crept up the slope, conning the Pequots' position and reporting singing and other signs of a celebratory party. Scouts found many traces of recently cleaned fish, which helped show the great numbers in attendance. This feast was apparently being held to hail the news that the English attackers had sailed away to the east. The Narragansetts had, so it seemed, been right in thinking that the roundabout plan of battle would confuse the Pequot leadership.

The ultimate fight at Fort Mystic, memorialized in Puritan literature and proclaimed by such monuments as the 1889 statue of Mason in West Mystic, has been regarded as the essential triumph that saved New England for future generations. The brief battle has been presented as a miracle: so few, so victorious. In recent times the revisionists have set that invincible, nationalistic interpretation on its ear. They maintained that the Puritans, having been informed that the fortified village at Mystic contained mostly women and children, with only a handful of Pequot warriors, knowingly and ruthlessly carried out the mass slaughter of the innocent residents despite the commandment of the Narragansetts that noncombatants be spared (a typical Algonquian provision). But modern social scientists urge us to reconsider the indictment.

Fortunately the exact site of the battle, where Mason and Underhill attacked just before daybreak on May 25, 1637, was discovered 350 years later, in 1987. With only a shadow of remaining doubt, evidence indicated that a two-acre plot atop an elevation known as Pequot Hill must be the historic location. Though archaeological investigations could not be complete or exhaustive because of centuries-long farming and occupation of the site, excavators found a number of revealing artifacts. From them it was easy to conclude that this commanding location, with its unblocked views to the west and south, had been crowded with a dense and carefully laid out community. As many as sixty or seventy dwellings had been constructed within the encircling walls; the commanders had planned a lofty encircling palisade and ordered it built according to the standards of the most rigorous engineers. They had apparently assumed that the women (whose domestic ceramics may be pieced together and studied from available shards) would provide necessary support for life within this essentially military installation. So the scholars suggest that some of the sting be taken out of the charge that the Puritans attacked a village of innocents.

Professor Kevin McBride's researchers also consulted local records to gain a historical perspective of the location. Their survey states:

> In 1875 Horace Clift reported that his father told him about a circular embankment several rods across a field on the summit of Pequot Hill, and that charred wood, corroded bullets and Indian relics were found whenever any plowing was done.

An available contemporary description of the fort is the woodcut that accompanied John Underhill's narrative of the Pequot War. This curiously stylized and symmetrical rendition looks almost too neat to be real. It is often used as an illustration by modern writers to show how quaint life and times were in the seventeenth century. But, on closer examination, it sets forth quite accurately what eyewitnesses had to say about the fort and its destruction.

Philip Vincent, a chronicler of the day, left perhaps the best architectural description of the fort. He said it contained

> at least two acres of ground. Here they pitch, close together as they can, young trees and half trees, as thick as a man's thigh or the calf of his leg. Ten or twelve foot high they are above the ground, and within rammed three foot deep with underminning, the earth being cast up for their better shelter against the enemy's dischargements. Between these palisadoes are divers loopholes. . . . The door for the most part is entered sideways, which they stop with boughs or bushes.

Those narrow and overlapping entrances can be seen in Underhill's sketch; it was through them that he (to the south) and Mason (to the north) entered with their tiny squads, according to plan. They surely knew, from the scouts' reports and from what their own eyes told them, that this was indeed an awesome fortification. Their only allies were the darkness and the Pequots' revelries of the preceding night.

Suddenly a dog barked, alerting the Pequot sentries. *"Owanus! Owanus!"* ("Englishmen! Englishmen!") they called. Mason and his sixteen soldiers, forcing their way through the fort's brush-blocked gate, nonetheless succeeded in taking the Pequots by surprise. They engaged a number of awakened inhabitants at close quarters, fighting their way down the narrow streets between the crowded "wigwams." But as the battle wore on and the fury of the Pequots rose ever higher, the English warriors began to tire in the face of stiff resistance.

Matters were going no better at the other end of the fort where Underhill and his men had broken through the entrance barricade. For here also the Pequots had refused to panic or scatter in the face of the English assault; as they fought back, their defense grew increasingly well organized. Underhill wrote of the fight as follows: "Most courageously these Pequots behaved themselves. But, seeing the fort was too hot for us, we devised a way how we might save ourselves and prejudice them." That desperate way, devised in fact by Mason, was to set the fortified community ablaze. Grabbing a firebrand from one of the wigwams along the street, he ordered his men to put all the nearby dwellings to the torch, moving in the windward direction, along the fort's northeast side. When Underhill, on his side, saw the smoke and understood the improvised tactic, his squad set afire the mats and rushes of wigwams in their sector. Soon a wind-whirled conflagration, rolling in on itself from two directions, consumed the entire village.

What then took place—the incineration of hundreds of inhabitants and the shooting of hundreds more who tried to escape—was both a human horror and, again, an abrogation of the Narragansetts' stipulation that women and children should not be harmed. *"Mach it! Mach it!"* ("Enough! Enough!") cried the Puritans' Algonquian allies, urging that the slaughter cease. But the fire continued to rage and, the English having withdrawn through the gates, the fleeing Pequots were ceaselessly cut down by the encircling rings of soldiers.

In the years immediately following the massacre, the Puritans sought excuses for their uncivilized, un-Christian behavior by claiming that this was the will of God. Underhill himself fell back on biblical references, concluding that "we had sufficient light from the word of God for our proceedings." And in this nearly contemporaneous account of the event, Plymouth's literary governor William Bradford somehow translated the event into a kind of joyous spiritual orgy:

> It was a fearful sight to see them thus frying in the fire and the streams of blood quenching the same, and horrible was the stink and scent thereof; but the victory seemed a sweet sacrifice, and

they gave praise thereof to God, who had wrought so wonderfully for them, thus to enclose their enemies in their hands and give them so speedy a victory over so proud and insulting an enemy.

Putting its manpower where its admiration lay, Plymouth then (the news of the victory having spurred hopes of total conquest) contributed thirty men to the campaign.

Later, when New England's historians had turned from God's will to Darwinism for their rationales of extinction, others took the action at Fort Mystic to be a splendid example of the way the world works. In his *Beginnings of New England*, John Fiske wrote:

> As a matter of practical policy, the annihilation of the Pequots can be condemned only by those who read history so incorrectly as to suppose that savages, whose business it is to torture and slay, can always be dealt with according to the methods in use between civilized peoples. A mighty nation like the United States is in honor bound to treat the red man with scrupulous justice and refrain from cruelty in punishing his delinquencies. But if the founders of Connecticut, in confronting a danger which threatened their very existence, struck with savage fierceness, we cannot blame them. The world is so made that it is only in that way that the higher races have been able to preserve themselves and carry on their progressive work.

Strangely, as the Puritan chroniclers and the nationalistic historians of later years retold the tale of the massacre, they chose to forget that the decision to put Fort Mystic to the torch had occurred not as a part of any master plan but as a matter of life-saving necessity. They preferred to see the war as all of a piece, ordained. But in fact the campaign had been launched by Boston and Hartford politicians for their own wild reasons, and the key episode at Fort Mystic had taken place as a kind of mistake, when the situation got out of hand. This ghastly victory gave no one at the immediate moment a sense of completion or satisfaction. With fresh memories of that single hour of carnage, Underhill wrote:

> Grat and doleful was the bloody sight in the view of young soldiers that never had been in war, to see so many souls lie gasping on the ground, so thick in some places, that you could hardly pass along.

Great and doleful indeed, with between five and seven hundred Pequots slaughtered and with scores of Englishmen exhausted or incapacitated. Though it was later claimed that but two of the English soldiers were killed, twenty of the seventy-seven were wounded; it was stated at the time that but a few dozen Englishmen survived unscathed.

What would history be like if the book were written by these horrified observers, then closed and not amended, one wonders? John Mason himself mused: "History most properly is a Declaration of Things that are done by those that were present at the doing of them." Perhaps, with only those pages in the book, war would seem less worthy, its workings less perfect; annihilation not ordained.

But back to the events of late May 1637. In addition to the awful carnage around them, Mason and Underhill faced immediate danger from the aroused Pequot army. From the other major Pequot fort, Weinshauks (at what is now called Fort Hill, above Noank, Connecticut), warriors rushed forth led by Sassacus, seeking to catch the westward-withdrawing Englishmen and their allies before they could attain the shores of the Thames River. There their own vessels and Patrick's forces awaited them.

Though exhausted from the battle, Mason's and Underhill's men still had the advantage of firearms. Responding to their officers' orders even as the Pequots fell upon them, the stronger survivors formed ranks and held off the attackers while the weaker struggled on to the river. Finally, with the entire English force in a defensive position on the riverbank, Underhill ordered the wounded carried on board the vessels for the voyage home. Mason and Patrick would march overland to Fort Saybrook, accompanied by Uncas's Mohegans and the Narragansetts who had fought by their side. This overland contingent, recovered from the battle, succeeded in routing the Western Niantics on the way through their territory and in brushing aside whatever bands of Pequots sought to impede their victorious march home.

As a part of the developing Puritan myth, traditional writers gave the impression that the Pequots were immediately liquidated by that one swift blow of the righteous sword at Fort Mystic. And, thus gone, who could grieve them? John William deForest, the nineteenth-century authority on Connecticut's Indians, wrote that, in this one event, the Pequots' "own barbarity had destroyed them." But in reality, a brutal and brutalizing campaign of three months was required for the English to overcome the Pequot warriors (and even then, and despite other attempts, they could not destroy this people). In the course of that summertime campaign in 1637, it seemed that something more savage than normal had seized the Puritan mind: a rush of vengeance, a passion for extermination; the kind of killing and enslaving associated with only the most barbaric of nations. One might also say that that was the time when New Englanders permanently concluded they should conquer the land they perceived to be theirs.

Among the Pequots, there was both resolve and despair. At the council meeting held immediately after the massacre, Sassacus received heavy criticism from the other sachems for the quality of his leadership. But though some dissenters chose to take refuge among the Montauks and others with the Narragansetts, Sassacus was able to persuade a large number to fight westward with him, aiming for Mohawk country. With eighty warriors and their families, he fast-marched to the Connecticut River, killing the English encountered on the way. Settlements along the shore braced for a storm of savagery, dreading most of all the possible alliance of the Pequots and the Mohawks.

Hartford and Boston, their rivalry intensified by imminent victory, threw all available manpower into the struggle for Connecticut lands. The residents of the three tiny river towns (Wethersfield, Windsor, and Springfield) managed to muster an additional force of 40 men, under the leadership of the tireless John Mason. It will be remembered that Massachusetts, back in April, had authorized a second, larger force to be sent to Connecticut upon Patrick's heels. This well-equipped group of 120 men, under the command of Israel Stoughton, now hurried south and west in pursuit of the embattled Pequots.

When Stoughton arrived at Pequot Harbor toward the middle of June, he was greeted by the news that one part of the Pequot community had elected to remain behind, avoiding the uncertainties of flight to the west. The men, women, and children had taken refuge in a swamp, hopeful perhaps that the English had had enough of slaughter. But after Stoughton's men had surrounded the swamp and he had demanded total surrender, the Pequots found how prisoners of war would henceforth be treated. First the men, numbering twenty-eight, were trussed up and led aboard one of the expedition's vessels for summary execution, the bodies dumped over the side. Then the women and children were examined and ranked for their worth as slaves.

Stoughton's letter of transmittal to Governor Winthrop tells the tale:

> By this pinnace you shall receive 48 or 50 women and children [he had already given many other captives to the Narragansetts], unless there stay any here to be helpful, etc., concerning which there is one, that is the fairest and the largest that I saw amongst them, to whom I have given a coat to cloathe her. It is my desire to have her for a servant, if it may stand to your liking, otherwise not. There is a little squaw that Stewart Calacot desires, to whom he has given a coat. Lieutenant Davenport desires one, to wit, a small one that hath stroaks upon her stummack, thus !!!

Slavery, a very profitable business (made all the more disgusting by Stoughton's attitude toward it), was tending to become another driving force behind the continuation of the war.

And along with slavery went further slaughter. At one stopping point in their westward flight along the coast, in a Quinnipiac swamp (near New Haven), a huddled group of Pequot women and children fell under the merciless guns of the pursuers. Chroniclers report that here the English muskets were specially loaded with ten or twelve balls, so as to expedite the mass execution.

The penultimate struggle of the fleeing Pequots took place as far west as Fairfield, where the people under Sassacus had taken refuge in yet another swamp. In a seemingly charitable gesture, the English sent in an interpreter to urge the noncombatants to come forth. Some two hundred of them responded to the offer, most of them later sold into slavery; but Sassacus's eighty skilled warriors remained with him. Fighting against the encircling might of a superior English force, the Pequots repeatedly attempted to break out. And at last they succeeded, with Sassacus himself eluding capture. It had been a major engagement, in which the Pequots again proved their martial skills. Appraising the unimpressive showing of the English force, Mason grumbled: "Captain Stoughton looked more for profit arising from sale of prisoners and other spoils of war, than he did for Indians to fight against."

Yet the end of the war came only when Sassacus, fleeing farther west with a cadre of twenty braves, finally reached the lands of the Mohawks. Though his plea for alliance may have been considered by the Mohawk council and his offer of five hundred fathoms of wampum taken under advisement, the Mohawks were too firmly committed to their own course of integration with the European trading nations to pay much attention to the Algonquian refugees. They killed Sassacus and his party without much hesitation, sending the scalps to Boston as evidence of the Mohawks' worthiness as partners in the international world of commerce.

In Boston, the bells rang. And the victory celebrations that then took place saluted not just the profitable triumph over the Pequots but also the simultaneous defeat of the liberally inclined antinomians and their pacifistic tendencies. Now the myths of the totally right, totally exclusive, and totally invincible Puritans could claim the New England soul. If the Pequot War itself did not twist New England toward native conquest, then the tribal memory of the war did.

Yet, in a strange way, the Pequot War, rather than wrecking the bicultural society that had been building before 1636, confirmed it and gave it solidity. With the Pequots out of the way (more or less) and power clearly in the hands of Massachusetts Bay, the "golden age" of wampum and furs could flower to its full splendor. The pragmatic historian Samuel Eliot Morison, brushing aside the brutalities of the war as typical of the time, wrote with satisfaction that the Pequot War had ensured peace and stability in New England for "nigh forty years." But a reconsideration of the terms of that peace (not to speak of the immorality of the war) shows that no sound political foundation for the postwar society had truly been laid. This war would beget further war, specifically that in the name of King Philip.

Among the shaky elements in the peace settlement for the Pequot War was the issue of how the native peoples would henceforth be regarded. Would they now be treated more equitably? No. Or would one or another of them, in the Pequots' absence, be given a role of dominance? Possible candidates for that position were the Mohegans and the Narragansetts, both of whom had fought on England's side. From the terms of the Treaty of Hartford (September 21, 1638) it appeared that both groups would be held in equal respect: the two hundred male Pequot captives and their people, whose destinies were determined by this war-concluding treaty, were divided almost evenly between the two native allies, swelling the respective armies and work forces. But Uncas, ambitious as ever and close to the sources of Puritan power, saw opportunities for a greater price. He awaited the time when he and the Mohegans could take the Narragansetts' share of the victory as well.

That time came but five years after the treaty (though the fulfillment of Uncas's scheme would have to wait until King Philip's War). Miantonomo, who became great sachem of the Narragansetts upon the death of his uncle Canonicus, had been summoned to Boston in the matter of land sales to a troublesome radical settler named Thomas Gorton. Two lesser Narragansett sachems had complained that Miantonomo had pressured them to sell the land—a small squabble but one that the Bay's authorities chose to take seriously. For them any land settlement issue was to be given serious consideration, particularly when it might involve an extension of the Bay's land resources. While Miantonomo was off on the humiliating mission of explaining his position and expressing his continuing loyalty to the English, Uncas saw that the time had come to strike provocatively at the Narragansetts.

Predictably, Miantonomo replied by preparing for war when he returned from the north. And, in equipping himself, he received a piece of armor from his friends the Gorton colonists, who wished him success. The battle took place on the Great Plain, in present-day Norwich, Connecticut. Uncas not only commanded his forces with cleverness and success, he also captured the routed Miantonomo—who could not flee with his usual swiftness because of the heavy armor on his back.

It must be said that Miantonomo, no less than Uncas, had been striving for postwar leadership, with his own agenda. Indeed, he had harbored thoughts of bringing all New England's Algonquian groups together in one federation. (In a curiously parallel move, the orthodox Puritan leaders succeeded at the same time [1643] in pulling together the exclusive four-colony federation known as the Council of New England.) When before his capture Miantonomo addressed the Algonquians on Long Island on the subject of native unity, his words, fortunately, were recorded (by Lion Gardiner, who had heard of them secondhand). The words live on both as proofs of one sachem's eloquence and as evidence of what was happening to native Americans in the wake of the Pequot War.

Miantonomo said to his neighboring Algonquians

> . . . you know our fathers had plenty of deer and skins, our plains were full of fish and fowl. But these English having gotten our land, they with scythes cut down the grass and with axes fell the trees. Their cows and horses eat the grass; their hogs spoil our clam banks; and we shall all be starved.

Make common cause, he urged, before all is ruined. These people with whom we are now associating ourselves will be the end of us.

Despite his eloquence, Miantonomo could get no fair jury when he was Uncas's opponent and prisoner. First Uncas took him to Hartford, making much of the ancient Algonquian tradition that the victor is entitled to slay the vanquished. For the reigning clergyman Thomas Hooker and the Hartford leadership, that proposition was morally disturbing; they therefore referred the case to Boston and to the first meeting of the New England Council, with its assembled clergy. When a discreet go-ahead was rendered as the verdict, Uncas went contentedly off on the trail home, understanding that he could kill Miantonomo en route (monitors accompanied him to make sure there would be no torture). According to legend, the execution took place at a clearing in the northern Connecticut woods known as Sachem's Plain: here, on a signal, one of Uncas's warriors buried his tomahawk in Miantonomo's skull. The Narragansett sachem having been slain, Uncas "cut a warm slice from the shoulder and greedily devoured it, declaring that the flesh of his enemy was the sweetest of meat and gave strength to his heart."

Understandably, the Narragansett people rose up in arms, formal warfare with Massachusetts being declared in 1645. But again the gentle offices of Roger Williams prevailed. He was able to persuade all parties that the greater interests of all would be served if peace were given another chance. Additionally, other less idealistic forces for peace were also seeking to stabilize the postwar world. As remarked by Samuel Eliot Morison and other historians, it appeared that the tensions of the commercial world in which New England found itself had been eased by the elimination of the Pequots. Perhaps the inner hostilities and the racial antagonisms could also be eased.

For example, one Richard Smith, a trader from Narragansett Bay associated with Roger Williams, strove with all his might to keep the respective partners in the trading world pulling to-gether for mutual profit. He maintained an office in New Am-sterdam and from there arranged for exchanges between the wampum-producing natives along New England's southern sea-coasts and the mighty Iroquois up the Hudson. It was the con-tinuing business of trade goods for wampum and wampum for furs, the producers and distributors linked in a precapitalistic system. With more tact and understanding than John Oldham, he was determined to keep New England working together in all its parts.

Furthermore, Massachusetts Bay became less aggressive. The stream of new wealth that had come with wave after wave of land-seeking immigrants dried to a dribble when, with the Cromwellian revolution in England, Protestant Englishmen found fewer reasons to leave home. Indeed, there was even a bit of spiritual uncertainty in Boston: would God's will perhaps be worked out not in the "Citty on the Hill" but in Cromwell's Commonwealth?

Global historians remind us that there were even larger forces of stabilization at work. The Iroquois of the Five Nations, hav-ing conquered the Hurons and extended their sway over the lands and waterways of the west, now threatened to take an even more dominant role in the destiny of the New World. The Iroquois raids disrupted both the native populations and the European settlers of New France and New England; now was not the time for the Puritans to stir up new difficulties with the natives.

In 1650, the very year of a second treaty session convened at Hartford—this one called to revise the borderline between New England and New Holland—a French Jesuit diplomat appeared in Boston. Overcoming mutual antipathies, Father Gabriel Dreuillettes made a proposal that commanded respect: an alliance of New France and New England, including the latter's Algonquian allies, against the threatening Iroquois. Now that Massachusetts Bay seemed to have overcome some of its internal problems—meaning the Pequot hostilities and the embarrassment with the Narragansetts—were the Puritans not ready for such a combined thrust? Did they not wish to claim the interior of the continent along with the French? The most attractive argument of all was that the beavers, which seemed to be diminishing in the East, were still thriving in western waters.

The Algonquians were particularly attracted by Dreuillettes's proposal. That winter four of the native and allied peoples in the northern and western territories of New England—the Pennacooks, Squakheags, Pocumtucks, and Mahicans—held a crucial conference to determine whether to go to war against the Iroquois on the European side, as proposed. The Squakheags, some of whose villages extended northward from William Pynchon's Connecticut River settlement at Springfield, came up with a positive verdict: the war that would secure New England against the Mohawks and their Iroquois allies should be pursued.

But Massachusetts Bay declined. There were less expensive and more profitable ways of bringing the Iroquois to the table than by war. And a strengthened alliance *with* the Iroquois might even work better: an alliance turned *against* the French, who clearly represented a worse devil, the pope himself. Furthermore, with the situation in England as delicate as it was at that moment—Cromwell's revolution had grown more conservative and Parliament was revoking colonial charters—now was not the time to take international risks.

Plymouth, to some small degree, was included in these discussions of the mid-1600s. But the time had passed when, as used to be said, "the Plymouth saddle rides the Bay mare." Nor did Roger Williams, left out of the New England Council and contending with new varieties of settlers in Rhode Island, exercise much power in the region. Both colonies, along with the proto-colonies in New Hampshire and Maine, seemed to be acceding to the stabilizing rule of the Puritans.

Suddenly, however, a new generation of ambitious and sophisticated Pilgrims began to assert themselves. They demanded and won from the United Colonies the rights to extensive territories on either side of the Kennebec River, south of the historic trading post that had been established at the site of present-day Augusta, Maine (originally called Cushenoc), in 1629. They would not let this post be overridden by settlers from the Bay, as had happened to them at Windsor. Furthermore, as they noted more and more Bay settlers streaming into the former Pequot territories in Connecticut, they too sought ways to enlarge their land holdings to the west. And if those gains could only be made by the sword . . . that seemed to be what destiny ordained.

Josiah Winslow was the eldest son of Plymouth's most able governor; for him, any diminution of the Old Colony (as Plymouth came to be called) was unacceptable. He revered his distinguished father and persuaded him to sit for a portrait (which still remains); he respected both the history and the potential of the colony. With the death of Myles Standish, the military affairs of the colony—and what was not military in a changing and competitive world?—fell increasingly into the hands of young Josiah. And first on his docket was the treaty, the long-lasting treaty of friendship and peace between the Pokanokets and Plymouth. For Massasoit (Ousamequin) had died in 1661 and the conditions of life in New England had changed; the Old Colony wanted to review this foundation document of harmony with their native neighbors to the west.

To Josiah Winslow came rumors, by way of Boston, of certain disturbing actions and attitudes on the part of Alexander (Wamsutta), Massasoit's oldest son and heir. When Wamsutta regally ignored the first invitation to come to Plymouth and discuss the troublesome situation with young Winslow, that proud heir of the Pilgrim fathers went out to arrest the native prince for questioning. He had learned from the historic Pequot War of 1637 and from the successful postwar actions of the Puritans how these obstreperous Algonquians must be handled.

3

"Until I Have No Country"

King Philip's War
in Southern New England

Soon after Massasoit's death, when his older son, Wamsutta, was establishing his sachemship of the Pokanokets, that young man made an "earnest request" of Plymouth that seemed very much in the mood of the day. Like many other native notables of this "golden age" of trade, he thought it would be appropriate to acquire an English name—marking him as a bicultural personage. The authorities at Plymouth duly complied: ". . . he shal bee called by the name of Alexander Pokanoket." His younger brother (previously called Metacom) would be "Philip of Pokanoket." These changes were quite in keeping with Algonquian practices—a new name for a new time of crisis was an ancient tactic. Also, equipped with such splendid names from European history, would the two young princes not be enabled to move all the more powerfully between New England's incompletely integrated societies?

This explanation of how Metacom became Philip came forth

for general readers only after the 1985 appearance of James Axtel's book *The Invasion Within: The Contest of Cultures in Colonial North America*. Before that, readers had been treated to various versions of Puritan chronicler William Hubbard's explanation; he reported that the New Englanders of his day had "nick-named" Philip after the classical Greek conqueror "for his ambitious and haughty spirit." Certainly the title "King" was bestowed on Philip as a jeer—from propagandists who wished to exaggerate his role in the war that bore his name—but the name Philip was given and taken in a way perfectly proper for a native prince of this time.

Today's ethnic historians also point out that among the Algonquians an individual's true name was known only to the most intimate family members. For an outsider to own that knowledge allowed him to own the person named. So to become Alexander or Philip was no personal surrender to the other culture. It was a mere showing of the cooperative face that these men of rank wanted, in 1661, to present to the world.

But unfortunately the decade into which Philip and his brother were then entering was the backside of the "golden age," radically different from when their father's interests and Plymouth's had come so harmoniously together. Gone were the days when a native prince or princess would wear bracelets, combs, and amulets whose value and design bespoke the brilliant, productive years of cooperation between the two peoples. Gone also were the mutual "feare" (in the sense of respect), the interdependency, the curiosity.

More than shining names and princely appearances would be needed to deal with the stresses that were then imposed on the Algonquian-settler relationships, and particularly on the Pokanoket-Plymouth partnership. The rumors of Alexander's plottings to make an aggressive, anti-English compact with his neighbors came at precisely the time when the mood in Plymouth was changing from passive existence to energetic expansion. The fact that Alexander had been summoned so roughly to explain away his campfire meetings with other sachems demonstrated the Pilgrims' altered attitude. When Josiah Winslow finally caught up with Alexander, the new sachem was discovered at his "hunting lodge" near Taunton, with perhaps eighty men and women in attendance. A pistol was thrust into his chest. If he stirred or refused to go along, he was "a dead man," Winslow is reported to have told him. In this decade, not cooperation and friendship but obedience and contrition were required. As the sachem's retainers watched in shock, Alexander was marched off under armed guard toward Plymouth.

It was indeed a time of crisis, both economically and politically. With beavers extirpated from southern New England rivers and the fashion shift away from beaver-fur hats for gentlemen, the Pokanokets and other Algonquians were dealt out of the commercial world. Wampum had ceased being an official medium of exchange. Boston merchants now directed their energies not toward obtaining and selling commodities extracted from the interior but toward the moving of international goods. Hartford and Springfield entrepreneurs concentrated on shipping their agricultural goods to seaside ports. The appearance and use of European coinage in New England marketplaces confirmed that transatlantic trade had triumphed over internal trade. However isolated it once had been, New England was now a part of the world.

With the restoration of the Stuart monarchs in 1660, a rising tide of altered political circumstances flooded upon New England. Foremost among the engulfing concerns in Massachusetts Bay and Plymouth was the status of their charters (or the lack thereof). Would the Catholic-inclined Charles II allow the New England colonies to retain control of their lands and peoples? The king answered the question by appointing a commission to explore the bizarre patchwork of grants and claims behind the colonial governments. Then in 1662 Plymouth was jolted by raids on their Maine holdings by marauding Mohawks, reaching even to the Pilgrim-established trading post on the Penobscot River. Politically this colony would henceforth be on guard, against native forces and royal agents alike. Its brash new leaders would stop at nothing to secure Plymouth's position in regional affairs.

In other ways, too, the Old Colony toward which Alexander was escorted in 1662 was a different, more aggressive place than the young settlement which had so cordially hosted Massasoit on so many visits. Although its population had increased along with the rest of New England's—doubling in size from 6,500 to 13,000 in the six years of the high-growth period preceding 1643—and although its hold on territories near and far seemed reasonably firm, there were inward as well as outward threats to this colony of self-proclaimed "Saintes." The original thatch-roof houses of the settlers were now encompassed by the ever-advancing sand; the houses looked, even in the eyes of contemporary observers, antiquated and impoverished in comparison to the planked and shingled dwellings of Massachusetts Bay's and Connecticut's new towns. Remarks were heard about "the ancient mother grown old and abandoned by her children." Even more damaging, the quality of intellectual and spiritual leadership in Plymouth, never high, was diminishing, the level of Christian education, even among the literate families, was appallingly low. What, in fact, were the true strengths of this old place?

Land was a part of the answer—especially the arable and well-watered acres that stretched westward, between Plymouth and Narragansett Bay—the easily cleared, deep-soiled meadows that made of this entire territory a real estate speculator's dream. Take, for example, the new town of Dartmouth: in 1652 the vast acreage embraced by its borders (over 100 square miles, from today's Fairhaven, Massachusetts, to the Rhode Island line) had been bought from Massasoit by thirty-four of Plymouth's "Old Comers"; these proprietors, Myles Standish among them, owned about two-thousand acres each, which they tended to regard not as personal plantations but as potential sale lots for such would-be immigrants as displaced Baptists and wandering Quakers from Rhode Island. Or take the new town of Swansea (1667): this community, at the very sticking point of Plymouth's contested, overlapping territories with Rhode Island, had been sold by Pokanoket rulers, under Plymouth's approving eye, to its proprietors and settlers. Both of these towns would assert Plymouth's interests in the direction of Narragansett Bay, and would also have the effect of pushing the Wampanoags out to the peninsulas the fringe lands where they could be more easily monitored.

For not just the Pokanokets but all Wampanoags had become, by the 1660s, dependents on rather than partners in New England's business. And that business, on the mainland, was strictly land development. Maps of the time show how the ancient native domains were being broken up by surveyors' lines and stone walls. Yet the Wampanoags, along with other native American groups, needed open reaches of land—for "swidden" (slash-and-burn) agriculture, for hunting, for moving about. Modern ecologists estimate that, for their land uses, the Algonquians required between sixteen and twenty times as much acreage as did the settler families. Alexander and Philip might choose to pay their debts by selling off Pokanoket land, but they could not go on selling land for long.

Weetamoo, wife of Alexander and sister of Philip's wife, was sachem herself of the Sakonnets (whose lands lay to the south and east of the Pokanokets') and understood the severity of the land-drain threat; she had to take legal action against her own husband to prevent his selling off her people's lands. Through the Plymouth court she was granted an order that halted that suicidal business. And, as the events of the 1660s rolled on, the younger generation of Pokanoket warriors stirred angrily against leaders who sought to enrich themselves from the sale of the people's land heritage.

Conservative historians emphasize that the exchange of real estate was by no means a "land grab" carried out by booted and spurred intruders from Plymouth, that sales were legally and agreeably conducted. Nor was land hunger the prime reason for the war that would break forth in the next decade—in which opinion they disagree with the revisionists. The conservatives, pointing to native dependency and to the natives' resultant restlessness as the cause, generally find in the records of land transactions instances of fairness and even generosity. Here is what the proprietors paid for the Dartmouth land: "30 yards of cloth, 8 mooseskins, 15 axes, 15 hoes, 15 pair of breeches, 8 blankets, 2 kettles, 1 cloak, a pound in wampan, 8 pair stockings, 8 pair of shoes, 1 iron pot, and 10 shillings in another commoditie." Quite a heap of trade goods. But, as against the long-term value of the land, the payment seems rather paltry. And the point was, each land sale left the Pokanokets with less capital, less power, less chance to be on their own.

*   *   *

The tragic separation of the Pokanoket and Plymouth peoples is viewed by Neal Salisbury and other historians of today as a strange affront to the successful, laborious efforts of Massasoit and Governor Bradford to structure a separated but bicultural society. Through times of plague and external assault, their ancient treaty had kept them in harmony, yielding strength to one another. Nonetheless, three events before 1660 stand out as dramatic exceptions to that historic harmony—events so fractious that they almost seem pointers toward the split that preceded King Philip's War.

The first of these events occurred in the very year of the 1620 treaty's signing, when one of Massasoit's shifty subsachems, named Corbitant, allied himself with the Narragansetts (who at that stage considered the Pokanokets subservient to them, and were outraged that the Pokanokets had entered into an independent treaty). But when news of Corbitant's imminent revolt reached Myles Standish, he persuaded both the Pilgrims and the Pokanokets that decisive action was called for. Strapping on his sword, he hurried to Middleboro and swiftly quelled the mutiny. To strap on the sword seemed the answer to any and all problems on the diplomatic front.

Squanto was the cause of the second disruption. This helpful but self-seeking translator continually tried to displace Massasoit, the tall and stately Ousamequin ("Yellow Feather"), in the Pilgrims' affections, to emerge, himself, as the Pilgrims' most trusted facilitator. After Squanto's last and most dangerous trick failed (a hoax in which one of his friends came running out of the woods, bloodied, claiming that Massasoit was on the attack), there was the awkwardness of protecting him from Massasoit's wrath. Finally, he died on an expedition, still the Old Colony's guide and translator among other

Wampanoags—a death-bed Christian. But forever after, the Pilgrims tended to believe that the natives were always, one way or another, pulling off some kind of scam.

The third and most threatening event took place when a band of adventurers from England settled at Wessagusset (present-day Quincy) and committed so many corn thefts and treacheries among their neighboring Massachusetts that those natives sought revenge against both Wessagusset and nearby Plymouth. Alerted to the Massachusetts' planned attack, Myles Standish sailed north to take charge. After assessing the situation in the face of the assembling warriors, Standish lured the dissident sachems into Wessagusset's storehouse and killed them with their own knives. Excited rather than satisfied by those executions, he ordered that the English kill every armed native they could find near the scene. The head of one warrior, severed from the body by Standish himself, was brought home to Plymouth and set on a pike, an example for all to contemplate. Proud as well as neurotic were the wearers of the sword.

Hearing of Standish's success, John Robinson, the saintly spiritual leader of the Pilgrims, wrote to his former flock from Holland, "OH! How happy a thing it [would have] been if you had converted some before you killed any . . ." Though he admired Standish for his military skills and thought that he, being sent by God, would continue to do good works if properly managed, Robinson concluded that the stubby, red-haired captain lacked "that tenderness of ye life of man which is meete." Further: ". . . to be a terrour to poor barbarous people . . . is a thing more glorious in *men*'s eyes than pleasing in *God*'s, or convenient for Christians."

Robinson's counsel went largely unheeded. In the Pilgrim's experience with the Pokanokets prior to 1660, blood and distrust came to outweigh peaceful intentions. No wonder that

Pilgrim-portrayer George Willison called the saints "ruthless"; disdain for the natives was built into the culture. And occasionally the fear of "heathen savages" that lurked in many an English breast expressed itself in orgies of slaughter—excesses such as those during the Pequot War, against which the civilized native allies had protested in vain. Although the conservative historians point out that this should be viewed as quite normal behavior for Europeans of the seventeenth century, to the natives the Pilgrims seemed bloodthirsty and, too often, untrustworthy.

Terrorized by Josiah Winslow's pistol at his chest and stung by the humiliating arrest, Alexander surely called to mind the history of English violences as the soldiers marched him toward Plymouth. *"Wotawquenange,"* meaning "cutthroats," had quickly become the common Algonquian name for these English ruffians. How could his father ever have called them friends? While contemplating the increased roughness of the English, he may also have seen among his own people a weakness, accompanied by desperation. He had probably concluded that only the most dire action would serve to reverse the tide of events. The continuing successes of the English had even intimidated the native powwows; the task of doing something about it seemed to be no longer in their hands but in those of the warriors. The pressure on all sides—from the farmers extending their fields, from the missionaries seeking more converts, from such outrages as this arrest of the sachem—could be relieved only by an uprising of the people before it was too late. So his thoughts may have run.

On the spiritual frontier, there had been many sharp confrontations between the old gods and the new. Both of the peoples believed that there was a centrally important connection between themselves and the spirits; if that connection failed, crops and culture and all would be lost. Roger Williams wrote of how Algonquian farmers in his vicinity watched as competing powwows strove to bring forth rain from the clouds in times of drought. "If the yeere prove drie," he reported, "they have great and solemne meetings from all parts at one high place, to supplicate their gods; and to beg raine, and they will continue in this worship ten days, a fortnight; yea, three weekes, untill raine come." And Uncas, though hostile to Christianity, had had to admit that one day he witnessed the awesome spectacle of how Norwich preacher James Fitch, who had been summoned after Mohegan rain dancers had failed to deliver, produced so much rain that "our River rose more than two Foot in Height." In addition to the economic and political struggles, Alexander surely appreciated that a struggle was taking place in this realm of the spirits.

To help us imagine how this era of declining native power might have seemed to Alexander and to Philip, we may be guided by the words of another great sachem of the time. Passaconaway, one of New England's most esteemed spiritual leaders as well as a powerful ruler, spoke both to his own Pawtuckets (who had moved to the mouth of the Merrimack River) and to all other Algonquians when he delivered this warning about the futility of trying to stop the English:

> I am now going the way of all Flesh, or ready to die, and not likely to see you ever met together any more: I will now leave this Word of Counsel with you, that you take heed how you quarrel with the English. For though you may do them much mischief, yet assuredly you will all be destroyed, and rooted off the Earth if you do . . . I was as much an Enemy to the English at their first coming to these Parts as any one whatsoever, and did try all Ways and Means possible to have destroyed them, at least to have prevented them

sitting down here, but I could in no way effect it; therefore I advise you never to contend with the English, nor make War with them.

Fighting back against Plymouth at this final moment may have seemed to Alexander and Philip, nonetheless, the only possible course. In the view of historian Alden Vaughan and a majority of other commentators across the spectrum of opinion this decision did in fact mature within the minds of the Pokanoket rulers during the 1660s. Then the issue was how best to effect that policy.

Alexander's aloof dismissal of Plymouth's first invitation to come and parley was probably not a planned gesture of defiance. More likely it was an attempt to evade responsibility for having commenced war-directed conspiracies with the Narragansetts. Caught at his lodge, Alexander must have protested, in his father's name. Winslow did have the grace, the day being hot, to offer Alexander a horse. But the young sachem declined, saying that he had no right to fare better than the women retainers who were forced to come along with him.

The heat and the terror and the humiliation pressed upon him; some say that the illness that struck him during the march resulted from an "inward fury." As they proceeded from Duxbury to Marshfield, Alexander's fever intensified. And after the harsh questioning and lecturing by Governor Thomas Prence (one of the colony's aggressive new leaders), he could barely support himself. Struggling on to Plymouth with the aid of his people and then turning toward home, Alexander died on the way to Sowams. The body of the young sachem was carried the rest of the way on the shoulders of his men, grim evidence of the dangers of undertaking any action against Plymouth.

*   *   *

Leadership—and revenge—devolved upon Philip. Though some chroniclers reported that Philip had concluded his brother had been poisoned by the Pilgrims, Hubbard scoffs that that tale was invented by the new sachem to assist his search for war allies against Plymouth. Today's more sympathetic historians, while continuing to examine the meager source materials about Philip in an effort to understand his personality and his motivation, speculate that he (born in 1640) and Alexander must have been children of Massasoit's later years, after the plagues of 1618–1619 had carried away so many of the Pokanokets' population and ruling class. But still little is known of the youthful character or formative training of Metacom-turned-Philip, the embittered younger brother who arrived at stage center at such a critical time in New England's settler-native relations. What has become known is more general ethnic information about the Algonquians, such as that the men were taller than the English; contemporary accounts picture them as lithe of limb, "the men fairer than the women." Let us assume, therefore, that Philip was physically well put together—a captive Englishwoman, during the war, did not object when Philip held her hand.

Additionally, something is known of the way native American societies at this time prepared their young noblemen for leading roles. Isaac de Rasieres, the Dutch trader-diplomat who visited Plymouth in the 1620s and who instructed the Pilgrims in the value of wampum, left this record of how worthy males in the native societies around Plymouth were subjected to a knightlike preparation for life:

> When there is a youth who begins to approach manhood, he is taken by his father, uncle, or nearest friend, and is conducted blindfolded into a wilderness, in order that he may not know the way, and is left there by night or otherwise, with a bow and arrows,

and a hatchet and a knife. He must support himself there a whole winter with what the scanty earth furnishes at this season, and by hunting. Towards the spring they come again, to fetch him out of it . . . until May. He must then go out again . . . to seek wild herbs and roots, which they know to be the most poisonous and bitter . . . which he must drink . . . And if he cannot retain it, he must repeat the dose until he can support it.

With some justification, we may therefore assume that Philip came tested and ready for his sachemhood, despite his junior status and the terrifying circumstances of his inheritance.

Not far away from Philip dwelled Canonchet, the recently emplaced sachem of the Narragansetts, who was equal to him in age (but greater in terms of eventual importance in the war). Son of the eloquent and unjustly executed Miantonomo, and veteran himself of many battles and intrigues, Canonchet was already a commanding figure in the tumultuous world of the 1660s. Though the Narragansetts had once been considered too wampum-wealthy for involvement with petty schemes and power deals, they now (since the post–Pequot War struggles) saw they must take an active part in those political maneuvers in order to survive. Canonchet's messengers had frequently been in Alexander's court at Sowams; his ambassadors undoubtedly attended the ceremonies surrounding Philip's accession to power. John Cotton wrote that this was a high and festive occasion, with "great feasting and rejoycing among the natives."

Nor was the new generation of Algonquians lacking in leaders who, like Uncas, chose the side of the English. First there was Uncas's own son, Oneco, who took command of the combined army of Mohegans and Pequots as his father declined into alcoholism and ill health. Then there was Ninigret, the now aged Eastern Niantic leader who had remained neutral in the

Pequot War. Alden Vaughan contends that Ninigret, who had acquired an impressive number of modern weapons from dealers in New York, became a key figure in the plots against Philip, eventually playing as central a role in the stirring up of King Philip's War as Uncas had played in the Pequot War with his whisperings against Sassacus. Ninigret's rumor campaign, calculated to rub Plymouth's most tender fears, all focused on the war preparations being made by the Pokanokets. For what other reasons would Philip be gathering such a band of warriors around him? And why else would he be holding those secret meetings with the Narragansetts?

But Douglas Edward Leach, author of *Flintlocks and Tomahawks: New England in King Philip's War* (1953), the first thorough history of the war in this half-century, provides balance for the native political scene by asserting that Philip was not far behind Ninigret when it came to plotting against a rival by playing up to the English. At one point Philip sent a letter to the settlers on Long Island, warning them of Ninigret's unscrupulous intrigues. That was simply the way diplomacy was waged between the peoples, their rivalries intensified by their increasing dependency on and desire to seem useful to the English.

But by 1670 the many rumors against Philip had accumulated and acquired such weight they could no longer be ignored; Plymouth now believed that the Pokanokets must be preparing for war, possibly in consort with the French. The evidence seemed irrefutable. Yet when a damning letter bearing Philip's own mark was shown to him, he was able to argue that the document had been forged by Ninigret or one of his agents. Still, the number of muskets known to be in Philip's arsenal at Mount Hope was frightening; like Ninigret, he must be receiving them from a generous outside source. Furthermore, his land sales to Rhode Islanders and other "strangers" continued, infuriating Plymouth's domain-conscious rulers. And his ceaseless complaints against those settlers in nearby towns who had not fenced in or restrained their farm animals demonstrated a rebellious querulousness. Rumors of conspiracy and reports of arms now became a terrifying fact of men on the march when Philip with an armed force paraded to and from Swansea early in 1671. Chronicler Hubbard saw that military display as the final bit of evidence, proving to the English that war was imminent. For with Philip "marching up and down, constantly in arms," who could prevent a confrontation?

Yet even Hubbard, for all his delight that the war was at last going to burst forth, and for all his certitude that the Narragansetts (having promised four-thousand warriors to the Pokanokets, according to his information) were in on it too, had to admit that the citizens of Swansea and nearby Rehoboth saw some justice in the natives' cause. That is, recognizing that their complaints about the New Englanders' crop-trampling farm animals had merit, they agreed to construct lengthy border fences and to fine trespassers on Pokanoket lands. But Hubbard then added that, in the face of the Indians' war fever, no such peaceful gestures could hold off the war for long.

Modern scholar Philip Raulet sees the matter quite differently. Writing in the *New England Quarterly* of March 1988, he states that the issue of the escaping farm animals was a very deep-cutting matter and that the attempt of the settlers to resolve it was a genuine move in the direction of better relations. He disagrees with Jennings and the revisionists that letting loose the horses and cattle had been a matter of policy among the aggressive settlers. He also disagrees with the revisionist theory that the English were totally uninterested in maintaining the peace. The missionary John Eliot was but one English Christian who, in Raulet's reading of the facts, believed that Philip could be brought around to a less bellicose stance. Even though Philip had once said that Christianity to him had no more value than the button on Eliot's coat, the missionary continued to have hopes for the sachem's conversion. Three of Eliot's "Praying Indians" were particularly active in trying to head off the war, urging that Massachusetts Bay take steps to cool Plymouth's ardor for the conflict.

Furthermore, the Wampanoags whose villages were sited within Dartmouth's borders and those whose land extended down to Sakonnet Point—both of which groups had once considered Philip's father as their great sachem—now urged that Philip's actions be moderated. Yet both they and the peace-minded English must have recognized that the situation was extremely fragile, the two societies well on the way to war. Plymouth, notified of Philip's march on Swansea, at once convened a conference of the United Colonies at Taunton, demanding that Philip himself attend.

The command performance took place in early April, 1671, a grand affair with the Pokanoket knights dressed in full finery and the Plymouth power structure armed to the teeth, determined to assert mastery in the manner of Myles Standish. Roger Williams also attended, trying to help convince the Pokanokets that this was an honest attempt at peaceful negotiation, not a trap sprung by the "cutthroats." But Philip, unconvinced of English good intentions, demanded that hostages be brought to his encampment outside Taunton. Only after that had been accomplished would he proceed to the conference.

All we know of the debate within that packed and tense meetinghouse at Taunton has come down to us through the Puritan chroniclers. From their narratives it appears that Philip at first sought to explain away the great number of weapons in his possession by a pressing need to be armed against the threatened aggressions of the Narragansetts. But when confronted with the known fact of his friendly and frequent meetings with Canonchet's Narragansett delegations, he ceased those dissemblings and confessed to plans for an eventual attack on the English settlements. The chroniclers then say he dismissed the importance of any settler incursions on his territories and any injustices on Plymouth's part, admitting that "it was the naughtiness of his own heart that put him on that rebellion, and nothing of any provocation of the English."

Yet one doubts that such a sin-laden confession would ever cross the lips of a proud, non-Christianized Algonquian. It seems more likely that Philip, knowing that he could only say *officially* what the English wanted to hear, merely consented to that statement as a way to gain more time. Neither he nor his Narragansett allies (who some sources say had agreed to join him in the spring of 1676) were ready to challenge the English at this moment.

Philip also agreed to surrender all his warriors' weapons and those of his allies—though, again, it's hard to believe that such a promise was real, given the true nature of Philip's limited command over the natives. Because he had little room to maneuver while in the same hall with the English soldiers, he made a show of immediately surrendering seventy token weapons. A more favorable part of the Taunton treaty, from Philip's perspective, was the contingency that, if there should be any abrogation of the terms, an appeal could be addressed to Boston. This was the provision that allowed Philip to make the later, desperate appeal to the Bay leaders . . . the scene that harked back to Philip's happier visit to Boston when a mere prince. At this stage in his diplomatic maneuvering it was important to Philip that he be recognized as the leader of a separate and integral society, not treated as a subject of Plymouth, wholly controlled by that colony's laws and regulations. He believed that Boston would still respect that critical difference.

In September—five months later—when he had failed to deliver any more weapons, Plymouth snapped the whip and demanded obedience. The Puritans in Boston—when he visited, according to Philip Raulet, on the urgent advice of those Wampanoags who still believed in peace—did little more than say that the matter should be put back in Plymouth's hands. Forced to make another gesture in the direction of surrender (so that he might proceed with his plans), he formally recognized his subjugation to Plymouth. In recognition of his revised status as a subservient puppet, he agreed to deliver a yearly tribute to Plymouth of five wolves' heads. When the English authorities also demanded that, to atone for his past transgressions, he pay a heavy fine in English money, he could only protest that he could not possibly come up with 100 pounds sterling. But as Plymouth insisted that the amount be paid one way or another, he won agreement to spread the payments over a five-year period.

Returned to Mount Hope from these diplomatic humiliations, Philip was subject to whispers that he was a "white-liver'd Cur." The murmurings of the warriors grew louder when he sold more Pokanoket land in order to pay the fine. And grimly over the years, biding his time, laying his plans, Philip paid all the demanded moneys. This was but a small part of what he trusted he would get back, if his plans succeeded.

Most historians regard the next four years, between 1671 and 1675, as the time when a "brooding" Philip completed his preparations for war by solidifying his relationships with various allies. Although they regard the outbreak of hostilities in June

1675 as occurring sooner than Philip had intended, they tend to focus on this man as the prime mover, doing all in his power to unite the Algonquians for total war. In this they essentially follow the lead of Hubbard and the Puritan chroniclers who needed a king (representing the Devil) to oppose them; otherwise, what was the war about? The revisionists, however, see the four-year period from a completely different perspective. They declare that this was the time when Plymouth's leaders, determined to take more land for themselves rather than see it all be swept up by the Bay, decided to attempt a localized war against the dependent Wampanoags, a simple war of annihilation. Only by this war could the Pilgrims secure their hold on the border territories that Rhode Island also claimed; only by this war would both the crown and Boston understand that the Plymouth enterprise remained in firm hands.

In these interpretations by historians old and new, one finds something excessively deterministic. The concept of inevitability would deny the humanistic possibility of anyone's setting things aright by the construction of, let us say, a political body that might have enabled both societies to live in peace. Or the strengthening of the very real bonds that had for so long kept the two societies more or less together, however influenced by economic patterns. Even Roger Williams was more of a trader than a saint; his view of New England as a region that should and could be kept at peace was the view of a practical businessman.

Among the cohesive forces that might have held the region together were the strong bonds between the Narragansetts and the Mohawks on New England's western and northern borders. As Roger Williams noted, these two people represented the "great bodies of Indians in this country . . . they are confederates, and long have been, and they both yet are friendly and peaceable [*sic*] to the English." Further, the war that the Squakheags had undertaken against the Iroquois at the urging of the French had been brought to a close by a treaty in 1671. As anthropologist Harald Prins points out, the larger forces in native North America seemed to have readjusted themselves to the revised economic conditions of the latter 1600s. They sought stability.

Strenuous labors, idealistic and otherwise, were undertaken within both Massachusetts Bay and Rhode Island to cool the hotheads in Plymouth. John Eliot renewed his attempts to tame Philip, instructed his emissary, a Praying Indian named John Sassamon (who had been sent to the Pokanoket court as translator and adviser some years before) to redouble his efforts.

Sassamon, from the perspective of the English, possessed the admirable qualities of being a second-generation Christian, of having fought alongside Israel Stoughton in the Pequot War. In fact, the self-revealing report that Stoughton sent home to Governor Winthrop, requesting permission to retain certain of the comeliest captured squaws as "servants," concluded with this sentence: "Sosomon, the Indian, desireth a young little squaw which I know not." That was Sassamon as a collaborator, however Christian, in the bicultural events of his early years.

More than thirty years later, Sassamon was still in the twilight zone between camps, both and neither. Yet Douglas Edward Leach concludes from the evidence that Sassamon was respected by both red and white cultures, no more compromised than any other realist of the day. Having worked as a teacher in John Eliot's villages, Sassamon went on in 1660 to become a functionary within the Pokanoket court. Some assert, of course, that he had been emplaced at Sowams and Mount Hope as a spy and troublemaker. Whichever opinion one fa-

vors, Sassamon was with Alexander during the last, fatal "hunting expedition" and march to Plymouth. He also accompanied
Philip to the crucial conference at Taunton.

A skillful counselor for the new sachem, Sassamon appears as
a named witness on several of the land-sale documents that
Philip negotiated and signed with his distinctive "P" mark.
Indeed, there's reason to conclude that Philip dismissed Sassamon from his court at about the time when the conflict began
to shape up not so much because he disdained the Christian
teacher's advice as because he disliked Sassamon's freewheeling
ways with the land sales. For Sassamon had tried to secure some
of the transacted land for himself, claiming an inheritance for
his heirs. So out of the court and back to Natick he went, then
to Assawompset, a pleasant lakeside village where his wife
(daughter of the "Black Sachem" Tuspaquin) held land. There,
halfway between Pokanoket and Plymouth, the aging Sassamon
fished and exchanged intelligence with passersbys, ever alert to
developments on both sides of the cultural border.

And there he acquired the alarming and definite-sounding
news that Philip, this time, was preparing his forces not for a
march-by but for a large-scale attack on Swansea. He took that
news immediately to Josiah Winslow, returning home only after receiving assurances that he would never be mentioned as
source of the intelligence. Word must have leaked out to the
bicultural community, however, for one day soon thereafter
John Sassamon failed to return from a winter fishing expedition. And when his body was discovered—bruised, with neck
broken, lodged beneath the lake ice—it was assumed that he
had been murdered, his well-intended ministrations brought to
a violent end.

Although it was difficult for Plymouth authorities to find a
link between Philip personally and the alleged murder, official

attempts to implicate the sachem eventually produced a native "eyewitness" who was willing to say the right things. This man, who had conveniently been within sight of the slaying on a nearby hill, identified the murderer: Tobias, a counselor of Philip's in the Pokanoket court. To try the charges against him, a supposedly balanced jury of settlers and natives was empaneled—though the natives were in the court only as observers and consenters, not as verdict-givers. Ultimately two more conspirators were rounded up for the trial and the three were hanged—their grotesque stringing-up accompanied by such otherworldly signs as blood spurting from the murdered man's body when one of the accused walked by. All of these signs the Puritans wrote into their chronicles; comets were reported in the sky.

What angered Philip most about the Sassamon affair, he said in his later complaints to would-be peacemakers in Rhode Island, was that conditions had reached the point where, in an English court, the word of any witness *against* an accused native was accepted; whereas a witness *for* the accused was not given a hearing. Who would listen to the fact that the "eyewitness" on the hillside had been heavily in debt to Tobias, the counselor accused of the murder? No one! Surely a fair-minded court would have ruled out testimony from such prejudiced sources. And so Philip's understandable complaints went on. But what in fact angered Philip, in the opinion of most conservative historians, was that the Sassamon incident provoked hostilities too soon, impelling combat several months before Philip or any of his Narragansett allies were ready. The miscarriage of justice, outrageous enough in itself, may have been responsible for Philip's loss of the war.

Douglas Edward Leach and other recent writers point out, however, that English authorities, recognizing that the Sassamon trial was more a lynch party than an act of justice and that native reactions would be swift and thunderous, hastened to put a peaceable face on things. Plymouth nervously informed Philip by messenger that, justice of sorts having been served, no further actions would be taken against the implicated sachem. Massachusetts Bay prepared to send emissaries to mollify Philip. And Rhode Island's attorney general, the Quaker John Easton, acting in place of aged Governor Williams, invited the Pokanokets to come to Providence and see if somehow wrongs could be righted. Despite his profound doubts that mere words would now do much good, Philip accepted the invitation, journeying to Rhode Island's capital with forty warriors and counselors. It was at this point that Philip's disillusioned complaints about English justice poured forth. At the same time he reviewed with bitterness the history of Pokanoket-Pilgrim relations and ended with a remarkable statement about his own attitude:

> The English who came first to this country were but an handful of people, forlorn, poor and distressed. My father was then sachem, he relieved their distresses in the most kind and hospitable manner. He gave them land to plant and build upon . . . they flourished and increased. By various means they got possession of a great part of his territory. But he still remained their friend till he died. My elder brother became sachem . . . He was seized and confined and thereby thrown into illness and died. Soon after I became sachem they disarmed all my people . . . their land was taken. But a small part of the dominion of my ancestors remains. *I am determined not to live until I have no country.*

Philip's words still seem tremendously powerful: he could not go on until his country was no more. Neither he himself nor his warriors would let him do that.

Hearing all Philip's charges (though he tried to stop the

torrent), Easton the peacemaker was finally moved to propose that the central issue of native governance by Plymouth be studied by a panel of mediators. To that panel he would name first and foremost the highest-ranking man in the English colonies, Sir Edmund Andros, recently appointed royal governor of New York. Easton suggested that Philip name the second personage on the panel, making his selection from among New England's most prestigious great sachems. He suggested further that Philip and his men should then return peacefully to their capital, leaving to Easton the matter of convincing Plymouth that such a negotiations board could effectively bring about and maintain peace.

Perhaps Philip was impressed by Easton's proposal. Raulet notes that, as late as June 17, 1675, the Pokanokets returned some horses that had strayed to their settler owners. Even amid the dire forces that drag societies into war and destruction, vital human gestures promise peace, one day.

Within but a few days, Easton was stricken by the dreadful news that Plymouth had already declared a state of emergency; it was too late for his panel to be brought together. Messengers from Plymouth to Mount Hope had found Philip surrounded by Pokanoket warriors armed and painted for battle; narrowly escaping (Philip himself intervening to prevent violence), the messengers had fled homeward with their terrifying report. Not much later (June 24) came word of Philip's warriors burning and ransacking houses at Swansea, as had been predicted by Sassamon. So the irreversible decision was then imposed by the prowar forces: the war would go forward, and the fifteen years of creative political maneuvering that had taken place since Alexander's accession would be rejected for all times as not worthwhile. John Easton and other peacemakers might as well put their recommendations back in their pockets.

. . .

Swansea—which the chroniclers also spelled *Swanzey*, the way it is pronounced—was reported to be a pretty little town in 1675, thirty or forty new houses, centered around a Baptist church. It stood at the head of tidal rivers that run down to Mount Hope Bay, just above the neck of land that connects the Pokanoket peninsula to the mainland. In threatening times like these, it seemed a long way from the military base at Plymouth, forty miles of complex trails away. Like Rehoboth (nearer Taunton) and Dartmouth, this town's farmer residents had grown prosperous on the bountiful but uneasy western perimeter of Plymouth's territories.

Swansea's scattered houses seemed ideal targets for any Pokanokets bent on mischief: farm tools and household objects were within easy reach of unemployed young braves. Though there had been years of cooperative exchange between the Pokanokets and the Swansea residents—exchanges of foods, of services, of agricultural labor—there were also annoyances: the pesky regulations about what could and what could not be done on the Sabbath and the eternally destructive farm animals were two. The situation had been livable if delicate; now it was incendiary.

Plymouth decreed that throughout its towns June 24 should be observed as a day of fasting and "Humiliation," in hopes that the God who determined all might be persuaded to aid his people, the English people, in this time of crisis. Swansea's settlers dutifully walked to meeting on that Thursday . . . and the natives, noticing unprotected fields and farms, contemplated their opportunities. Some may also have contemplated the saying of Wampanoag shamans (as reported by anthropologist William Simmons) that the natives could win the imminent war only if the English fired the first shot.

At one Swansea farm a boy and an old man, excused from church services and charged with guard duty, looked out and saw in the field beyond the barn just what they dreaded most: Pokanokets slitting the throats of cows let out to graze. The boy did as he was told; he fetched the musket and opened fire. He had no idea that he'd be the one held responsible by history for having shed the first blood in what would become King Philip's War.

His shot fatally wounded a marauding Pokanoket (who was dragged away by his people). Later, in swift reaction, other Pokanokets killed three, then six Swansea citizens returning from church services. The day of prayer had become a day of vengeful death.

Throughout New England the hue and cry was raised; the Swansea killings were magnified into an attack by a monstrous army, the opening assault of an implacable enemy. The apprehensive emissaries who had been sent from Massachusetts Bay in order to mollify Philip happened to arrive in Swansea at this moment. Aghast, they turned around and raced homeward with their report from the front. Propagandists preshadowing Hubbard broadcast that the Indians had "slaughtered all the English they could find." In Boston as in Plymouth, bells rang militia units to arms. England's God was repeatedly invoked, the men sent forth with a prayer that the Lord "Blesse, succeed, and prosper them; delivering them from the hands of his and our enemies; subduing the heathen and returning them all in safetie to their families and relations againe."

In Rhode Island, the quest for peace was transformed into prayers for a brief war—Philip trapped and dispatched. A flotilla of boats was promised to aid in surrounding the sachem of Pokanoket on his peninsula. In Connecticut, however, panic reigned when the news of Swansea arrived. Officials struggled after the fact to see if peace could be restored or if guarantees could be obtained that the Narragansetts, much wooed by Philip, would remain neutral; with hopes of peace dashed, they called for forces to be sent to the strategic southeastern corner of their colony.

At Fort Saybrook, a curious event then occurred which showed that King Philip's War, for all its isolated and regional beginnings, was taking place in a world of other large-scale issues to which some say it was related. This was, as has been pointed out, the post-Restoration era, when the crown sought to bring all its domains into one smoothly functioning, imperialistic whole: the East Indies, Virginia, and New England, by this plan, would each have its special, complementary role to play. And when New York's Governor Edmund Andros decided to demonstrate the Duke of York's total command over a territory perceived as extending all across southern New England (and thence to Maine), he sent out a two-vessel mini-invasion to take over coastal Connecticut. But he made the mistake of communicating his intentions to John Winthrop, Jr., who had been made governor of Connecticut.

So when Andros arrived at Fort Saybrook on July 8, 1675, he was first challenged by the local militia and then opposed by a sizable force sent downriver by the governor. After a period of blustering and declaiming, Andros realized he was in the wrong place at the wrong time. He withdrew to New York, deeply embarrassed. It was only this contretemps, in the opinion of Francis Jennings, that dissuaded the Connecticut Puritans from jumping aboard the "invasion" of Pokanoket territory along with the Pilgrims and the militarists from Massachusetts Bay. They stayed warily home, on defense against the crown and any rebellious Narragansetts on the border.

*   *   *

In their varying ways all parts of New England organized themselves for the war that would mark the end of bicultural society
in the region. Yet this turn toward war, for both settlers and
Algonquians, was such a momentous psychological wrench that
it caused reverberations in their respective heavens, contemporary sources tell us. Cultural anthropologist William Simmons brought many of those brink-of-war reports together in
this recapitulation:

> The weeks prior to King Philip's War were an ominous time for
> English and Indians as both sides anticipated war. The English near
> Boston heard a gun go off in the air, bullets whistle overhead, and
> the drums of ghostly armies marching through the woods, while on
> the same day at Plymouth they heard invisible troops of horses
> riding back and forth. . . . Some visions are a kind of collective
> dream.

For the nondreamers, this was the time to pursue the military
objective of trapping and dispatching New England's most troublesome native leaders. In settlers' towns it was the time to kiss
the wife good-bye and buckle on the rusted sword. Old soldiers,
conscripts, men who needed a new chance, prisoners desperate
to be free, bumped shoulders on the way to the green. To shape
up this mixed bag of men required leadership from colonies in
which most officers were aged and bloated, distinguished more
for ripened memories than for present skills.

In the troop of 110 "volunteers" sent immediately south from
Boston marched a dozen pirates released from death cells, led by
Captain Samuel Moseley. He also brought along three Christian Indian guides and a couple of hunting dogs; he himself was
described as a "buccaneer from the West Indies." That troop
aimed for Attleboro, where they were to join up with a company of foot soldiers led by Captain Daniel Henchman and a

cavalry squadron under Captain Thomas Prentice. A brief delay was occasioned by an eclipse of the moon—a bad omen, opined some of the more superstitious. Not until the afternoon of June 27 did they all come together with the two companies sent to Swansea by Plymouth. This contingent of indifferently armed Pilgrims proved to be even worse trained and more terrified of the Indians than the variegated group from the Bay. Soon after arrival, two of Plymouth's sentries were killed by unseen raiders.

Then appeared out of the woods a housebuilder named Benjamin Church—the man demanded by the times. Though possessing no military credentials (his father had served in the Pequot War), Church had enough woods sense and what might be called native intelligence to understand how to move men effectively across the southern New England terrain. Interrupted by rumors of war from his intention of building himself a house at present-day Little Compton (near Sakonnet Point), he had gone to Plymouth to find out what was going on, and found himself drafted.

Tall, broad, and proud of his woodland capabilities, he took it upon himself late in life to publish his field notes. With the aid of son Thomas he produced in 1716 the remarkable narrative called "Entertaining Passages Relating to King Philip's War which began in the month of June, 1675. As also Expeditions more lately Made against the Common Enemy, and Indian Rebels in the Eastern Part of New England: With some Account of the Divine Providence towards Benj. Church Esq; by T.C." Although later editors foolishly gave a shorter and more professional-sounding title to his memoirs—*Church's History of King Philip's War*—no one who reads a page or two could believe that the author was seeking to pass himself off as a professional writer, least of all as an historian.

At Plymouth, Church was ordered by Major William Brad-ford and septuagenarian Major James Cudworth to lead the Pilgrims to the Swansea battlefront as a scout and advance guard. But so laggardly was the pace of the Pilgrims at the rear of the column and so swift his own, that Church had time to kill, flay, roast, and eat a deer with his men before Plymouth's officers caught up with him. Then Church had occasion to meet the equally pompous officers from Massachusetts Bay who (Church reported with tongue in cheek) "had entered into a confederacy with their Pilgrim brethren against the Infidels." Not one bit cowed by the pious militarists, Church suffered the foolishness of the mighty as well as he could.

Another engaging quality of the Church memoirs has been pointed out by Alan and Mary Simpson, editors of the 1975 reissue of the work for the Little Compton Historical Society. The editors stress that Church was much more an admirer of the natives and their way of life than he was a racially biased storm trooper. He liked to negotiate with, test the mettle of, and be true to his Indian friends. So it is through the eyes of this sympathetic carpenter-warrior that we are given rare glimpses of the bravery, nobility, and ultimate misery of the Algonqui-ans at war, as well as firsthand images of cross-country combat.

Not long before Church's trip to Plymouth and back, he had been witness to a crucial encounter among the Wampanoags near his own building site. His memoirs enable us to see these people as they dealt with each other in crisis—and also to take the measure of Church himself in those tension-filled days be-fore the attack on Swansea. He had been invited by Awa-shonks, "squaw sachem of the Sogkonate [Sakonnet] Indians," to attend a great dance conference at her village. Philip had sent a half dozen of his most impressive Pokanoket strongmen down the coast in order to persuade his cousin Awashonks and her three hundred Sakonnet braves to join him and his cause. Church took it upon himself, in accepting Awashonks's invitation, to counter Philip's ambassadors. To help him, he took with him to the dance conference young Charles Hazelton, son of his tenant, "who well understands the Indian language."

Church and the boy found Awashonks already dancing "in a foaming sweat." But upon their arrival, the ceremonies ceased and the serious business began of hearing each side out and deciding whether to join the Pokanokets or the men of Plymouth. Church, who at this point had just returned from an earlier trip to Plymouth, could declare that the Pilgrims then were *not* preparing for war. Would he have begun to build his house if he had suspected anything of that nature? He also vigorously resisted the strong-arm tactics threatened by the Pokanoket ambassadors against Awashonks, threats to make her join Philip. He urged the squaw sachem to make an immediate alliance with Plymouth, the only secure course of action. All the while, he stood up against Philip's towering emissaries, questioning them eyeball-to-eyeball about their intentions, giving them back challenge for challenge. Here was a man willing to tough it out for peace.

In those crucial days back in the middle of June, Church had also met another crucially important squaw sachem, Weetamoo of the Pocassets. Once the wife of Alexander, this remarkable woman was presently married to a rather ambiguous intercultural character whom the English called Peter Nennuit. It was from him that Church learned of Philip's difficulties in restraining his hot-tempered braves; and it was subsequently from Weetamoo herself (at Tiverton Heights) that he learned of the Pocasset braves' inclination to fight alongside the Pokanokets. Though Church now urged the sachem to take herself across the river to safety and to an alliance with the English on Rhode

Island, he doubted that she or they would follow his advice. Philip's campaign for allies was being effective; he apparently had the personal power and credibility to take on the leadership role, at least in this corner of New England. That having been determined, Church anxiously departed for his next fateful meeting at Plymouth.

In the very last days of June, with the armed and mounted English forces finally in place at two garrisons near Swansea, the incipient war did take on the look of a real war. Telling strikes were made by both sides. But these first engagements also had their comical side, according to Church. He had to beseech the Massachusetts soldiers *not* to leave a wounded man in the field after a brief encounter at the causeway leading to the Pokanoket peninsula; someone (namely Benjamin Church) would have to go out and bring in the victim. But then, with the regulars disinclined to join him in the attempt, and all native shots and arrows directed his way, he too had to retreat. "The Lord have mercy on us if such a handful of Indians shall thus dare an army!" he exclaimed.

Eventually the uprising subsided to the point where the English could summon enough courage to cross the causeway and march their army down the peninsula toward Mount Hope, from which site they found the Pokanokets had safely and skillfully removed themselves by canoe. Counting that failure-at-arms as a victory, the army's officers chose to spend whatever time it would take to build a fortress at Mount Hope. It was at this time that London broadsides flashed the word that Philip had escaped into the "Pocasset Swamps."

Church was at length given a small number of men to take across to the Pocasset shore, using boats supplied by Rhode Island. Relying on his tracking skills, and spying traces of where the enemy had passed, Church was able to promise his bloody-minded men that they would "soon see Indians enough." Hurrying south through Pocasset country, they came upon a broad field on which the rows of spring-planted peas were now blooming and ripening nicely. Here, on this "pease field" below Punkatee's Neck, Benjamin Church demonstrated both his courage and his tactical abilities (not to speak of his good luck).

Attacked by a native force first estimated at sixty warriors but enlarged subsequently to nearly three hundred (possibly these were warriors from Philip's nearby hiding place), Church and his twenty men ran before the musket blasts of the well-emplaced enemy. Some of the more foolhardy Englishmen paused to pick a peapod or two before responding to their leader's orders to form up. Without loss, Church was finally able to secure his squad behind stone walls and outcroppings above the river. And when Church learned that the powder supply was dangerously short, he instructed his men in the fine art of making every shot count. As the afternoon dragged on and the situation of the English grew more desperate with the mounting number of attackers, salvation winked at them in the form of a friendly vessel sailing down the river. But the wary skipper found the hailstorm of bullets not to his liking and steered away from the imperiled soldiers. Fortunately, when a second vessel approached, Church was able to persuade her skipper to come to their assistance. Though the ferrying back and forth from shore to ship had to be accomplished with but one small canoe, all the men got safely aboard, two at a time. Then Church insisted on going back himself to the contested field in order to reclaim a hat and cutlass abandoned during the retreat. With that mission accomplished and finally back on board, he delivered a farewell musket blast at the enemy, only to see that the remaining powder was so slight that his ball was propelled only half the distance. In writing many years later, he recalled the encounter as more invigorating than terrifying.

Most readers of the war, rather than being treated to the lively memories of Benjamin Church, have been subjected to the blood-curdling prose of the Puritan chroniclers and later nationalists. Historian John Fiske, for example, portrayed the next several weeks of the war as a time of dehumanizing grisliness. After telling of Philip's escape from Pokanoket, Fiske goes on to describe how

> a party of savages swooped down upon Dartmouth, burning thirty houses and committing fearful atrocities. Some of their victims were flayed alive, or impaled on sharp stakes, or roasted over slow fires. Similar horrors were wrought at [the Plymouth towns of] Middleborough and Taunton; and now the misery spread to Massachusetts [Bay], where on the 14th of July the town of Mendon was attacked by a party of Nipmucks.

Within the context of these tales of horror, Fiske's use of the word "savages" is revealing: he does not know who these people were or what they were about. And as his tales go on to emphasize the generalship of Philip, does he really know that Philip personally was engaged on this or that front? Other Victorian writers call Philip at this time a "will-o'-the-wisp," moving swiftly from scene to scene, inspiring the warriors with whose sachems he had allegedly made alliances. So we are urged to imagine a carefully planned war, moving in grand coordination from the Rhode Island frontier into Massachusetts; not a series of separate raids by provoked people but a brilliantly orchestrated war, conducted by a devilish military genius.

Local historians of the New England towns often (but not

always) fell into the same trap of repeating, even embroidering the propagandistic stories of William Hubbard, Increase Mather, and Nathaniel Saltonstall. Dartmouth historian Leonard B. Ellis wrote of the "untold violence and horrible torture from the Indians" that had been inflicted on his town's settlers. By contrast, it is instructive to visit Dartmouth and to be led not by the ancient mythmakers but by the modern students of land records and dwelling sites. This provides a somewhat different view of what actually happened there in July 1675.

Dartmouth, in reality, turns out not to be the typical idealized Puritan community, but quite the opposite. The unorthodox purchasers of the large, subdivided lots had come here from a diversity of places, each choosing to pursue a rather individualistic destiny. The settlers built thirty-six "substantial, two-story dwellings," one source verifies, the houses spread down along the banks of the Apponagansett and other gently flowing rivers. Fields were fertile and not excessively rocky; Quaker and Baptist farmers flourished by hard work. Entrepreneurs developed dams for millponds, forges for ironmaking, sheds for shipbuilding. One writer left a picture of an interior scene in a Dartmouth home at wintertime: boys warming themselves in the central fireplace, perched on the ends of the burning logs and looking up through the chimney at the stars.

Against the possibility of an attack by the natives, three sizable houses had been designated "garrisons": one in present-day Fairhaven, one on Palmer's Island (New Bedford), and one on the Apponagansett. There food and ammunition were stored, and to them would flock the widespread inhabitants when a danger signal was given.

But the Wampanoags nearby seemed peaceful enough. They were named the Acushnet, Apponagansett, and Acoaxet peoples. Directly across the Apponagansett from the garrison house of John Russell was a little native village called Indian Town. We may wonder what tensions existed between this dependent, ghettoized subcommunity and its mastertown. In the somewhat similar town of Little Compton, Benjamin Church described those tensions by saying that the settlers, as they prospered, became "very jealous [meaning suspicious] of the Indians."

A pertinent story preserved in Dartmouth memory (and in a faded newspaper clipping from the 1930s) tells of a young malcontent in Indian Town who decided, one day, that he'd had enough of servility. Standing on a wall and turning toward the garrison, he made a vigorous and rude gesture. Immediately he was shot—obviously by a superior marksman, for the cross-river distance is about an eighth of a mile. Later, after the alleged massacre, Church rendered his own report on Dartmouth in which one can find implications about the sour relationships between settlers and natives here. But even without it, when you stand in the field before the garrison house site and gaze across the river, you gain a feeling of the people-to-people distances, the resentments and hostilities (of which the young malcontent was the embodiment) that existed here before a shot was fired.

When news of the uprising at Swansea reached Dartmouth, it surely caused instant alarm, among the Wampanoags as well as the whites. For the Wampanoags years of repressed anger must have then burst forth with passion and swift action— whether or not Philip himself or one of his lieutenants led the people to their task of vengeance.

The native assault first hit the outlying houses, it appears. Then, success building on success, more and more houses were put to the torch. Apparently most of Dartmouth's terrified residents had withdrawn to the garrisons, from which they watched the rising pillars of smoke as surrounding houses were set ablaze. At least one family is known to have been caught at home, where all were killed. These, most probably, were the victims who received the ghastly treatment recorded by Increase Mather of having been "barbarously murdered." He went on to describe the attackers' behavior: "Such also is their inhumanity as that they flay off the skin from their [victims'] faces and heads . . . and go away with the scalps of their enemies." Yet Mather remained curiously vague about the specific people and the particulars of who struck whom when.

After burning the Dartmouth residents' thirty-six homes, the attackers seem to have concentrated on the Russell garrison, a holdout point from which the defenders fought back with courage and vigor. Leading the defense were Captain Samuel Eels and Ralph Earl. By the time Benjamin Church arrived, these two and their men had succeeded not only in driving off the Wampanoag attackers but also in taking quite a number captive. So perhaps this was no wholesale massacre after all. Church found the natives securely under guard and peace restored. We can read that part of his description with some satisfaction. But we also shudder as the rest of the soldier's tale transpires. He and his men,

> coming to Russell's garrison at Poneganset . . . met with a number of the enemy that had surrendered themselves prisoners on terms promised by Captain Eels, of the garrison, and Ralph Earl, that persuaded them (by a friend[ly] Indian he had employed) to come in. And, had their promises to the Indians been kept, and the Indians fairly treated, 'tis probable that most, if not all the Indians in those parts, had soon followed the example of those that had now surrendered themselves, which would have been a good step towards finishing the war.
>
> But, in spite of all that Captain Eels, Church, or Earl could say, argue, plead, or beg, somebody else that had more power in their

hands improved it; and, without any regard to the promises made them on surrendering themselves, they were carried away to Plymouth, there sold, transported out of the country, being about eightscore persons—an action so hateful to Mr. Church that he opposed it to the loss of the good will and respect of some that before were his good friends.

Researching this disgraceful abandonment of principle some two centuries later, New Bedford's Thomas Rodman found confirmation of Church's account in the records of Plymouth. A court order under the appropriate date referred to 112 men, women, and children who had been brought in to Plymouth, presumably from Dartmouth, "natives now in custody." After "serious and deliberate consideration," the court decided that, because some of these people had been

> actors in the late rising and war of the Indians against us, and the rest complyers therein . . . which Philip with others completed against us, which has caused the destruction of severall of us, by loss of lives and estates . . . the council adjuged them to be sold and devoted into servitude.

The phrase "Philip with others" seems a giveaway: Philip in fact could not be named as chief for he was then known to be in the Pocasset Swamps. Yet it was by using his name that this outrageous act of enslavement could be justified.

Meanwhile, the English army at Swansea continued to solidify an already strong position. The soldiers also destroyed some one thousand acres of Indian cornfields and rounded up hogs and cattle from Philip's recently enlarged, now demolished home base at Mount Hope. Certain squads also conducted inept probes into the Pocasset Swamps, seeking Philip and his sister-in-law, Weetamoo.

Additionally, a large force had been detailed to march to

Wickford, there to pressure the Narragansetts into a treaty of neutrality (which became known as the Treaty of Pettaquam-scutt Rock). With Philip having eluded the English and the dangers of an enlarged war now apparent, Massachusetts Bay authorities wanted to do whatever possible to keep the Narragansetts out of the conflict—and to prohibit their providing a haven for Pokanoket war refugees. Certain aged sachems were found by the Bay delegates to sign the proffered treaty under force (and under the eyes of Roger Williams). The sachem Canonchet was then praised and flattered by the English, a splendid gift pushed at him. This was a silver-trimmed coat, a special incentive for delivering the fleeing Weetamoo into English hands (which would be a total violation of traditional Algonquian rules of honorable behavior) if she was caught. A ruler as sophisticated and principled as Canonchet was probably not much impressed by these oafish diplomatic tactics, whatever his feelings at that point about the long-debated alliance with Philip.

During this time of English maneuvering, Philip and Weetamoo decided to make their move away from the delimiting safety of Pocasset and to broader freedom among friends and relatives to the north. Perhaps they might have been discovered and disarmed, brought swiftly to account; Church believed that, if the pursuit had been less incompetently managed, the war could have been ended then and there. But Captains Daniel Henchman and Samuel Moseley found the task beyond them. Philip's and Weetamoo's superior knowledge of the land allowed them to slip the English leash, finding a safe way through or around the search parties. And, after the next few days of cat-and-mouse fighting, with the English constantly returning in exhausted condition to home base with nothing accomplished, the natives' contemptuous view of the Puritans' capabilities seemed justified.

Major Thomas Savage, newly arrived at the front and appointed commander-in-chief, allowed his men to be ambushed
in a shadowy valley. A large number of English having been
killed and wounded in that encounter, Philip took advantage of
the victory by moving swiftly across the Taunton River, heading north. Unfortunately for him, one of the three Pokanokets
killed in the darkened valley was his next-in-line brother, Sun-
conewhew.

There was other bad news for the fleeing Philip: Uncas, the
unfailing Mohegan friend of the English, had stirred himself
and sent fifty warriors to aid the settlers' cause. His son Oneko,
having gone first to Boston then to Plymouth for orders, was at
this moment approaching Swansea and Rehoboth with a large
force. Eagerly he undertook the pursuit of Philip and Weetamoo, whose progress was slowed by baggage, animals, and children. A tremendous battle of opposed native warriors resulted,
Philip having positioned his most valiant men to conduct the
rearguard battle to the end.

The Mohegans might have actually overriden Philip's rearguard fighters if the desire for plunder had not held back the
victors as they looted through the Pokanoket camp. Then,
when Daniel Henchman arrived with additional English troops,
the pursuing army was saddled with official indecision. Henchman also heeded the request from his farmer-soldiers that they
must soon be allowed to get home to harvest their crops. Concluding that Philip and Weetamoo had already escaped up the
Blackstone River, he called off the chase on August 3.

The Mohegans were sent back to Connecticut with com-
mendations. But what had been an abrasive and vicious contest
between two neighboring people now looked like a regional
war, a war beyond the capacities of the English colonial forces.

4

Frontier Rebels and the Narragansett Gamble

The War in Western New England and Rhode Island

Somewhere along the course of Rhode Island's Blackstone River, Philip and Weetamoo decided to take separate trails through the forests. Weetamoo and her Sakonnets, accompanied by a number of aged and infirm Pokanokets, headed southwest, seeking refuge among the Niantics of Ninigret, the troublemaking neutralist. "Unto Ninnicroft she went," in the words of a contemporary writer. There she hoped to find that protection which the Massachusetts Bay authorities had sought to deny her by their treaty with the Narragansetts at Pettaquamscutt Rock. But Philip, presumably seeking both safety and a way of carrying on the conflict, headed northwest. There he would be in the land of the Nipmucks, with whom his alliances and family connections were as strong as their mutual resentment of the English.

As depicted on William Hubbard's map (the medieval-styled woodcut of early New England), Europeans tended to regard

Algonquian groups as nations, with regal dominion over definite territories. Yet the Nipmucks—whose name means "Fresh Water People," designating that they hailed from the interior—added up to not much more than the changing sum of whichever interior villages chose to work together at a given time. When Philip arrived in Nipmuck territory, however, the combined villages were dominated by a small number of dynamic personalities who provided some central leadership for the peoples.

One of these sachems was Muttawmp of Quaboag (near Brookfield); another, Matoonas of Pakachoog (Worcester). Though Matoonas had once been the faithful chief officer, or "constable," of his Praying Indian community, he had acquired an everlasting hatred of the English when they executed his son for a murder of which he was clearly innocent. Matoonas's first opportunity to put that hatred into action was a raid on Mendon immediately after the Swansea uprising. Then, with the success of Mendon behind him (six settlers killed and many farm buildings put to the torch), he could look forward to other strikes in company with his Nipmuck and Nashaway associates.

Shortly before Philip's arrival in Nipmuck country, Matoonas and Muttawmp had executed the next move, a much bolder and larger-scaled attack on Brookfield. It alerted all southern New England, as Swansea and Dartmouth had not, to the horrifying reality that New England's Algonquians were on the march, with the means and the might to hit any desired target. It also displayed the natives' strategic intelligence: Muttawmp, who like Matoonas had forsworn his conversion to Christianity, apparently viewed Brookfield as a worthwhile objective because of its well-stocked farms and a sensible one because of its isolation from defended towns. Toward Brookfield he directed the burning energies of some two hundred warriors.

Earlier, Massachusetts Bay's Governor John Leverett (appointed in 1673 and elected eternally thereafter) had been informed of the increasing alienation of the Nipmucks, especially the younger braves. Hoping to rectify the situation, Leverett, a veteran of the Cromwellian wars, had sent out a number of carefully selected spokesmen to attempt negotiations. The first of these, a hunter and trader named Ephraim Curtis, had returned with word that Matoonas's Praying Indian community of Quaboag had been abandoned, that the Nipmucks were gathered at council fires in the hills, but that the possibility for peaceful talks still existed. Next to go out was Captain Edward Hutchinson (son of the banished Anne Hutchinson), who maintained a large farm in Nipmuck territory and employed many presumably grateful native agricultural workers. He was to lead a troop of thirty booted and helmeted horsemen—evidence that the English were prepared to fight if negotiations failed (or possibly prepared to seize hostages).

Hutchinson's force was preceded by three Christian Indian guides and by Ephraim Curtis, who continued to play the role of go-between. But though Curtis again succeeded in finding and talking with Muttawmp and in arranging a meeting place for the next day's conference with him and Captain Hutchinson, no Nipmucks showed up at the appointed time (August 1, 1675). To Hutchinson's native guides, the signs on the ground were suspicious . . . signs of many marching men. But the captain pushed on, waving aside the suggestion that a trap might be waiting around the narrow trail's next turning. The Brookfield men who had joined Hutchinson agreed with the audacious captain, believing that the Quaboag natives, good Christians and trusty laborers, would surely not turn treacherous after so many years of harmonious living.

The trap was sprung soon after the English had passed a tight place between a swamp on the right and a cliff on the left. Up out of the swamp grasses swarmed a force of hidden braves; immediately, eight of Hutchinson's troop were killed and he himself given a wound that would later prove fatal. A portion of the English horsemen escaped Muttawmp's skillfully prepared trap by dashing up the hill and finding a little-used trail back to Brookfield, thanks to the aid of their still-loyal guides.

The siege of Brookfield that followed this sharp encounter lives on in spooky legends and hair-raising art. There is a story of a God-sent deluge that extinguished the flaming contents of a farm cart that the Nipmucks had pushed up against the side of the garrison house into which the settlers and soldiers had run. And there is also an early-twentieth-century engraving of the leanly muscled native warriors, each one blessed with a superb feather headdress, firing flaming arrows at the garrison in the midst of the storm and waiting to take another potshot at someone foolish enough to poke a head out of the shutters. Two of the English did attempt a sortie; they were the first victims of the siege.

Relief came not in the form of another Puritan miracle but in the person of an aged cavalry officer, Simon Willard, who galloped overland with a force from Lancaster. The battle that ensued on the fourth of August was fierce and inconclusive, each side withdrawing with a share of victory. But the ambush and siege at Brookfield gave warning to all New England that Algonquian discontent and military coordination had reached the point where any community throughout the region might expect to suffer from an expertly led attack in force. It also forewarned that negotiations for peace, if ever they were to be conducted in the future, would have to be held under conditions of guaranteed security for each side; passions were raised too high for any other course.

It was at this moment, when Muttawmp and Matoonas and their warriors were celebrating their victory in the newly constructed Nipmuck fort at Wenimisset (west of Brookfield), that Philip, the first rebel of them all, appeared with his company of forty or fifty men plus their women and children. According to Leo Bonfanti, author of several booklets on native Americans, Philip then gave each of the victorious Nipmuck leaders a "peck of unstrung wampum" to demonstrate his appreciation for their deeds. Certainly his hope was now stronger that the joint objective of punishing the English heavily might be achieved.

But was there a larger hope—such as to push the English into the sea? Or to strike so many of the outlying communities that the settlers would be driven out of the interior? And, on the other hand, was there a decision by the United Colonies (formal or otherwise) to take this opportunity to exterminate these troublesome Algonquians? Or to divide and conquer them on one front after another? Over the years all of these hypotheses have been put forth by historians. But as we have seen, both societies fought as they could, in each theater, strategy developing as the struggle went along. Each side hoped, out of misery or fear or suspicion, to change the balance by battle.

The best illustration of this as-it-went-along procedure is the non-campaign that developed on the Bay Colony's western frontier—a theater that reacted in panic and excitement to the news from Brookfield. Here, eighty miles from Boston and forty from Lancaster and twenty from Brookfield, there were neither English military forces nor hope of swift assistance if the natives should take up arms. To these communities northward along the Connecticut River from Springfield no Major Simon Willard could come galloping upon word of attack. Recognizing their importance and their fragility, Governor Leverett set about sending the towns what supporting forces he could find.

The stakes were high. For since John Oldham's day this bountiful valley of meadows between sharply rising hills had become the breadbasket of New England and other English colonies. Though Springfield had been founded by William Pynchon as headquarters for the fur trade in the golden era of the 1630s, and though fur and wampum continued to power the local economy for the next two decades, that productive combination of resources and peoples had disappeared by the 1660s. Then wheat and other English grains became king. John Pynchon (William's capable son) was shipping 1,500 bushels of wheat annually from the Connecticut River valley to his coastal clients in the decade before King Philip's War; it was in fact New England wheat that relieved the Virginia famine of 1674.

To this temperate and fertile valley streamed colonial farmers, bent on attaining the English dream of a family homestead. And, moving into the baronial role of land dispenser, John Pynchon eagerly and conscientiously knit together the would-be land purchasers and the River Indians by means of a series of mutually agreeable land deeds. His purposes were to develop products for his shipping systems, to inhabit the valley in the face of possible French and Dutch threats, and perhaps to construct in the wilderness a biracial society that would enjoy freedom from both Bay and crown. He continued to represent the flexible, constructive peacekeeper in the midst of destructive social and racial pressures. Responding to his invitations, homesteaders made their way through chestnut-dense forests to the meander-carved valley of the Connecticut.

The native population had been stressed by decades of European contact and consequent change—stressed not so much from disease and brutality (though those had both occurred) as from tribal conflicts related to increased competition for European contacts. Typical of the River Indians who had suffered punishment at the hands of other Algonquians in company with the shifts in trade economy were the Pocumtucks, whose main village was located at present-day Deerfield. After the Pequot War—which, as seen, was fought to put in place an English-Mohegan monopoly where once the Pequots held sway—the Pocumtucks suffered for their ages-old antipathy to the Mohegans. John Mason himself came upriver to collect the fine of one and one-quarter fathoms of wampum per man, the price of being caught on the wrong side.

The Pocumtucks were then able to regain prominence by means of an alliance with the Narragansetts to the southeast and the Mohawks to the northwest. Sited in the central position, they grew in strength and went on to broaden their federation to include the Pennacooks and Abnakis in New Hampshire and Maine. But, for reasons unknown to modern historians—perhaps the urgings of the French or perhaps arrogance, as one historian suggests—the Pocumtuck-Mohawk connection snapped in 1664: that summer the Pocumtucks committed the international crime of murdering a visiting princely Mohawk ambassador. War could be the only result.

In order to meet the Mohawk army that then stormed in from the west, the Pocumtucks built a sizable redoubt overlooking Deerfield at Fort Hill (a yet-to-be-excavated site). But neither the fortress nor skillful field tactics succeeded in holding the Mohawks back; the Pocumtucks were decimated. Then the enemy from the west continued to rage eastward, battering other segments of the Pocumtuck Confederacy, including the Pennacooks and the Abnakis. Even the Squakheags in present-day Northfield (who had long ago found protection from native rivals by welcoming a European trading post in their midst) and their close cousins the Sokokis in

Maine felt the sting of the avenging Mohawks, in a war not ended until 1671.

The ferocity of these recent native battles must have been recollected as the settlers heard from their preachers' pulpits of the horror at Brookfield: God under fire from the devils of the wilderness. Yet many of the Connecticut valley farmers must also have nursed the hope (as had the townspeople of Dartmouth and Edward Hutchinson of central Massachusetts) that the natives who worked in *their* fields, helped grind *their* corn and build *their* houses were far too thoroughly cowed to attempt any insurrection. The time of equality between settlers and natives had obviously passed with the phasing out of wampum, but was there not now a convenient and well-established master-servant relationship? Or would that relationship prove so corruptive as to wreck the frontier society John Pynchon worked to advance?

Deerfield, which would be the scene of the first military activity of King Philip's War in the valley, gives one small answer to that large question. Today the town's central village stands as a restored historic site, designed to bring alive the social history of the seventeenth and eighteenth centuries. It also affords an opportunity for visitors to ponder the still-pertinent realities of local native-settler relations. What went wrong here, and is that flaw a built-in part of the New England tradition?

Like the newly arrived planters who rejoiced in the liberality of these fields and the drama of these hills, present-day visitors to Deerfield are swept by the feeling that, in such a paradise, all natural and human forces must be benign. The river loops through the broad valley; the hills block out the rest of the world; the houses with their tiny, seventeenth-century windows and handsome "Valley" doorways stand graciously back from gently ascending Main Street. The Deerfield River, while picturesque, is peculiar: it runs *north* in an abnormal way; only when it gets three miles past the village does it succeed in breaking through the chain of hills and turning east for a confluence with the thunderous, *south*-running Connecticut. Local historian George Sheldon referred to those blocking, interlocked hills as "two strands of an enormous cable." And the Pocumtucks referred to this topographically taut location as *Pemawachuatuck*, "at the twisted mountain."

The circumstances by which the English settlers got here is also a bit peculiar. Back in 1651, when John Eliot was laying out his first Praying Indian village at Natick, he ran into a problem with the town of Dedham; its selectmen had said that the experimental Christian community of Natick was being built illegally, on their land. The case was eventually heard by the General Court. In a classic verdict of nobody loses, the Court decreed that, although the Praying Indians of Natick should not be displaced, Dedham deserved to be given eight thousand acres by way of compensation—acres to be found somewhere to the west. After a few false starts, and after John Pynchon had been retained to help with the search, the Dedham selectmen chose Deerfield, a strangely quiet place after the Pocumtucks' defeat by the Mohawks, a place that would figure importantly in King Philip's War.

By 1667 the land had been officially acquired: a sachem by the name of Chauk had been found to sign the deed with his mark, on behalf of all Pocumtucks. By 1669 the first purchaser of a land plot, a farmer named Samuel Hinsdale, was plowing his land. By 1670 the main street and subsidiary ways had been laid out. And by 1673, after independence was won from Dedham, the first church was established. With the meeting house framed and roofed, Samuel Mather was called in 1675 to be the first minister. There were more than twenty families in the village to greet him when he rode up Main Street.

In the open meadows on the south and west and north sides of the settlement, farmers planted crops of wheat and rye, flax and peas, Indian corn and beans. In their yard gardens they grew vegetables and fruits (apples, pears, and quince). At the heart of town was a fenced-in common; livestock was allowed to forage on the hillsides during the grazing season, and the natives did not seem to mind. The fact that the settlers were in the middle of a "savage" wilderness—the nearest English community being the former trading post at Northfield (Squakheag)—seemed to cause no trepidation.

As for the remaining Pocumtucks and other regional Algonquians, it appeared that they had made adequate provision for themselves in the initial land deeds. The Pocumtucks had retained for themselves the rights to hunt, fish, and gather wild fruits and nuts even on land staked out by the settlers. Their deeds' provisions generally gave "Liberty of fishing [to] ye Indians in ye Rivers or waters and free Liberty to hunt Deere or other Wild creatures and to gather Walnuts, chestnuts and other nuts, etc. on ye Commons." Although the deeds seemed fair, they concealed a heavy-handed paternalism. The natives were imagined to be frozen in their own, primitive economy. Although they would pick up whatever they could forage and would work for the settlers when needed, playing a marginal role at the fringe of this prosperous, new-agricultural community with its improved iron tools and strong marketing ties to the commercial world beyond, they would own no part of it. Psychologically or physically.

"Did [the Pocumtucks and] the Squakheags have the *technical* ability to withdraw from the fur trade [of old] and still meet their basic material needs?" asks the regional ethnohistorian

Peter Allen Thomas in a recent study. Yes but no, he replies to his own question, pointing out that the iron plows and the English seeds and the agricultural techniques that made Deerfield's soil yield so richly were not easily available to all. Dr. Thomas's thesis—entitled "In the Maelstrom of Change: The Indians Trade and Cultural Process in the Middle Connecticut River Valley, 1635–1665"—goes on to demonstrate at length how and why these River Indians did *not* successfully make the transition from the fur-trading era to the new agricultural age.

Instead, up and down the valley there was an unhealthy pattern of unequal and discriminatory relations between the thriving settlers and the displaced natives. Now that they could no longer barter venison or beaver for the needed and desired English goods, the women tried to sell baskets or birch brooms, the men to work at menial agricultural tasks they despised. In the words of a perceptive nineteenth-century writer, the natives "saw themselves sinking in degradation and subservience before the rising power of their white neighbors." Or, in the cruelly apt phrase of nationalist historian George Bancroft, they came to depend on and even love "the crums [*sic*] from the white man's table."

In regional court records George Sheldon found sad evidence of how the native population responded to this life of enforced dependency.

In 1665, Nenawan was fined "40 shillings or 20 fathams" for breaking into Praisever Turner's mill. In 1667 Quequelett was "whipt 20 lashes" for helping Godfrey Nims and Benoni Stebbins [presumably bond servants] "about running away to Canada." Indians were fined 40 shillings for a "breach of the Sabbath, in traveling to and fro," at Springfield. For "bringing apples from Windsor, and firing a gun" on Sunday, a fine was imposed on a party at Warranoco.

Sachem Umpachala and Wattawolunskin of Pocumtuck were fined for drunkenness.

Such details help project a sharp-featured image of the Algonquian here as a member of the subproletariat, fit only to consort with other servants and to suffer the law's lash for imposed poverty. It was into these troubled waters that the revolutionary news from Swansea and Brookfield was dropped.

Perhaps an imaginative and unprejudiced society would have been able to soothe the tensions. Instead, in the Connecticut valley, every move made by the settlers seemed calculated to heighten them. With Hadley named headquarters for the three troops sent by Massachusetts Bay to secure this vital region in early summer of 1675, settler-native relations grew even tenser. John Pynchon urged everyone around him not to overreact to the news from distant Swansea, but few listened. He protested his unfitness for any military position, but had to agree when the title of commander in chief was forced upon him.

Then in August came the report of the Brookfield siege. The military at Hadley immediately demanded that the neighboring, "threatening" Norwottocks surrender their weapons—which would, among other things, prevent them from hunting and supporting themselves. When, briefly, after the Norwottocks came up with the ingenious idea of joining the soldiers in a search for any westward-wandering Quaboags (the presumed attackers of Brookfield), the weapons were returned to them. But it seemed to the three commanders at Hadley—Captains Watts, Lothrop, and Beers—that the Norwottocks had been less than enthusiastic in their search; neither any Quaboags nor any other hostile Nipmucks had been found. Indeed there were signs that the Norwottocks were fortifying their village on the west bank of the Connecticut, all too close to Hatfield, turning it into a strongpoint for their own warriors and for other River Indians. So the commanders decided to get the weapons back.

A swift-footed native informer carried the news of the English commander's decision to the Norwottocks' camp, causing the people to gather around the council fire to debate their possible options. One choice was to forget about the remarkable success of the Wampanoag and Nipmuck raiders, to disband the fortress, and to turn a peaceful face to the English, bowing to each new demand. The other choice was to take up arms and to make a war alliance with the other Algonquian warriors who were now massing in the region.

An elderly Norwottock stood up to suggest that, if patience were applied, surely the current contentions would pass away and the former times of mutually advantageous harmony would return. At once a loud argument developed—or so the incident is recalled by local historians—with younger braves demanding action against the English. When the elderly sachem stood up again, he was killed with a blow from a young brave's tomahawk. Thus was the decision made: they would fight the English; with no further discussion, the Norwottocks abandoned their village and moved north, with the thought of joining the equally discontent Pocumtucks.

Captains Lothrop and Beers, on finding the native fortress evacuated, set off in pursuit of the Norwottocks with a force of one hundred. But native tactics proved a match for English might. As the soldiers hurried along the trail, climbing the ridge that rises between South Deerfield and the river (Sugarloaf Mountain), they fell into a trap carefully prepared by the Norwottocks' rear guard. In the sharp action that followed, nine of the English soldiers were slain, and the bulk of the fleeing natives were able to reach the Pocumtucks' village. Yet in the prose of the Puritan propagandists, this battle at South Deerfield, this initial episode of King Philip's War in the Connecticut valley, was counted as a victory for the English. Had not the marauding savages been driven away by Lothrop's dauntless men? The successful combining of two armed and ready native groups was quite ignored.

At virtually the same time (August 24–25), raids were carried out by roving Nipmucks on Springfield, much to the consternation of John Pynchon and other peacefully inclined settlers. They had believed that the local Agawams, unlike the Norwottocks and the Pocumtucks, would remain loyal. But, as a cautionary move, the settlers decided that they should take the Agawams' weapons and hold some of their children as hostages. That move so angered the Agawams that they reconsidered their neutrality; later, after a subsequent and dazzlingly successful Nipmuck attack on the town, they swung their entire support to the rebels' side.

The valley frontier burst into flames: Deerfield was struck again and Northfield was subjected to a large-scale attack in which eight settlers were killed and wide damage done to farms and crops. When a relief expedition of thirty-six troopers and teamsters under Captain Beers rolled up the valley to Northfield, it was virtually wiped out at a ford south of town. The siege that followed, staged by the local Squakheags plus other allies, was finally broken by Connecticut's Robert Treat and his force of downriver colonials.

For the Puritans used to seeing God's hand in everything and his predetermining favor at the root of all events, the black news from the valley was doubly discouraging. The fields and orchards now under attack were ripe with crops for harvesting; food would be short that winter. And it appeared that a divine judgment of some disturbing sort was being rendered. In the distressed and fearful mood of the day, hatred of the enemy became a racial matter. Even Praying Indians were seized or hanged or driven out into Boston's Deer Island for internment. Popular approval supported wild Captain Samuel Moseley when he, returned from the search for Philip, burned to the ground two native villages in New Hampshire, villages that had been under the protection of the peaceful sachem Wonnalancet. Though there was some official outcry against his action, Moseley's family relationship with Governor Leverett protected him from punishment. Then he capped the New Hampshire action by storming into the Praying Indian villages of Nashobo (Littleton) and Okammakamest (Marlborough). There he roped together fifteen of the inhabitants, conducting them first to Boston, where they were nearly lynched, then to Deer Island, where they were interned in conditions of starvation and misery.

The purported deviltry of Philip of Pokanoket was sufficient excuse for any attack on native Americans. Philip's hand was seen even in the uprising of the Abnakis on the Maine coast in the early fall of the year. It was specifically against him that Robert Treat's force of Connecticut soldiers had been sent forth, first pursuing him and his Wampanoags as they fled northward into Nipmuck territory, then chasing the spirit of his rebellion all the way up the Connecticut River to Northfield. Though these soldiers did not find their great enemy in the ripening fields or brilliant forests of the autumnal valley, they felt happy enough to be assigned to guard duty in one or another of these upriver towns. For they were keeping *him* from their homes.

Massachusetts Bay propagandists, too, combined fact with fiction to give its citizen-soldiers a keen sense of the Devil they were opposing. Holiness itself was on the battle line, it appeared. Perhaps the best example of the Puritan writers' creative efforts was their tale of how a saint appeared in the midst of a wholly imaginary battle for Hadley on September 1. As John Fiske repeated the tale:

> The inhabitants were all in church keeping a fast, when the yells of the Indians resounded. Seizing their guns, the men rushed out to meet the force; but seeing the village green swarming on every side with the horrid savages, for a moment their courage gave way and a panic was imminent; when all at once a stranger of reverend aspect and stately form, with white beard blowing on his bosom, appeared among them and took command with an air of authority which none could gainsay. He bade them charge on the screeching rabble, and after a sharp skirmish the tawny foe was put to flight. When the pursuers came together again, after the excitement of the rout, their deliverer was not to be found.

Just who was this figment? He was, the romanticists went on to repeat, the "regicide judge" William Goffe—that is, one of the British magistrates who had ordered the severing of King Charles I's head. He had been hiding in the New World, the story went, ever since the restoration of the Stuarts. For Puritans, Goffe was as close as a man could come to being a saint—and so it was small surprise that he had materialized in New England at a time when his supernatural power was needed for a town's defense. Historian Fiske explained away the odd fact that certain Puritan chroniclers (namely Hubbard and Mather) had not chosen to mention the saint's fortuitous appearance by saying that those writers' concern for Goffe's personal safety from royal authorities overrode their desire to credit him with Hadley's salvation.

A story more factual and far more threatening to the Bay was then written regarding actions on the western frontier—again at Deerfield, shortly after the momentous decision was made by the military to withdraw all settlers from Northfield. The event took place over the course of several days and opened on September 12, a Sunday, when watchful Pocumtucks fell upon worshipers returning along Main Street to the Stockwell garrison from Deerfield's meetinghouse. As settlers swiftly took cover, only one man was killed, but two houses were burned and a number of horses and wagonloads of beef were taken. A force of English soldiers, dispatched to round up the local raiders, could find no one as they combed the nearby hills.

Military leaders and settlers alike pondered the deteriorating situation. Just as there seemed to be a host of Nipmucks in the area poised to make massive strikes from without, so there were close-up enemies within waiting to make subtle and knowing raids upon farms and settlements. Could the valley resist this double threat? Would Deerfield, too, have to be abandoned (as John Pynchon urged, depressed by the regional crisis and by the low response to draft calls in Massachusetts Bay)? If Deerfield were evacuated and all the region's settlers huddled into a few, heavily fortified bastions, the scene would indeed be depressing, like England in the Dark Ages.

Pynchon wanted nothing more than for the war to end. His mill and trading businesses were in ruins, his self-admitted inadequacies as commander in chief all too clearly revealed, his dream of a bicultural society smashed. Responding to Pynchon's pleas for an end to the war not with a far-reaching policy toward peace but with more boots-and-helmet warriors, Governor Leverett sent forth Captain Samuel Moseley, his dogs and his reputation preceding him. The Bay's strategy, if it can be called that, was simple: while Captain Lothrop was ordered to Deerfield to protect the harvest from local attackers, Moseley and his gang would seek out the mightier enemies, the Nipmucks, wherever they might be.

Among those who watched the new English troops arrive at Deerfield was Muttawmp, Nipmuck victor of Brookfield. His forces had been augmented by Pocumtucks and Norwottocks flocking to his cause. But his seven hundred warriors, for all their numbers, were not enough to counter the armed might that the English could muster. Far better to continue fighting the hit-and-run battles he knew how to win, the destructive ambushes and assaults for grain and cattle, than to risk any large-scale confrontation. His mission was clear: he would take away from the English whatever they harvested and whatever they needed to support themselves; that would lead to victory. Deerfield continued to be his perfect target.

The landscape viewed by Muttawmp, upon the fields beyond the town, could have been painted by Breughel: the soldiers, shedding shirts and weapons because of the heat of the day, had set off in search of wild grapes to slake their thirst; the farmers piled hay on the wagons and put their own weapons aboard too, getting ready for the leisurely ramble south. Muttawmp saw at a glance how to stage the most effective attack.

Captain Lothrop should have suspected what lay ahead when his wagons encountered a large number of trees that had been felled across the southward track at Muddy Brook. The train of carts halted, those in the rear piling up on those in front. Amid the shouting and confusion, the first musket shots were heard. It was an ambush. Lothrop was slain within the first few minutes; most of his soldiers fell with him, before they could grab their weapons. A few of the teamsters, lying low and wriggling through the underbrush, escaped to tell of the slaughter. The victorious Algonquians leaped upon the wagons, ripping open the English bed sacks that protected the grain, searching the bodies of the fallen for anything of value. But suddenly they were caught themselves in a rain of bullets from the surrounding woods; Moseley's seventy troopers, alerted by the sounds of battle, now charged down from the hills.

Muttawmp's men successfully fought off the counterattack, however, killing a number of the troopers. Then, recognizing the infamous Moseley as their opponent, they baited him to come forward again, to continue the battle here in the sun-and-shadow dappled woods where the advantage was still theirs. "Come, Moseley, come!" they called (as Hubbard described the encounter). "You seek Indians, you want Indians? Here is Indians enough for you!" So Moseley and his men fought on until nightfall, finally leaving the field of battle to the Algonquians.

Too late by several hours, Connecticut's Robert Treat made an appearance. By then Muddy Brook had won its new name— Bloody Brook. Along with Treat marched a company of one hundred soldiers and sixty Mohegans (including Uncas's second son, Attawanhood); they might have had the woodland skills, alongside the firepower of Moseley's troopers, to vanquish Muttawmp. But now they could only wait until daybreak and serve as gravediggers. In summarizing the loss of seventy-one soldiers at Bloody Brook, Hubbard called it "the saddest day that ever befell New England."

Soon thereafter, on October 5, a combined force of Agawams and Nipmuck veterans freely attacked Springfield, burning thirty houses at what had been proudly viewed as the English capital of the region. Treat, again arriving too late, was surrounded by the enemy and broke free only when assistance arrived from Hadley. It now appeared that the Puritan commanders of the west would be no more effective in winning battles or concocting strategies than their colleagues in the east had been in capturing the man who supposedly began the war.

As anxiety increased across the Puritan commonwealth, the rage of intolerance against all other philosophies intensified.

Many of the devout even concluded that it was God himself who had "let loose the savages, with firebrand and tomahawk." It was apparently his purpose "to punish the people of New England for ceasing to persecute 'false worshippers and especially idolatrous Quakers.' " More of the hapless natives were hanged on Boston Common, more Praying Indians sent off to the West Indies in slavery, more Christian villages closed down, their inhabitants crowded onto Deer Island, where neither adequate food nor housing existed.

At Marblehead, some months later, women returning from church services happened upon a group of captive Algonquians. Raising the cry against them, the women proceeded to beat the natives to death. A certain Mrs. Mary Pray of Providence recommended to the authorities the total extermination of "the red race." The Quakers—who resisted the draft and some of whose members had been forced to run the painful gauntlet between angry Puritan paddlers—were now forbidden to hold any meetings whatsoever, under penalty of fine and imprisonment.

Even as church and state authorities struggled to overcome subversives by tightening the controls of orthodoxy, the colonists showed increasing signs of disunity. The settlers of the western frontier towns loathed the brutal-minded soldiers who occupied the garrisons; the soldiers deserted, plotted to be elsewhere. Robert Treat, nominally second-in-command of the entire force, had taken it upon himself to march away from the battlefront; on September 30, he and his Connecticut citizen-soldiers and their Mohegan allies had simply headed south. His excuse was that, being under orders from Hartford, he must heed a cry for help from Wethersfield, where panic reigned after rumors of a native attack; the upriver valley towns could fend for themselves. Treat was finally persuaded to return. And Major Pynchon, his pleas finally heard, was replaced as commander in chief by Samuel Appleton.

Muttawmp must have been aware of the English command's disarray. The October air was now sharp, the blaze in the hills dying, the time right for the assault that might crack the English. In his versatile mind a move took shape that could be followed by a final blow. And so on October 19, Muttawmp's forces hit the center of the English-occupied valley towns— Hatfield.

The initial plan was both shrewd and of a piece with broader strategies. Muttawmp staged affairs so that great fires were ignited in the south, creating the impression that a major attack was under way in the direction of Northampton. But Samuel Moseley, then in charge of the Hatfield garrison, had become native-wise: he declined to send out a significant exploratory force, one that would leave the town exposed. Finally yielding to the alarmed citizens, he sent a squad of ten men to ride out and investigate. As Moseley had expected, the riders soon fell into a murderous ambush; only one of them escaped, returning with news of the disaster. Fortunately for the English, his return coincided with the arrival of Major Appleton, who had come to the relief of Hatfield even at the risk of the Hadley headquarters.

Now the surrounding Algonquians faced a concentrated and reinforced English military corps. They launched several attacks, charging at times into the very center of the town, burning a number of houses, capturing prisoners and taking livestock. But as the day drew to a close, Muttawmp concluded that he could not overwhelm the English. He ordered his men to withdraw, content with the victory of the moment.

Though hungry and harassed and thoroughly dispirited, the English garrisons held on at Hatfield and elsewhere. Their invented-on-the-spot bastion strategy had preserved them when all else failed. The Algonquians departed for winter quarters, recognizing that their plan had fallen short. They hoped now to consolidate their food supplies and their households against what would prove to be one of the region's coldest and most punishing winters. On November 19, Major Appleton released his men, declaring the "Western Campaign" at an end.

But there had really been no campaign, despite the posturings of the would-be-Cromwell commanders or the Bible-thumping myths of the chroniclers. Nor was this pieced-together military effort of the English what it has been called by the revisionists—a drive by the Puritans (superior in population and in military might) to annihilate New England's etiolated native Americans. Instead, it was a rather fitfully staged reaction to native rebellion, a reaction distinguished more by confusions and failures than by policies and victories. Yet, what can one say about the phase of the war that followed immediately on the heels of these dustups in the west—the campaign against the Narragansetts? At first this impressive drive looks like the very model of a premeditated campaign by seventeenth-century Europeans, out to get territory. But it is only when the foolish, nearly disastrous campaign is examined in greater detail that it reveals itself for what it was: an ultimate gamble taken by a badly shaken and failing society.

Ironically, it may have been the peace-seeking John Pynchon who, inadvertently, came up with the concept of a wintertime strike against the powerful Narragansetts. For it was he who advised that *after* the falling of the leaves was the best time to attack any Algonquian group. Then they would be more visible, better targets for European marksmen. And that advice fell gladly upon the ears of Governor Leverett. His populace of the

Historical Portraits of the Pokanoket Sachem, blamed for New England's fiercest war, range from Paul Revere's hideous 1772 engraving entitled *Philip, King of Mount Hope* (top left) to Thomas Hart Benton's organic 1930s painting of the native leader (top right). In the 1800s, painters showed Philip, always with crown, as either forgettably ridiculous (bottom left) or broodingly romantic (bottom right).

The New World of Privileged Native Americans in the seventeenth century can be imagined from a revealing 1681 (?) portrait of Ninigret II, sachem of the Niantics (also know as Nehantics) after King Philip's War (left). The wampum-rich headdress, gleaming medallions at throat, handsome blanket over right arm indicate the esteem in which cooperative natives were then held—Ninigret II's father had been a pliable neutral during the war. Native artists flourished during this time of peace-or-war between white and red societies, producing such splendid works as "Princess Ninigret's Haircomb and Bracelet" (top left and right) and the alleged "King Philip's Belt" (bottom).

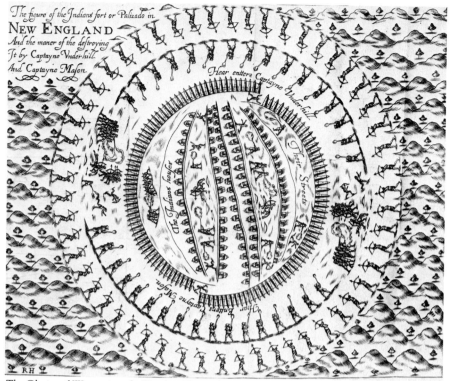

The figure of the Indians fort or Palizado in
NEW ENGLAND
And the maner of the destroying
It by Captayne Vnderhill
And Captayne Mason

Hear enters Captayne Vnderhill

Their Streets

The Indians houses

Their Enters Captayne Mason

RH

The Glories of War against the Heathen Natives have continually been hailed by colonial
and nationalistic American artists. This curiously symmetrical woodcut (above) served
as an explanatory diagram for John Underhill's account of his participation in the climactic
battle of the Pequot War (1637), the war that set the tone for racial politics in that century.
The very model of rampant English militarism, Major Thomas Savage (who took part in the
Pilgrims' and Puritans' first attack on Philip in 1675) was heroically portrayed by contemporary
artist Thomas Smith (top right). Nineteenth- and twentieth-century accounts of King Philip's
War usually included exaggerated, propagandistic scenes like the one at bottom right;
this depiction of the August 1675 attack on Brookfield, Massachusetts, focuses on the
moment when a rain squall extinguished the Indians' flaming assault wagon, interpreted as
divine intervention.

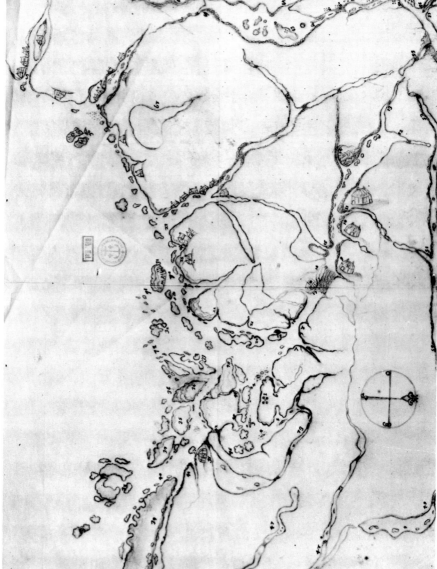

To French Eyes New England was correctly viewed from north to south, as in this map prepared for the French governor from native sources just before King Philip's War. The cross at left center marks headquarters fort at Pentagouet (Castine, Maine); English houses on the Merrimack River are marked by number 29.

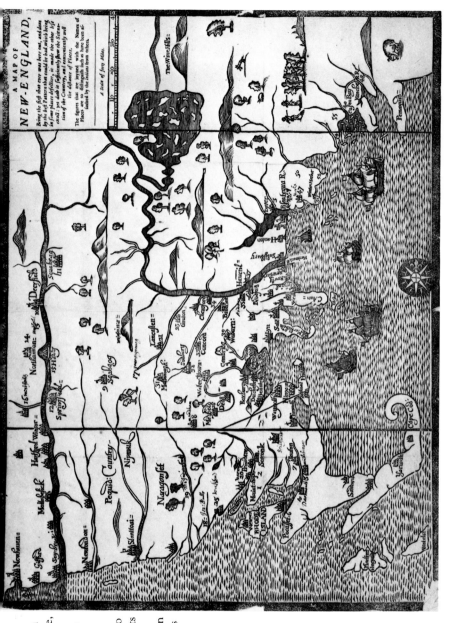

To English Eyes New England was perceived from east to west, as in the woodcut map above, an illustration for William Hubbard's history of King Philip's War. The large river at center offering access to the interior for colonists and traders is the Merrimack; numbers on the map indicate towns attacked in the war.

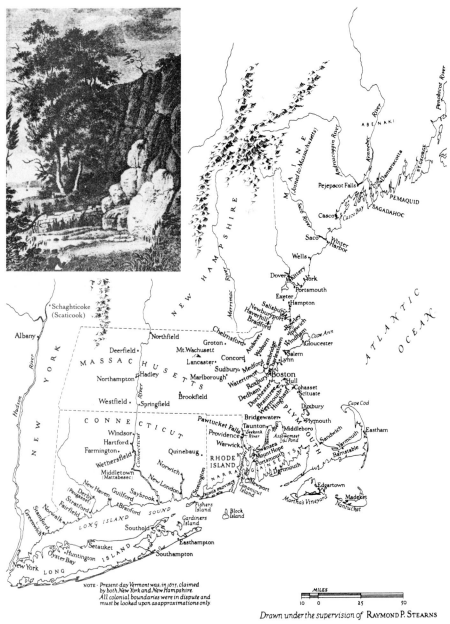

Theater of King Philip's War. New England of 1675 is accurately limned in this modern map based on historical sources. It ranges from Fairfield, Connecticut, where the Pequot War ended, to Pemaquid in Maine, where England's royal command sought to stop the region-wide rampage that Philip was alleged to have masterminded. The inset engraving of "King Philip's Seat" reflects more accurately the nineteenth-century desire to endow Philip with kingly attributes and faculties than the specific rock formation that still exists at his beloved Mount Hope site in Rhode Island.

Massachusetts Bay Colony was at this moment (early winter, 1675) "desperate," according to historian Samuel Eliot Morison. The people were starved of funds, of food, of favorable reminders that God was on their side.

The Narragansetts, with whom ambiguous diplomatic exchanges had been going on since the imposed neutrality treaty of July, represented a rich possibility of relief from all these anxieties. Their wealth, in terms of territory and goods and corn approached grandeur (indeed, native sources reported that the summer and fall just passed had been a time of extraordinary harvests, with many additional fields planted and reaped). And their potential menace, if they should choose to listen to Philip's beseechings and join the Wampanoags and the Nipmucks, was formidable. Canonchet, their renowned leader, was able to put more than three thousand warriors into the field; their independence was an insult to Puritan New England.

Even Roger Williams, an admirer of the Narragansetts for so many years, had wearied of this people's arrogance. Just as there had been a critical shift of sentiments within the Pilgrim/ Wampanoag alliance after the death of Massasoit (dramatized by the suspicious behavior of his sons), so had there been a change in Rhode Island/Narragansett relations after the death of Canonicus and the execution of Miantonomo. Miantonomo's young descendants had pressed their case so far as to claim that the island of Conanicut—where Roger Williams harvested his hay and set his livestock out to graze—had not been legally transferred to its English owners. For the elderly Williams, whose whole dispute with the Puritans had stemmed not so much from theological differences (though they were great) as from differences regarding the ownership of New England's land (he thought it was patently the natives'), this youthful arrogance was too much to bear. His reaction against the Narragansetts' "Scandalous Pap" sounded like a typical salvo of Puritan outrage.

Further, when the young Narragansett sachems complained that Williams and his business partner, Richard Smith (who shared the ownership of their trading post after 1651), had been able to grab Conanicut only because the native owners had been befuddled with English-supplied drink, Williams replied:

> [This] distinction of Druncken & sober honest Sachims is both lamentable & ridiculous: Lamentable [in that] all ye Pagans are so given to Drunkenness. It is ridiculous allso [in that] these two dissenting Sachims should be esteemd such sober honest men. . . . it is notoriously knowne what conscience of all Pagans make of lying, stealing, murthering, etc. And as for Drunckeness also, they will not say themselves (especially ye youngest of these two) but [that that] is their frequent and delightful practice.

In other words, they're all a bunch of drunks. Roger Williams by this time was obviously in no mood to prevent would-be attackers from doing what they would with the Narragansetts. He had not, finally, been able to live with them (a fact that must trouble many of Williams's admirers).

But while the increased strains of the 1660s had disturbed the Narragansetts and their historic friends, there also seems to have been at the same time a remarkable reinforcing of their traditions and their ancient religious practices. Even as other Algonquians surrendered to life changes associated with European technologies, the Narragansetts resolutely strengthened their covenant with their god and his universe. This conservative turning of the seventeenth-century Narragansetts was investigated recently by two creative anthropologists. So sensitively did they analyze the findings at two Rhode Island burial sites that the historic Narragansetts have appeared in a new light: they have come to be regarded as not only the most populous but the most sophisticated of New England's seventeenth-century natives.

The first of the anthropologists' books, Dr. William S. Simmons's *Cantantowwit's House*, reviews the contents of approximately sixty burial sites of Conanicut Island. The positions of the entombed bodies seem to show that the Narragansetts still believed during the 1660s in their ancestral heaven—which they thought lay somewhere to the southwest—and in that heaven's divine ruler, Cantantowwit. Similarly, Dr. Paul A. Robinson's researches on behalf of the Rhode Island Preservation Commission at another nearby burial ground (Burr's Hill, in Warren, Rhode Island) clearly supports his thesis that the Narragansetts' religious practices *intensified* rather than diminished as the people came into more stressful contact with the European settlers during the 1670s. Additionally interesting is that Conanicut (the first of the anthropologists' sites) was the very island whose possession provoked the argument between Roger Williams and Miantonomo's heirs.

A third excavated site was but a few miles south of Williams's trading post at Cocumscussoc (Wickford). Here the missionary-trader, removed from wife, six children, and the political wrestlings of Providence, was able to find enough "beloved Privacie" to concentrate on business and meditation. And here, he and Richard Smith unintentionally contributed to the physical deterioration of the neighboring natives. For though Williams and Smith would not sell liquor or guns—items that the Narragansetts could get quite easily elsewhere, particularly from the Dutch—they did sell them refined sugar and molasses as well as starches, all of which increased physical weaknesses, including dental difficulties. High percentages of the adults suffered from severe tooth decay, as the disease-marked jaws in this mainland site's tombs indicate. And among the juveniles at this site, the proportionate death rate is abnormally high (28 percent), many of the youngsters having perished from tuberculosis, an illness that seems to have arrived in Rhode Island only with the settlers. These findings tempt scientists to take another look at the Narragansetts and to conclude that, while strong, they were at the same time vulnerable.

In the golden era when the Narragansetts had been spared from European-induced plagues, one explanation for their good fortune was that religious tradition bade them burn a dead man's house, possibly killing the germs that had caused his death. But now neither those traditional burnings nor their beneficent spirits prevented them from suffering increasingly from the peculiar medical problems of the bicultural world. And whereas Roger Williams had once found that kindly dealings with the Narragansetts encouraged them to contribute to the maintenance of peace, he now saw in their behavior nothing but betrayal and deceit. By their purchase of arms, their sheltering of fugitive Wampanoags (who stole livestock and stirred up the region), and their loud and angry demands, the Narragansetts "threaten to render us slaves," he complained. Once he'd lived in an interracial haven; now he felt he was on the edge of chaos.

Early in August 1675 came the shattering news that a number of Richard Smith's cattle had been "killed by stealth." This seemed the final evidence that the Narragansetts had swung toward a policy of active harassment of the white settlers. A few days later a Wampanoag claiming to represent Philip himself approached Roger Williams for negotiations. The aged peacemaker, while mistrustful, heard the visitor out hospitably: "I carried him and Mr. Smith a glass of wine . . . and a bushel of apples for his men." Still, things had gone too far and the meeting ended with nothing resolved.

Even when Canonchet went to Boston in October to confirm the treaty made at Pettaquamscutt the previous summer, Williams was not convinced that peace was possible. A gesture by the supposedly neutral Ninigret—who with great show handed over two Wampanoag scalps—also failed to make the case that stability could be maintained in the region. As the war went on in other parts of New England, Roger Williams was skeptical that either the Niantics or the Narragansetts would be content with their dependent, deteriorated condition.

When the pronouncement came forth from Massachusetts Bay of war against the Narragansetts, it sounded grand, reasoned, and power-packed. But it was none of these. Issued in the name of Charles II, king of England, Scotland, France, and Ireland, the document was dated the seventh of December, *Anno Christi* 1675. The Puritan authors of the declaration felt obliged to review the whole course of the war thus far and to point out in those events certain signs that the Narragansetts had been conspiratorially involved, even while they were ordered to disassociate themselves from the evil King Philip. But as the authors went on, reiterating that the Narragansetts had been guilty of "succoring" and "harboring" the enemy, their argument sounded less and less convincing. Yes, the Narragansetts had "favored, abetted, and assisted" Philip "and his whole Crew," but was that proper cause for a military invasion? Perhaps a show of force was called for—but an armada and wipe-out army?

The issue behind the charges of assistance was that the Narragansetts had so much to assist with, and no one else (least of all the Puritans) had much of anything. The English settlers and their government could not tolerate either the supply of food during the forthcoming winter to the hibernating rebel forces or their own deprivation. And the Narragansetts were obviously guilty, with their bulging reservoirs of corn, of being at the heart of the problem. Furthermore, if the rebels were able to grow in strength and organization during the winter, they might be able to turn a summer and autumn of small triumphs into a spring of total victory.

Even so, were the Puritans willing to risk their not-exactly-invincible army against the mightiest people of New England for several sacks of corn—at a time when many towns in the region were either wiped out or reeling from the latest attack? Yes; they were desperate enough to gamble, it would seem. The possible benefits from the war against the Narragansetts (new land, plenteous supplies, numerous slaves) outweighed the hardships or the consequences that would be incurred. They were worth gambling for.

This was indeed a call to adventure to which all New England eagerly responded (except for the Quakers and other such radicals). Major Appleton of western-frontier fame led Massachusetts Bay's army of 527 men; Captain Samuel Moseley (not to be excluded if pelf might be had) also eagerly responded to the call. And representing the Old Colony of Plymouth, Major Bradford rode forth with a force of 159 men; the Pilgrims had no intention of being left out of this action on their border. On behalf of Connecticut, the occasionally tardy but constantly valiant Captain Robert Treat reported for duty, at the head of 300 well-armed settler-soldiers accompanied by 150 Mohegans. In recognition of his premier role in the fight with the Wampanoags, Josiah Winslow was made general of this impressive combined task force of 1,000 soldiers—the mightiest army yet put into the field of North America. Winslow wisely requested that Benjamin Church join him as a kind of freelance captain.

Yet despite the strength and diversity of the Puritan-Pilgrim task force (as well as the royal seals and divine invocations), it was from the beginning a fairly shoddy crusade, launched against a foe largely innocent of having made war. Even the Victorian historian George Ellis termed the campaign against the Narragansetts "an unprovoked invasion." Indeed, it continues to seem not so much an intelligent and rational preemptive strike—none of the Puritans themselves called it anything like that—as a simple act of desperation when all else seemed to be failing.

As for what the Narragansetts thought of it when rumors of the task force's approach come to them, their reaction can perhaps be understood against the background of one of their most ancient and most honorable traditions: for them (as for all other Algonquians), it was established that the aggressor must always give warning to his enemy of the imminent attack. This unannounced move by the English was obviously unethical and uncivilized; there would be no way to protect the women and children. In discussing that and other aspects of the historic event with anthropologist Paul Robinson, a present-day Narragansett leader observed that his people still tell successive generations of the outrageous nature of the assault. Like Pearl Harbor, it will never be forgotten. "So far as we're concerned," he told Robinson, "what the Puritans began here has never ended. The war's still on."

The invasion began with some precision and few illusions. General Winslow marched his Plymouth contingent into Narragansett country over an inventive pontoon bridge across the Sekonk River. The message he delivered to his men before they turned their drive south reveals the clear-eyed philosophy of the Pilgrim command at this point. Winslow told all ranks that if they "played the man, took the [Narragansetts' fort], and drove the enemy out," they would receive a generous award of land as well as their promised wages. Not a holy war this, but a sneak campaign for goods and property.

The Bay army's first attempt to capture a notable Narragansett sachem, the "wily Pumham," failed—he simply was not there, for the country was now alerted. But Moseley (who had crossed the Narragansett by ship and thus was one of the first to arrive at the front) did succeed in getting his hands on fifty-four prisoners. These he prepared to sell as slaves, which procedure was understood to be another motive for the campaign. Thus he was commended for his efficiency when the army joined him at Wickford on the western shore of Narragansett Bay.

That rather remote location on the frontier, Roger Williams's former trading post, had been designated as the rendezvous point for the colonies' respective commands. From there, on December 13, the joint force moved inland, south and west, intent on reaching Canonchet's fort (that is, rumored fort) as soon as possible. A fort did indeed exist, though it was neither Canonchet's own headquarters nor a strongpoint comparable to any other Algonquian military post the Puritans had ever seen or heard of before. Captured Narragansetts began to give them a rough idea of its size and significance, though the reports were at first believed exaggerated. It was being built on an island in the middle of the Great Swamp; it was, in effect, a fortified city, able to withstand any attack with weapons of that day. The site, historians now agree, was near South Kingston, Rhode Island; but the exact position, the particular hummock, in that vast, mirey territory is yet to be identified.

For the Narragansett warriors and their families, the fort, still under construction as they assembled there, must have seemed the last and best hope against the onrushing English. Many of these Narragansetts had come here after having fought along-side the Wampanoags or with the Nipmucks now quartered at Mount Wachusetts (fifty miles to the north). Here was a secret, defensible safety point for hibernation, with Canonchet's military post, bristling with warriors, but a few miles to the south.

The Narragansett engineers had pressed into construction service a former native employee of Richard Smith, a man understandably nicknamed Stone-Wall John, for he was well trained in the English art of masonry. This craftsman and a team of laborers, probably working under Canonchet's directions (and those of Canonchet's self-described English "slave," Joshua Teft), hurried to complete the virtually impenetrable wall around the perimeter of their swamp island. The wall, as Teft later described it, was to be topped by a spiked stockade; only one felled tree across a moat would provide access to the gateway leading into the fortress. At either side of the entrance-way, block houses and flankers had been designed. Much remained to be done, but time was running out.

More than a thousand Narragansett men, women, and children crowded into the five-acre patch enclosed by the masonry and earth wall. Each family constructed its own wigwam, of which there were several hundred; the women lined the wig-wams' interior walls with food-storage tubs and sacks against possible musket shot. As the families completed their structures and prepared themselves for what might come, word arrived that the English forces had organized themselves at Wickford.

Perhaps some time could be won by the negotiations. Stone-Wall John was among those sent out, across the frozen swamp and over the snow-deep trail, to parley with General Winslow under a flag of truce. Negotiations would also give the Nar-ragansetts time to assess the size and capabilities of the invading force. Yet when the delegation arrived, protesting the lack of a formal message of warning and demanding explanations, the meeting soon broke up in an exchange of shots. The English had not come to parley. The warriors accompanying Stone-Wall John took off at great speed, heading south—perhaps to entice the English in that direction, toward Canonchet's military post at Pettaquamscutt. But Stone-Wall John himself returned at once to the fort, determined to close the remaining gaps in his construction.

There was little chance for any such final labor, however, for the English had found a guide who professed to be familiar with the swamp and the fort's location; with him leading the way, they immediately prepared to march. This captured Narragansett, named Indian Peter, did his work so well (whatever his motives) that his timely assistance must be compared to that of the renegades who had successfully directed John Mason to the Pequots' fort forty years earlier. And, just like those guides, Peter took the English directly to the concealed entrance, then stood back in horror to watch the result: the setting afire of the houses and the slaughter of his people. For this proved to be another massacre which the English might not have been able to effectuate without native support. But it was a battle that would have no victor, only victims.

Benjamin Church's narrative of the action is all the more memorable because of its personal details. He had noted, for example, that the soldiers from Plymouth, notoriously ill-supplied, had "not one biscuit left" before the battle. He wondered if that had been a part of the reason for the pell-mell attack; they hurried it along so they could get back to their supply base. Yet Church did not claim that he could see or understand all that was going on around him; his view was obscured by the blizzard that burst upon the combatants at the time of attack. The raging storm and the fire blasts and the smoke from torched buildings as well as the confused and milling warriors all combined to make it impossible for him to bring back a coherent report to General Winslow. But Church did perceive that the first wave of attackers had been badly mauled by the Narragansett defenders and that there was chaos among the reserves who had finally penetrated the fortress via a break in the wall, but then had been stalled.

Church at length crossed over the log that led into the fort, teetering across the swamp waters. Inside, he came face-to-face with a certain Captain Gardner of Salem, "amidst the wigwams" and the confusions of the fight. But at once the captain collapsed. Church stepped up to him and,

> seeing the blood run down his cheek, lifted up his cap, and called him by name. He looked up in [my] face, but spoke not a word, being mortally shot through the head. And, observing his wound, [I] found the ball entered his head on the side that was next the upland where the English entered the swamp. Upon which, having ordered some care to be taken of the Captain, [I] dispatched information to the General that the best and forwardest of his army that hazarded their lives to enter the fort, upon the muzzle of the enemy's guns, were shot in their backs and killed by them that lay behind.

Another military snafu.

At the time when the officers (remembering the lessons of the Pequot War) had decided to set the Narragansett community ablaze, Church and his men were outside, seeking to capture those who had fled and to defend against others who might even then be forming to strike back at the English. Out in the icy, rimed forest, in the tumult of hostile and friendly natives, he suffered three wounds—one in his thigh, another "through the gatherings of [my] breeches and draws." As for the third, the bullet had "pierced [my] pocket and wounded a pair of mittens that [I] had borrowed of Captain Prentice, [which], being wrapped up together, had the misfortune of having many holes cut through them. . . ." With his good humor intact, Church survived that ghastly day of battle.

The exhausted English commanders then faced the grim decision of whether to stay in the smoldering fortress. Or, with rumors of Canonchet's army's approach making all apprehensive, should they attempt the rugged march back to Wickford even as the winter's day died around them? Church vigorously argued that they should remain where they were, as the several unburned wigwams and the walls of the fort were a better bet for the scores of wounded then the snowy trail through the forest. But Moseley, in his customarily abrasive way, "replied that Church lied, and told the General that if he moved another step towards the fort he would shoot his horse under him."

When the army's battle-addled doctor added his consenting opinion to Moseley's, the decision was forged: the survivors would drag their wounded and dying companions through the night's snows to Wickford. But first, before leaving, the English made sure that the Narragansetts' wealth—those baskets of corn and tubs of provisions—was burned and totally destroyed. Much as they would have liked to carry the corn with them, that task was now beyond them.

The campaign was completed at great human cost. Most of the fort's inhabitants were destroyed—six hundred killed and three hundred taken prisoner. More than a quarter of the English soldiers were killed or wounded during the struggle. Of the wounded, many perished during the march to the coast or after reaching Wickford; forty were buried there during the next few days. Ninigret, as eager as ever to demonstrate his neutrality, dispatched some of his men to bury the English dead at the battle site—for which he requested prompt payment. The timely arrival of a supply ship from Boston in Wickford harbor prevented the death of many other English soldiers. Of the three colonies' contingents, the Connecticut force suffered most heavily: eighty of the three hundred men in Treat's command were killed during the first rebuffed assaults against Stone-Wall John's fortress.

Yet the gravest result of the Puritans' unprovoked assault upon the Narragansetts was that now Philip and the Nipmucks had a fresh supply of warriors to fight on their side—enraged Narragansetts by the thousands (for only a few hundred had been stationed in the swamp fortress). How strange it seems that the *prevention* of the Narragansett alliance had been a prime objective of the invasion (the objective emphasized by conservative historians who see this as a preemptive strike), yet that alliance is exactly what was caused by the invasion. Canonchet, leaving the Great Swamp battle behind him, now embarked on the road to war. And Philip (who, according to some, had been at this time in Narragansett country beseeching the sachems to give him men) now found his political efforts toward alliance fulfilled, thanks to the Puritan militarists. An officer on General Winslow's staff, Joseph Dudley, claimed in his report that, yes, "Philip was seen by one . . . under strong [body]guard."

The Puritans neither won their gamble nor got away with entering the game, for all the civilians they'd killed. Just as Lion Gardiner had protested forty years before that Endicott's sally against the Pequots would leave Saybrook in the midst of aroused bees, so now formerly peaceful Rhode Island (whose borders had been violated by the Puritans' task force) was in jeopardy of its very life. When General Winslow called his campaign to an official end on February 3 and sailed back to

Boston, but a few weeks were required for the aroused Narragansetts to lay Wickford to waste and to threaten all the colony's outlying settlements. Yet the total folly of the Narragansett campaign must be measured not only by its backlash within one sector under attack but by its effect on New England as a whole. The aroused bees, wise enough to understand the nature of the enemy, were now streaming forth to attack the home territory of the intruders.

However Canonchet worked out with Philip and the other leaders the structure of military command, modern historians believe that the Narragansett sachem soon won recognition as the main figure in the new alliance. Only the highest rank would be appropriate for the sachem who supplied so many warriors. Similarly, it appears doubtful that Philip, whose men numbered in the neighborhood of eighty, would have been accorded a prime position at the council fires.

The Pokanoket prince's status was further diminished by a pivotal episode that occurred far from the native allies' central encampment at Menamaset (New Braintree, south of Mount Wachusett). Philip had determined that, for him, the best place to pass the winter was in the distant northwest at Schaghticoke (Scaticook) on the Hoosic River above Albany, beyond the territory of the Squakheags, where he might attempt an additional alliance with the "Magnes" (as he called them), the Mahicans. Here, across today's Massachusetts–New York border, he might also obtain additional weapons from the peoples who traded with the French. It was a creative plan, even if it did not represent the main thrust of the natives' military effort. But it backfired. For Philip, far from finding new strengths that would provide more power for his command and more personnel for the springtime attacks, succeeded only in igniting the ancient enmity of New York's Mohawks. And backing up the armed might of the Mohawks—who had not forgotten their fierce war against New England's Algonquians—was the authority of the British government in Albany.

Governor Andros's imperialistic ambition, though perhaps frustrated from asserting itself eastward along the Connecticut coast, now sought to embrace all the west-reaching Iroquois territories, as well as whatever lands east of the Hudson he might be able to grab. Nor did this vision seem impossible, given the vanquishing of the Dutch and the disorganization of the French. Although Andros had seemed to be against the Puritans in their mismanaged war with the Algonquians (his attitude being one of political disagreement, not war), he was certainly not going to aid New England's enemies by tolerating the incursion of troublemaking Wampanoags into his colony and its native federations. He therefore let it be known to the Mohawks that an attack on Philip would be quite in order. And they, far more interested in consolidating a trade position with the English than in entering into New England's war for freedom, swiftly obliged the governor.

The Mohawk warriors struck Philip in a brutally effective surprise attack. Only forty of his four hundred men survived, many of them badly wounded. In the words of a Puritan chronicler, "They drove said Philip quite away." And, in the opinion of later commentators, this was the key battle that prevented Philip either from becoming the chief commander of the warring Algonquians or from widening the alliance so the fight for freedom might be won. If ever his dream had existed of clearing New England of its Pilgrim and Puritan settlers, now he could play no major role in effecting it. Nonetheless, the war that went on to rage more intensively after the western and Narragansett campaigns continued to bear his name and to be focused on him from the English perspective. Nor would his own struggles, for his own people, cease.

Recognizing that they knew but little about the plans and capabilities of the native alliance, the Massachusetts Bay Council and Governor Winslow enlisted two Christian Indians to undertake a daring intelligence mission. They were to set out in January and get close enough to the Menamaset command structure to find how many men were in arms and what settler towns were slated for attack when winter eased.

These scouts, undertaking a month-long excursion that deserves notice for its individual courage and for its strategic importance, penetrated to the heart of the natives' encampment. They found at Menamaset that the Algonquians' battle plan had become more centralized, more directed toward key objectives. The Narragansetts (who continued to arrive in this northern fortress) had lost but a small part of their strength in the Great Swamp battle and were all the more determined on revenge. The Nipmucks boasted of their victories on the western frontier. The spies heard all, but even more chilling: immediate attacks were planned on the settler towns that lay in the exposed valleys between Worcester and Boston. The war would swiftly be advanced to the very homes and hearths of those who had brought it into being.

5

Victory's Trail to Defeat

The Bitter Death of King Philip

Lancaster, Massachusetts, both looks and sounds like a place of proud tradition: the Bulfinch-designed church on the green with its high-arched portico and its noble belfry appears on most top-ten lists of American colonial architecture; the town's very name bespeaks an ancient English connection. One would never suspect that at one desperate moment in February of 1676 every structure at the center of town, including the meeting-house, had been burned or leveled in the furies of King Philip's War. Lancaster was abandoned on order of Massachusetts Bay officials. One can imagine the bells tolling hollowly as the survivors of the attacks were carted away to garrison towns closer to Boston. Rather than a symbol of colonial pride, Lancaster then was a smoldering symbol of defeat, of the shattering reality that the English settlers were being pushed back into the sea.

In terms of the evolution of the rebellion, Lancaster also

symbolizes how a series of disconnected uprisings had become something else, a total war of committed native Americans against a blundering religious-military officialdom. For the attack that overcame Lancaster and led to its later reduction to ashes was the *second* in that Nashua valley town's history during King Philip's War. The first had occurred back in August of 1675 when the amazing news from Swansea had excited, but not united, native leaders all across southern New England.

"One-eyed John" was the dismissive nickname the settlers had given to Monoco, the Nashaway sachem who had led a small group of his discontented people in the 1675 attack. Their score had been modest: one house burned and seven settlers slain. But when One-eyed John stormed the town in February 1676, assigned to this mission by Canonchet and Muttawmp, he commanded an allied force of some four hundred warriors. This power-packed thrust had the character of an onrushing army's blitzkrieg upon a strategic target. The fact that One-eyed John was prevented from destroying all of Lancaster on that bitter February day, blocked by a late-arriving squad of English cavalry (a squad that, for its efforts, was ambushed and wholly wiped out but a few weeks later), says also that his forces were as adept at getting out as they were in getting to their target.

As a prominent Nashaway sachem, One-eyed John carried with him to war a full collection of bitter memories of what had happened to native-settler relations in the past several decades. It was a typical story of a New England locality in the seventeenth century, all the more poignant for that reason. His home ground in the Nashua valley—which wends northward toward the river's intersection with the Merrimack in New Hampshire—had once been prime trading territory. With both red and white societies playing contributory roles, this had been an outstanding example of the diversity and integrity of the mid–New England settlement pattern during the golden age of trade. The destruction of Lancaster seems particularly grotesque when the harmony of those earlier years is recalled.

The Nashua valley's native saint was the patriarch Nashawhonan (spellings of his name vary), who had invited the English to become his neighbors for a variety of reasons, including protection from the tribute demands of the wide-ranging Narragansetts. Nashawhonan ranks with Sequassen of Wethersfield as a founding father of this second period of settlement. Both had been respected and flattered by the English as if they and their heirs would forever be included in the construction of a mutual government; both would be betrayed.

Thomas King, the first trader to move to this crossroad location of Nashaway, established his "trucking house" here in 1641, a dozen miles beyond the successful post at Concord, thirty-two miles from Boston. Though some might have viewed King's location as lost in the wilderness, to him it was where pelts and trade goods might be most advantageously exchanged, within easy reach of both the Concord and the Merrimack rivers. He seems to have been a representative frontiersman, canny and exploitative, plagued with legal difficulties associated with his "defilement" of the woman who later became his wife. He had all the qualities and few enough scruples to run a smart trading post. Records show that his operations quickly became profitable; they also show that the Nashaways, who had energetically swapped their trapped furs for guns and liquor and other European goods, fell increasingly into King's debt. They supplied more and more for less and less.

As the beavers dwindled and trade with native hunters declined (making them unnecessary), the white settlers expanded into both larger-scale farming and mining for metals. When acceptable-quality iron was found in nearby bogs, the town became site of the first ironworks in central Massachusetts. Early settler John Prescott took on the role of the area's leading blacksmith, in addition to remaining a sometime trader. He was often visited by the aging Nashawhonan. Settlers and natives were still at peace with each other, despite the economic dependency; in the words of a later writer, the settlers found the Nashaways "convenient neighbors," presumably as servants and field hands. In 1653, as new English settlers flocked to the prosperous location, it was formally established as a town; its name was changed, from Nashaway to Lancaster.

The leader of these newly arrived successful farmers was John White, generally regarded as Lancaster's foremost civic personage of the era. He was a virtual Abraham, siring a plentitude of children including one, his daughter Mary, whose fame would eclipse his own. It was she, as wife of the town's first minister (Joseph Rowlandson) and as a captive of One-eyed John, who would write the most popular secular book of the seventeenth and eighteenth century. Mary Rowlandson's narrative of her enslavement following the February 10 assault—that is, the second and main assault of King Philip's War—became a publishing classic in its own time.

The disaffection of the Nashaways from the white settlers' civilization may have begun with the questionable practices at Thomas King's trucking house. But that seed of discontent put down deep roots and matured when the enlarged fields and pastures of the amazingly prolific settlers crowded all other land uses out of the valley—though the original deeds, like those for Deerfield, had stated that the English would not molest the Nashaways' "fishing, hunting, or planting places." And when, upon the death of Nashawhonan, Massachusetts Bay's General Court sought to ensure the passivity of the Nashaways by imposing the Court's own sachem, the wildflower of discontent grew and bloomed and bore the bitterest fruit.

The imposed sachem was Matthew, a nephew of Nashawho-nan, who had taken the culture-crossing step of conversion to Christianity. Another nephew (or possibly grandson), Shosha-nin, had a stronger claim on the sachemship because of his leadership qualities and popularity. But that claim would not be heard; the settlers called him "Sagamore Sam" and the Court ignored him. John Eliot and Increase Nowell were then re-quested by the Court to see to it that Matthew won, one way or another—an interesting example of racial politics in New England.

Cheated of his inheritance, Sagamore Sam took note of the hostilities which had just burst forth between the Pokanokets and Plymouth. Joined by One-eyed John and other Nashaways, he went off to augment the ranks of those in rebellion. The Nashaways had a history of affiliation with the Wampanoags; now they were united in disaffection from the English rulers.

During the winter of 1675–1676, rumors had swirled like snow-flakes about the hostile plans being made by "the Narragan-setts" in their camps beyond Lancaster. These winter camps at the foot of Mount Wachusett were swollen with warriors and refugees from the western and southern battlefronts; they hummed with plans for attacks on certain targeted towns, Lan-caster among them. It was on January 24 that the word came to Governor Leverett from his Christian Indian scouts that the native allies would fall upon Lancaster in twenty days. Their plan was first to destroy the town's bridges so that none of the inhabitants could escape, then all would fall beneath their wrath. But even with that specific date and description, the governor concluded there was nothing to be done to help the distant town. He thought in terms of armies; he had no army to send. Lancaster's fifty families, organized into five or six garrisons, defended by but a dozen soldiers, would have to take care of themselves.

The leaders of the town, particularly Pastor Joseph Rowlandson and his brother-in-law (the appointed military leader, Lieutenant Henry Kerley), frantically besought Boston to change its static policy and send what troops were available. Then, even while Pastor Rowlandson and Lieutenant Kerley were in Boston making a final plea for help, an exhausted messenger arrived at the doorstep of missionary leader Daniel Gookin in Cambridge. The messenger, who had hiked eighty miles through the snow from Menamaset, brought definite intelligence that the blow on Lancaster would fall the very next day, February 10. Although it was obviously too late to send out an effective defense force from Boston, orders were dispatched to Concord and Marlborough that mounted squads there should ride to Lancaster's assistance. At Marlborough, an apprised Captain Samuel Wadsworth hustled to get his forty men saddled up and on the ten-mile trail to the threatened town.

One-eyed John and his men attacked with a vengeance at "about sun-rising," in the words of Mary Rowlandson's justly famous *Narrative*. She watched his assault on the houses of neighbors who belonged to another garrison: one neighbor, before he could reach the garrison, was knocked down, stripped naked, and disemboweled. Then the fury of flame and shot and ax fell upon the Rowlandson home—the six dogs who'd been left behind by their master declined to rise in their mistress's defense. It was "the dolefulest day that ever mine eyes saw," she wrote.

What Mrs. Rowlandson could not observe was that, as her family reeled before the blows of the "savages" or were taken captive, other garrisons elsewhere in the spread-out town were also losing many defenders but were holding firm. And while Mrs. Rowlandson reported that thirty-seven persons were killed or seized in her immediate area (less one who escaped), other trustworthy contemporary accounts put the total number at forty-eight, including soldiers and others killed nearby.

But statistics do little to convey the horror of that day. As Mrs. Rowlandson described it, the carnage was made slightly more bearable for her by the knowledge that God could not let her down. Yet it was ghastly.

> There was one [friend or relative] who was chopped into the head with a hatchet, and stripped naked, and yet was crawling up and down. It was a solemn sight to see so many Christians lying in their blood, some here, and some there, like a company of sheep torn by wolves. All of them stripped naked by a company of hell-hounds, roaring, singing, ranting and insulting, as if they would have torn our very hearts out; yet the Lord by his almighty power preserved a number of us from death, for there were twenty-four of us taken alive and carried captive.

She herself had been wounded, as had the infant she carried in her arms. But though she once thought that she should "choose rather to be killed by them, than taken alive," she was sufficiently daunted by "their glittering weapons" to opt for captivity among "those (as I may say) ravenous bears." Her captivity as a hostage against the future lasted for eleven weeks and five days—and was the source for an unsurpassed portrait of daily life and behavior among the native peoples at this time in their conflict with white society.

Mrs. Rowlandson's narrative also gives hints of how a Christian gentlewoman of her upbringing could possibly have endured those seemingly endless weeks, not to mention the death of her child-in-arms, the constant specter of starvation, and the rigors of being force-marched some 150 miles along a snow-deep forest and swamp trail past Mount Wachusett to Vermont and back. She herself suggests that her Bible reading sustained her; furthermore that a loving God imposed this trial on her so that she would be chastened. She could say, along with King David of the Old Testatment: *It is good for me that I have been afflicted.* And never, even on the most miserable of the eighty-two days, did she (according to her account) despair of God's care for her and her family. A remarkable testament of endurance.

But in the down-to-earth opinion of historian Nancy Woloch (author of *Women of the American Experience*), Mary Rowlandson should be seen first and foremost as a survivor by virtue of her feminine practicality—and all the more heroic for it. Professor Woloch points to Mrs. Rowlandson's needlework and to her can-do attitude as the attributes that made her seem valuable to her captors, and to herself. She could make a shirt for Quinnapin (the Narragansett sachem who purchased her from One-eyed John), a pair of stockings for his wife (or for another woman who might pay for the product with something to eat), or a shirt or a cap even for Philip's son. And because she had value as a contributor—which value she herself had to estimate in terms of pounds sterling when the debate began on how much ransom should be demanded for her return—she was enabled to survive.

Other captives complained, others proved such a burden they could not be allowed to live by their stressed warrior hosts. Mrs. Rowlandson told of a pregnant woman with several children who imposed an excess of grief upon her captors. And who contributed nothing. The Indians, vexed with her importunity, gathered a great company about her and stripped her naked and set her in the midst of them. And when they had sung and danced about her (in their hellish manner) as long as they pleased, they knocked her on the head and the child in her arms with her. When they had done that, they made a fire and put them both into it and told the other children that were there with them that if they attempted to go home, they would sever them in the like manner.

Many of the hostages abandoned hope—like the male captive whom Mary Rowlandson succeeded in rescuing from an incapacitating depression. But she herself had the inner steel and the frontier hardiness to make it through. "Housewifery and trade were [Mary's] second nature," according to Professor Woloch. She bartered well, and at one point acquired a handsome knife which she gave with great pride to her master, Quinnapin. And she kept a running mental record of every ground nut, every kernel of corn that came her way. She also had sufficient confidence to stand up for that in which she believed: despite the harassments of Quinnapin's wife, she *would not* work on the Sabbath; she *would* read her Bible.

Yet life among "the Narragansetts" (as she called all the Algonquians) by no means filled her heart with a love for her tormentors or a preference for their wilderness way. In her pages neither a revisionist nor a romanticizer of the native Americans can find much good news: the Puritan way of life is noble and the natives are base. But though Mrs. Rowlandson disliked her captors' unwashed "greasiness," she might have admitted that her contemporary Englishmen were not very fond of bathing either. At one point it was Philip himself who offered her water for washing. She scorned the natives' constant lies—or were they possibly joking at her? And she dreaded their treachery—

though she seemed to make an important distinction between the *machit*, or bad, Indians and others more honest.

Despite these understandably negative feelings, Mrs. Rowlandson came to admire the Algonquians' survival skills and (in some cases) personal attitudes. There was along her trail a great dearth of food, relieved only by raids on English towns or by journeys down to Rhode Island to bring back some of the Narragansetts' cached supplies, supplemented by what nuts and roots they could dig up from the icy ground or find on the banks of the rivers. Nonetheless, there was no fear of starvation; she never heard of a native who had starved. Beyond this, she admired her captors' ability to function and move as a smart military team, as opposed to the English. The heavily armed, well-supplied Puritan force that was supposedly chasing along in pursuit of One-eyed John and his party was halted by a river which the natives crossed with few problems. To her surprise, she reached the conclusion that the "providence of God" also preserved the heathen.

Her personal admiration for Quinnapin seems almost a case study in the psychology of hostage and captor. "My master . . . seemed to me the best friend I had of an Indian," Mary Rowlandson wrote. When he was away from camp, life seemed less possible to her. Quinnapin, it should be said, may have had a special nobility about him (if one believes in genetics); he was Canonchet's first cousin, a grandson of Canonicus. Perhaps it was for that that Mrs. Rowlandson considered him a cut above all others, or perhaps it was for his kindliness. His wives she considered unworthy of him.

The most prominent of the three wives was Weetamoo, squaw sachem of the fierce Pocassets. When last encountered in these pages, she and her people had been fleeing with certain Wampanoags away from the pursuing forces of Plymouth, in the direction of the Niantics. At that time she had severed her relationship with Peter Nennuit, the neutralist whom she had married soon after her first husband, Alexander of Pokanoket, had died (of poisoning, she believed along with Philip). But the Niantics also proved too pro-English for her tastes and, after the Great Swamp battle—which she had endured and from which she had barely escaped, according to some reports—she had joined the Narragansetts and gone north with them for the alliance with the Nipmucks and the Nashaways. In the course of those embattled months she met and married Quinnapin, who had been one of the commanders in charge of the fort at Great Swamp.

> A severe and proud dame she was; bestowing every day, in dressing herself neat, as much time as any of the gentry of the land, powdering her hair and painting her face, going with necklaces, with jewels in her ears, and bracelets upon her hands. When she dressed herself, her work was to make girdles of wampum and beads.

Thus, for all her "insolence" and haughty imperfections in Mary Rowlandson's eyes, Weetamoo the squaw sachem was a working woman. This was a quality which Mrs. Rowlandson, with her Protestant work ethic, could understand if not admire (in the sympathetic view of Professor Woloch). Another captive remarked in later years that, despite their hard work and because of their more naturally harmonious life, Indian women had things easier than did the wives and mothers of settlers. For the natives, work was not regarded as an end in itself.

The best of the Indians, as seen by Mrs. Rowlandson, did indeed appear to have some praiseworthy attributes. Toward them, she felt a certain sympathy, saying, "I fared better than many of them." These were, presumably, the battle-widowed, the refugees with no homes to seek out, the desperately hungry and the incapacitated. Her rare sympathy for them will be remembered as long as her own endurance; by no means did she feel that they were to be driven from the face of the land.

And so one wonders how she felt about the man who, in the view of most contemporaries, epitomized the native rebellion— King Philip, whom she met a number of times. She never addressed the subject of his character directly. But here is her revealing account of one meeting which took place when Philip was on his way east from the defeat at Schaghticoke. Though battered and humiliated, he was presumably trying at this time to get his strength back and to join with the other Algonquians (particularly the Narragansetts) for their springtime forays against the English.

> At last, after many weary steps, I saw the Wachusett hills, but many miles off. Then we came to a great swamp through which we travelled up to the knees in mud and water, which was heavy going to one tired before. Being almost spent I thought I should have sunk down at last and never get out; but . . . Philip who was in the company came up and took me by the hand and said: 'Two weeks more and you shall be Mistress again.'

She did not shudder at his touch. On the contrary, he and his sudden news gave her much-needed courage, as did a remembered psalm: "When my foot slipped, thy mercy, O Lord, held me up."

Mrs. Rowlandson was then heading eastward, conducted back from Squakheag and from Coasset, near present-day Vernon, Vermont. In the weeks before, she had crossed over the Connecticut River to Coasset in a canoe, though on other occasions she had had to rely on a raft hastily put together by the hurrying natives as they sped so fluently over land and water. It was at the bustling meeting place of Coasset that Mary

Rowlandson had first seen Philip (very soon after his punishment by the Mohawks). As she anxiously observed the
struggling-in of his men and the purposeful chargings about of
other warriors, her hopes rose and fell. Rumors of defeats and
victories affected her as well as everyone else in the camp. She
grasped desperately at any news, particularly at word of what
might have happened to her husband or her children (two of
whom she had encountered by chance during her journeyings).
She always kept one ear cocked for any intimations of her being
ransomed. But it was not until she heard that one sentence
uttered by Philip that she had reason to hope there might be
plans in the wind for her release.

When she was finally turned over to the Massachusetts
Bay authorities upon payment of ransom, on May 2, 1676,
Mary Rowlandson had been witness not only to a terrifying
("chastening") personal experience but also to a mind-boggling
view of how the tides of war can shift. In her words: ". . . the
strange providence of God in turning things about when the
Indians were at the highest, and the English at the lowest," and
then the other way. For amid the Algonquian warriors that
late winter and early spring she saw a curious reversal of for-
tunes and of spirit—a swing from arrogance to exhaustion.
With them she walked victory's trail to defeat. And thus in
her account of that time she allows readers to see and hear how
it happened that King Philip's War was, by the natives, won
and lost.

Following the attack on Lancaster, the string of early spring
victories exploded like fireworks. Cleverly executed, physically
devastating, psychologically terrifying, they seemed to prove
that the Bay Colony's Old World military stratagem of war-
by-bastion was simply not going to succeed. Among other na-

tive leaders, Muttawmp of the Nipmucks was loud to proclaim that the English would be driven into the sea. And it appeared that that bold intention of the native allies could be fulfilled. But as the spring sun rose higher in the sky, that purpose withered.

First of the native victories was at Medfield, sixteen miles from Boston. As at Lancaster, there were few soldiers here, commanded by one lieutenant, Edward Oakes. He may have been an adequate officer in many respects but he suffered from compassion for his soldiers. Heeding their complaints that the constant strain of patrolling back and forth between Medfield and Marlborough was exhausting, he let them all retire early on the night of February 21, without guards. At dawn that morning, a force of three hundred "Narragansetts" attacked the town, killing twenty men and women, and taking a large number of captives. It was claimed that Philip was seen on a black stallion, untouched by whatever bullets came his way.

With Satan himself battering once more at their gates (in the view of the Puritan chroniclers), the Puritans' imaginations projected new images of doom. But modern historians have concluded that the leaders here were, again, One-eyed John and Sagamore Sam, responding to the instructions of Muttawmp, as they had at Lancaster. And it appears that here, as earlier on the western frontier, a weakness of the Nipmuck and/or Nashaway attack strategy was that it was so costly in manpower.

No records reveal how many warriors fell at Medfield, but a piece of propaganda the victors left behind nailed to a fence post offers some clues. It read:

Know by this paper, that the Indians that thou hast provoked to wrath and anger, will war this twenty-one years if you will; there are many Indians yet, we come three hundred at this time. You must consider the Indians lost nothing but their life; you must lose your fair houses and cattle.

Why was so much of the message devoted to the Indians' loss of life? It would seem that this is a self-revealing admission that the loss of men was deeply disturbing, their vainglorious words to the contrary notwithstanding. And no wonder that this concerned them, for in losing lives, the Algonquians lost their only asset. Houses and farms could be rebuilt by the English, but the natives could never replace their slain young men. The new generation was their last possession, their commercial position and their land having been lost. To sacrifice that for a few stolen cows and nicked soldiers was no victory, particularly when they had begun the contest at a population disadvantage. One wonders if the English were becoming aware that their triumphant enemies were bleeding themselves to death.

After Medfield, the Narragansetts and Nipmucks turned upon Groton (north of Lancaster) in a series of increasingly weighty attacks. In the last of these, sixty-five homes were burned and one settler killed. One-eyed John had been at the head of these raiders, more interested in destroying English property than in manpower exchanges.

At the back of his mind there seems to have been a program for utter eradication of the settlers' towns. For, as the smoke rose from Groton's destroyed buildings, he yelled a message across the fields to the garrisoned survivors. "Watch what I'll do next," he said in effect. "My five hundred men and I will burn the following towns *in this order*: Chelmsford, Concord [again], Watertown, Cambridge, Charlestown, Roxbury, and Boston itself." Then, as the chronicles report, his final words rang out: "What me will, me do!"

Bowing before the strength of One-eyed John's boast and the inadequacies of the Puritan armies, Groton was soon evacuated, under the orders of Major Simon Willard. As the aged officer and his men urged the citizens along the road to their haven nearer Boston, two more of their number fell into an ambush and were killed.

On the eighth of April near Sudbury, a far greater loss was suffered by Captain Samuel Wadsworth, who had arrived with his troopers across the river from Lancaster just in time to save that town from total destruction two months earlier. Though by now a veteran Indian fighter, Wadsworth was lured into an ambush with his force of 60 men. Surrounded by the five hundred Algonquians he'd set out to pursue, he and his entire company were cut down after a brutal struggle. Again, however, Muttawmp's victory over the English was scored at too great a cost: 120 of his men were lost.

The grim pattern of unaffordable victories continued to impose itself on the native allies; as reckoned by modern historians, they could not long endure the negative ratio of two of their young men lost for each settler or soldier killed.

From her own perspective as a witness in the camp that had sent the young braves forth into battle, Mary Rowlandson considered and reconsidered the rumored results of the Sudbury battle. Those results seemed rather ambiguous in the minds of her captors.

> . . . they came home as with a great victory. For they said they had killed two captains [Samuel Brocklebank of Rowley as well as Wadsworth of Milton] and almost an [sic] hundred men. One Englishman they brought along with them. And he said it was too true, for they had made sad work at Sudbury, as indeed it proved. Yet they came home without that rejoicing and triumphing over their victory, which they were wont to show at other times, but rather like

dogs, as they say, which have lost their ears. Yet I could not perceive it was for their own loss of men. They said they had not lost above five or six, and I missed none except in one wigwam. When they went they acted as if the devil had told them that they should gain the victory; and now they acted as if the devil had told them they should have a fall.

Most puzzling, she thought. And she wondered what this meant to the native allies' religious leader, the powwow who had sent the men forth with such assurances of their invincibility. He was looking, she reported, "as black as the devil (I may say without abuse)."

On the ring of towns around Boston the war continued with a ferocity that could only be called climactic—though the towns were hit not precisely in the order forecast by One-eyed John. Weymouth, even closer to the capital than Medfield, was blasted along with other neighboring towns; then Marlborough, Mendon, and Chelmsford. Worcester was destroyed. Here, April had become the cruelest month.

On the western front, a particularly powerful attack had been launched a few weeks earlier against Northampton by Quin-napin, Mary Rowlandson's gentle master. He had taken on this assignment as a result of the command conference at Squak-heag on March 9—the conference at which Philip had sought to rejoin the allies after his Schaghticoke defeat. After the conference and the subsequent battle, Quinnapin returned tri-umphantly to nearby Coasset, where his wives and Mary Row-landson awaited the results: the mounds of captured beef and the numbers of seized horses. Mrs. Rowlandson enjoyed the brief hope that, because Quinnapin and the other commanders now seemed to be making such ambitious and far-ranging plans, she might be taken to Albany for ransoming, riding one of the newly captured horses. Possibly she'd be exchanged for the powder badly needed for the planned attacks. What a relief it would be to ride—"I was utterly hopeless of getting home on foot, the way I came."

But that hope, like so many others, failed her: there was to be no horse. Nonetheless she derived one benefit from the excitements associated with Quinnapin's successful attack on Northampton. In all the wigwams at the victors' encampment at Coasset, preparations were under way—food cooked and packed for the ready-to-march warriors. The tantalizing smells of cooking groundnuts (a woodland tuber) and corn and meats hung in the air around the family fires. Philip, for whose son Mrs. Rowlandson had first made a shirt, then a cap, invited her for dinner.

> I went, and he gave me a pancake, about as big as two fingers. It was made of parched wheat, beaten, and fried in bear's grease, but I thought I had never tasted pleasanter meat in all my life.

In turn, she invited Quinnapin, on the point of his departure for battle, and Weetamoo for dinner, planning to give them the peas she had earned by making a shirt for another squaw's "sannup" (husband). The couple attended the event and apparently Quinnapin behaved himself with all politeness. But Weetamoo, "the proud gossip," would eat nothing "except one bit that he gave her upon the point of his knife." This social tiff seemed to result from Mrs. Rowlandson's having committed a dinner-table gaffe: she had served both of her guests from the same dish.

What the rather strange dinner party at Coasset may not have realized on the brink of another battle in this early spring-time of seeming victories east and west was that, in fact, Northampton had been but another too costly triumph. Too many men had been lost with too little gain. Although the slain and captured animals had indeed filled the natives' stomachs and aided their war preparations, only three or four settler houses had been burned and six Englishmen slain. The town had recently been palisaded, with the officers getting smarter about bastion tactics; each soldier's musket shot was expected to bring down one of the attacking braves. Another reason for the relatively successful defense of Northampton by the English was the arrival in the valley of a new breed of fighters, men determined to take the war to the natives. The colonial who stands forth as the epitome of this more aggressive breed, a man whose imprudent daring would have a major effect on this cockpit of war, was William Turner.

Quite the opposite of the static Puritan militarists whose old-fashioned policies had employed only small forces and had concentrated on defensive strongpoints (with the exception of certain large sweeps, such as the thrust against the Narragansetts), Turner believed in moving large numbers of men into the heart of native territory. He came by his unorthodoxy honestly; he had been persecuted and excommunicated by the Bay authorities in 1671, having attempted to start a Baptist church in Charlestown. Eventually he was allowed to worship as he preferred, but Bay tolerance went only so far: his application to lead a company of volunteers against the rebellious natives was summarily rejected, along with his military theories. By 1676, however, Bay authorities were desperate enough to make him a captain.

Many of the one hundred men that he gathered for his new company were as irregular as he, marginal members of the Bay's citizenry. They had arrived in Northampton only a few days before Quinnapin's assault. The most obvious result of their presence on the battlefront was that (in the words of a Victorian historian) scores of the raiders "bit the dust." Another result was that, rather than sitting back in boredom to wait for the next attack, the English soldiers prepared to ride forth from the bastion's gates in pursuit of the enemy. There was an enthusiasm for killing here that would play a major part in turning this feast-time of native victories into a time of discouragement and defeat, the time that would yield Mary Rowlandson's release.

A similar turnaround of affairs was taking place on the southeastern front. Here the Wampanoags were pressing upon the outskirts of Plymouth even as their Nipmuck and Narragansett allies pressed upon Boston. At Plymouth, the colonial authorities had held a council of war on February 29, immediately after receipt of the grim news from Lancaster and Medfield. Benjamin Church had been among those summoned for the conference, and his advice had been characteristically forthright.

If asked to lead an English military force, he said, he would never "lie in a town or garrison," waiting passively for the enemy to strike, but would "lie in the woods as the enemy did." Furthermore, the colonies should never send out *small* companies, for that tactic would result only in deadly ambushes, like the one in which Captain Wadsworth had been cut down. Instead, he said, the English forces should be accompanied by as many friendly natives as possible; only by this bolstering of English troops with woods-smart natives would the enemy be defeated on his own ground. The council's reply to these recommendations

> was that [the Pilgrims] were already in debt, and so big an army would bring such a charge upon them that they should never be able to pay. And as for sending out Indians, they thought it no ways advisable and, in short, none of [Church's] advice [was] practicable.

The fixed mind of the colony's leaders received a rude shock less than two weeks later when a Wampanoag sachem named Totoson launched a daring and successful raid on one of Plymouth's supposedly impregnable outposts, Clark's garrison on Eel River. It stood but three miles from the capital itself. In the assault, which began on Sunday, March 12, when most of the settlement's inhabitants were in church, the garrison was totally destroyed, with Mrs. Clark and all other occupants killed. Totoson and his small task force disappeared into the surrounding woods. The council began to recognize that new policies—even Benjamin Church's expensive proposals—might have to be considered.

It happened that Church himself, just as pleased to be apart from the fray, had been requested by his in-laws to leave his very pregnant wife with them at Plymouth, at Clark's garrison, shortly before Totoson's assault. He had fortunately declined. A few days later, as the Churches took the risky route home to Rhode Island by way of Taunton, they met Captain Michael Pierce, who was leading a small force of exactly the sort that Church had advised against. His company of sixty-three English soldiers was supported by but a handful of friendly Indians—who had been enticed to join the pursuit of Totoson by promises of four coats for his capture, plus one coat for any other "merchantable" captive.

With word widespread of the recent attack on Warwick by the Narragansetts, and with rumors flying of Canonchet's having appeared along the Blackstone River, Pierce and his mixed company marched cautiously toward Rhode Island. Near the border they were demolished in a classic ambush, with all but twelve English and nine friendly Indians killed by the unseen enemy. Subsequently, Canonchet's men assaulted Rehoboth, burning sixty-six residences and destroying numerous other farm buildings. So here in the southeastern part of New England it appeared that spring would bring an onrush of additional defeats for the English.

The colonies' military leaders now had no choice but to revise their original policies. The fact that time and numbers were on the English side was apparently not enough to save New England from destruction. Plymouth sent a message to Benjamin Church that his advice would be heeded; Massachusetts Bay released large numbers of natives from confinement on Deer Island—men who had never been on Philip's side, but who were locked up anyway just because they were Indians—and delegated them to army units. And in Connecticut, whose eastern border was threatened by Canonchet with an army of six or seven hundred warriors, the decision was made to put all possible armed men, red and white, into the field.

Even in Rhode Island, where the pacifism of the Quakers had once reigned, the mood was swinging toward the pursuit of war to the end. That switch of mood was forced upon the inhabitants by the destruction of Providence on March 29, perhaps the grimmest month in this part of New England.

Shortly before the attack on the capital, a distinguished group of Narragansetts had appeared on the outskirts of town, demanding a conference. Canonchet led the delegation, for rumors were true: he had indeed returned to his home country in keeping with decisions reached at the wintertime conference at Squakheag. Also recognized in this group of war-bent Narragansetts—who had come here, true to the ethical traditions of their people, to give warning of the attack—was the face of Stone-Wall John. Revenge for the disaster at Great Swamp was what had called him forth.

Canonchet appeared at Providence's gates in the full majesty of his command and with his already formidable reputation enlarged by a recent and great victory over the English at Central Falls, Rhode Island. Following that wipe-out of a significant Massachusetts Bay force, his triumphant warriors had staged a massive bonfire and dance to celebrate the qualities of his generalship. Given that loyalty and the undying hatred of the Narragansetts for the English who had invaded them, it was clear that only the most credible and convincing statesman could be sent forth to make the case for Providence. The aged Roger Williams was selected.

Helped by others, leaning on his cane, he struggled to the confrontation. Although he had recently been elected to command the town's "traine band," his authority drew upon his many years as friend and counselor to successive generations of Narragansetts as well upon his success in holding together all of Rhode Island's disparate elements. But as Roger Williams, eloquent as ever, spoke of peace and moderation, he knew that his pleas fell on deaf ears.

In reply, Canonchet stated that this was now war to the end. He himself would not cease to make war until Plymouth had fallen. For had it not been Plymouth that had started the war and had violated the most ancient of treaties with its unjustifiable strike against the Pokanokets? Now the time had come to get on with this war that the English had brought upon themselves. And with those words, Canonchet's men moved out, putting Providence to the torch; in that one day of fire, seventy houses and thirty barns were burned. Roger Williams was forced to leave the town he had founded, a refugee of war.

With such smoky signs on the horizon, it became apparent in lands even beyond New England that the Pilgrims and Puritans were no longer able to control the territory they had once ruled with such independent pride. The sympathetic citizens of Dublin, Ireland, sent across the waters a gift of food and funds; Protestants everywhere pondered anew what this connoted about God's plan for his people. But London remained aloof. The Restoration court of Charles II was not about to forsake its revels and give regard to those Roundheads in New England whose cruel and irrational policies toward other peoples had provoked this storm of vengeance.

Among New England's native societies, there was also at this time a recognition that one side or the other must be chosen—the war had reached such a pitch, with both sides now aiming for total victory, that neutrality was no longer an option. Thus even Ninigret of the Niantics decided that he would have to join the Mohegans in their historic alliance with the English. He made that decision at the time when Hartford's two newly authorized companies were being formed under the command of Captains James Avery and George Denison. To their companies—in a manner that would have satisfied Benjamin Church—were added considerable numbers of Mohegans and Niantics, in a ratio of forty-odd Englishmen to eighty native ancillaries. No longer would the native ambush rule the day as the battlefield's most successful tactic.

Marching east into Narragansett country, Connecticut's Captains Avery and Denison learned through scouts of the general whereabouts of Canonchet. Though historians sought to unify the story of the war by giving it Philip's name (pulling it together in the person of one villain), modern analysts credit Canonchet with supreme leadership among the native allies at this point. Canochet's war? Undoubtedly Avery and Denison saw this Narragansett sachem as their main target, whatever news there might be from the other battlefronts. So into Rhode

Island territory they pushed, following the intelligence reports of their native allies.

But as the two Connecticut companies approached Canonchet's rumored camp in the valley of the Pawtucket River, they were spotted by Narragansett sentinels. And when Canonchet heard the first report of the closeness of the oncoming English forces, he realized that there was no time to form a defensive battle line. He therefore took flight, running as swiftly as possible away from the approach route of the English. He was apparently counting on the English to follow their usual plan of attack—that is, to move upon an enemy position head-on. But what he did not realize was that Avery and Denison, coached by their ancillaries' woodland wisdom, had already sent flankers ahead and had totally surrounded his camp.

Immediately when Canonchet spotted a band of encircling Mohegans and Niantics, he turned and ran downriver, counting on his swiftness alone. But his pursuers were equally fast. Struggling to cross the river ahead of them, Canonchet slipped and fell, dunking his musket and powder horn in the water. He knew that his fight was over.

Canonchet's captor was a young Mohegan, who (according to storytelling historian George Bancroft) was quite awed by his prisoner. To the youth's stammered questions, the great sachem replied: "Child, you do not understand war; I will answer to your chief." But, brought before Avery and Denison, he said contemptuously that their offer of his life for the surrender of all Narragansett forces made no sense: the Narragansetts would go on fighting, thousands of them, with or without him. The captains' reaction to those proud words was to slay the forty-three Narragansett captives they had taken along with Canonchet and to chain the sachem himself for the voyage to the nearest Connecticut town. There, in Stonington, he would be war-tried.

Condemned to death on April 2, Canonchet requested that his executioner be Oneco, son of the Mohegan who had killed his father so many years ago. Before the ax descended, he had a chance to say that he was content with the swiftness of the judgment. "I like it well; I shall die before I speak anything unworthy of myself." The Mohegans, eager to demonstrate their continuing fealty to Connecticut, sent the great sachem's head on to Hartford.

William Hubbard was so impressed by Canonchet's stoicism that, despite his cultural prejudice, he wrote it was as if "some Roman ghost had possessed the body of this western pagan." But then, pious apologist that he was, he referred to Canonchet at the next opportunity as "that damned wretch."

In saying that thousands of Narragansetts would continue his war, Canonchet had both overestimated his warriors' numbers and underestimated his own value to the native cause. No other leader could supply his combination of personal authority and strategic wisdom. Philip may have possessed considerable skills as diplomat, as guerrilla, as leader of his own men, but it was to Canonchet that military leaders of the day gave the laurel for his generalship of combined native forces. Now the battlefronts he had dominated—and which he had trusted would lead to overall victory—would fall before the new combination of native-supported English fighting groups. And although Captains Avery and Denison would continue to lead their mixed red-and-white companies on to future successes (as would Captain William Hunting, the English officer who would avenge the ambush of Wadsworth at Sudbury), the most effective of these field-wise officials would be Benjamin Church. Although he was not restored to command until July 1676, the policies that he had long espoused were fully demonstrated as effective in the late spring months of that tragic year.

In the Connecticut Valley another innovative captain, William Turner, continued to be vexed and frustrated by the set-piece strategies of Massachusetts Bay's high command. These policies did nothing but encourage the native allies to make such bloody raids as the one launched on Hatfield on May 12. Led by Pumham, the venerable Narragansett sachem, this raid succeeded in taking seventy head of cattle from the embattled town—whose defenders seemed totally uninterested in pursuit. They were there for guard duty, they had been told.

Then, through the report of a settler's son recently released from captivity in a native village called Peskeompskut, Turner learned some intriguing details about that upriver encampment. In the first place, Peskeompskut had become the supply base for the western division of the Algonquian army. Here the native women engaged in the essential (and traditionally joyful) springtime task of catching salmon and other migrating fish. To this bustling center were brought the cattle taken at Hatfield and other raided towns; here those meats and other supplies would be divided among the community. It was a place of food and resuscitation. The ringing sound of blacksmiths' hammers could be heard above the roar of the river. As at nearby Coasset (twelve miles upriver), smoke curled above the wigwams of the gathered families, but here the wigwams numbered in the hundreds.

Secondly, the place was poorly guarded, the warriors off on their missions and the women virtually defenseless. As Turner presented his argument for an immediate attack on Peskeompskut he must have explained away the natives' laxness in defense by saying that they had learned the wrong lesson from the

English military's bastion-minded lack of aggressiveness—they had concluded that the English would never dart forth and take a distant village by surprise. But now he and his band of free-thinkers, accompanied by a number of settlers who yearned to get the war over with so they could plant their fields, would execute this smashing surprise attack.

Captain Turner was quite correct: this was a tremendous opportunity to wipe out at one blow the upriver camp that was at the heart of the natives' war effort. But among the things he incorrectly estimated was his own strength (not to speak of his military fitness). Although he had been so weakened by a recent illness that he had had to write the council requesting to be relieved of the command for which he had struggled for so long, he could not bear to let the opportunity slip by. And when the days went by without the arrival of the promised professional support from Connecticut, he left his sick bed, determined to set off on his own. His espousing of the campaign had captured the enthusiasm of so many other volunteers that his strike force finally numbered 150 men in all, though some of these were more interested in the possibility of booty than in observing proper military procedures.

Turner and his men, planning to attack after a nighttime trek, were assisted by the wet spring weather. A thunder shower at the end of the day had persuaded the native sentries that it would be far preferable to concentrate on that night's feast of captured beef than to maintain their guard. So the approaching task force, having followed the directions of the recently released captive, successfully made their way on horseback and by foot to the first of the several native camps at Peskeompskut. Here at daybreak on May 19 they discovered nothing stirring, the effects of the feasting on beef and salmon having kept the sentries long abed. Turner commanded that the soldiers leave their horses at this point, lightly guarded; the bulk of the force advanced to the attack on foot.

When viewed today, the site of the Peskeompskut battle looks every bit as awesome as it must have in the time of the captain who conquered it and whose name it now bears (Turner's Falls, within the town of Montague, Massachusetts). The Connecticut River at this point roars down through a giant S-turn, crashing over great rock islands. Here centuries later was built the first hydroelectric plant on New England's largest river; sportsmen still fish within the spray and thunder of the falls. In order to spear the salmon three centuries ago, the native women leaned out from delicate stagings built upon the rocks. The blood-red fish that they were fortunate to have speared, weighing between four and six pounds, no longer appear at Turner's Falls.

In the complex encampment at Peskeompskut there were many other resources besides the forges to repair the antiquated muskets and the hearths to bake the breads and corn patties. There were the fast-growing children who would replace the fallen braves; there were the older family members and the religious leaders who emphasized the cultural values that made the struggle worthwhile (or who spoke for peace). To destroy this rich and productive base—where early spring seemed to give such a secure promise to the gathered people—would be to blast both the spirit and the supply system of the native warriors.

When the occupants of the first camp were awakened from their slumbers at sword point, they thought at first that they were under attack from their ancient enemies to the west. Chroniclers report that the cry of "Mohawk! Mohawk!" was heard before that voice was silenced by the thrust of the blade. The English attack was swift and brutal, with no prisoners taken. Turner's men advanced on the base itself, then set the wigwams ablaze, hurling the forges into the river, decapitating the women and children and oldsters. Panic-stricken people dashed for the canoes, overfilled them in their haste to cross the river. As the canoes capsized in the waves, the passengers were thrown over the falls and dashed upon the rocks by the might of the river. There was hardly time to fire a shot in defense; it was a total slaughter of the villagers.

But suddenly native warriors were seen nearby, on the op-posite bank. Now it was the turn of the English to panic. Running back to where their horses had been tethered, the farmer-soldiers found the horseguards under attack, ambushed by encircling natives. And, as Turner and his men straggled south in disarray, away from the scene of easy slaughter, they fell into additional ambushes. One of Turner's officers, Lieu-tenant William Holyoke, had his horse shot out from under him. But as the native came forward to slay the stunned officer, Holyoke raised himself and shot the brave; his men then found him another horse.

Turner himself, still suffering from his illness, lost command of his men. Some went this way, some that in flight. He himself was ambushed crossing the Green River. He fell with thirty others, leaving the command in Holyoke's hands. Though the nationalistic historians were rather discreet about this unseemly rout, the revisionists take great comfort from the defeat of the "amateurish" bloodthirsty attackers.

Yet, despite the death (and possible disgrace) of the auda-cious Turner, the English had reason to count the incident at Peskeompskut Falls as a sizable victory. They estimated the number of natives slain at two or three hundred—now there would be fewer children to walk the warpath of their fathers and brothers. And the most important native position in western

New England had been destroyed—not by the master plan of the Puritan armies, but by rampageous settlers. The Narragansetts, the Nipmucks, and whatever other Algonquians had been in the west preparing for the new season of war now scattered in varying directions, foodless, with diminished hope.

May was a time when, across the region, there was mention of peace; hostages were exchanged or returned. In a curious reversal of the English sale of captives into slavery (a practice that blossomed into a major industry before the war was over), the native Americans made some business out of ransoming their hostages. It was as a small but not insignificant part of this business that Mary Rowlandson had bought her way to freedom. First she had been challenged to set the price for her possible release. Torn between the knowledge that her husband was penniless as a result of Lancaster's fall and the recognition that her captors would not think the matter worthwhile if the price for her redemption was not high enough, she calculated that twenty pounds was reasonable. Her captors nodded, and negotiations went ahead. The money was soon "raised by some Boston gentlemen," Mrs. Rowlandson wrote gratefully in later years. She was also grateful to John Hoar, the courageous and much-abused negotiator who moved back and forth between the two parties.

It seemed to be a time when such across-the-cultures conversations, even a cessation of hostilities, were again possible—which is not to say that a resolution of antagonisms might come to pass. In Mary Rowlandson's detail-rich description of the encampment near Mount Wachusett (her twentieth "remove," as she called the stopping points along her journey's way), one has a sense that Quinnapin and the other warriors, so recently full of confidence, were now played out. Had the loss of their men and the death of Canonchet taken away their will to go on fighting? No longer were there boasts of future conquests around the council fires, only a kind of empty silence, broken by foolishness.

Quinnapin, as the negotiations for Mrs. Rowlandson's release went on, let John Hoar know through one of the Christian Indian interpreters that a pint of liquor might enable him to view the matter more favorably. The pint having been obtained, Quinnapin (who had spent the night before dressing himself elaborately for and taking part in a great dance) then proceeded to drink himself into such a state that he harassed Hoar and made a spectacle of himself chasing after the squaws.

Philip, too, seemed to have his mind elsewhere than on the serious business of pursuing the war. Though he had succeeded in reentering the company of native commanders, his authority was slight. Now recognizing that a deal was about to be made for Mary Rowlandson, he put in a special request for himself on the side: two coats and twenty shillings and half a bushel of feed corn plus some tobacco would win his cooperation. Then, when the consensus seemed to be swinging in the direction of letting Mrs. Rowlandson go without any such deference payments to him, he petulantly absented himself from the discussions of the natives' general court. If ever he had been "King," that time had passed.

The warriors at Mount Wachusett were more intent on holding their dance, having their last fun, glorifying their past victories, than in planning for the future. The hunger they were feeling in their bellies, a hunger that would be intensified by the defeat at Peskeompskut, urged them not in the direction of additional, costly raids but toward the bargaining table. The native allies on the western front, disgusted with Philip's failure among the Mahicans and aware of his power as a symbol to the

English, threatened to cut off his head and send it to Boston as a prelude to negotiations.

Recognizing the loss of his credibility and prestige among the allies, Philip made the only decision possible: to return to his own territories. So at the same time that Mary Rowlandson was conducted homeward, through her charred and ruined town of Lancaster to friends in Boston, Philip was also following the trail home, away from the so recently victorious warriors who had once hailed him as their inspiration. Those brave men, now plagued by disease and short of weapons, without shelter as well as hungry, had not been able to take time out this spring to prepare their fields for planting. They could not do that and fight. So now they were caught on the sword's edge, with nowhere to go but deeper into defeat. Philip and his few companions must have left them with a heavy heart.

Yet from the perspective of the English, the sudden silence on the battlefields of central and western Massachusetts must have been rather astonishing. The ferocities of March and cruelties of April had led to . . . this silence. There was a bit of action at Hadley when a weak force of raiders was pulverized by a newly emplaced cannon. But otherwise there were few natives to be seen, no reports of their stirring. So the authorities closed down the western battlefront; the settlers were told to go ahead with their planting.

In southeastern New England, other unforeseen events were taking place; one involved Benjamin Church, after he had been notified of his policies' vindication but before he resumed his command. The episode demonstrated both his own imaginative and courageous approach to the local people and the natives' willingness to accept and work with an honorable proposal. It took place when, upon rounding Sakonnet Point in the canoe that was taking him from Cape Cod to Rhode Island, Church spotted some Sakonnets fishing from a rock. He asked his paddlers to bring the canoe within hailing distance, then opened up conversations with "the enemy."

Trusting in his own reputation among these people, he went ashore and attempted to see if the Sakonnets might be persuaded to abandon "Philip's" cause. To his pleasure, he found that one of the fishermen was a lieutenant of the squaw sachem Awashonks. With him he worked out a meeting date for a discussion with Awashonks about the possibility of peace. He would go to the meeting alone—a decision that horrified his Rhode Island neighbors.

The meeting took place at the famous Treaty Rock, which still may be seen in Little Compton, Rhode Island. In preparing for this discussion on equal terms, Church made sure that all weapons were laid aside and that his route back to his vessels was secure. Awashonks, for her part, seemed determined that no harm should come to her former friend. Yet the situation at first was quite formal. As Church (who always wrote in the third person) later described it, he had

> pulled out his calabash and asked Awashonks whether she had lived so long at Wetuset [Mount Wachusett] as to forget to drink *occapechees* [a little dram of brandy]; and, drinking to her, he perceived that she watched him very diligently. . . .

Soon she joined him and, the ice broken, they proceeded to discuss the rights and wrongs of the past months' warfare. Finally Awashonks's

> chief Captain rose and expressed the great value and respect he had for Mr. Church; and, bowing to him, said, "Sir, if you'll please to accept of me and my men and will lead us, we'll fight for you and will help you to [get] Philip's head before the Indian corn be ripe."

It was at length agreed that Awashonks's son Peter would go to Plymouth to present the Sakonnets' submission for peace and their petition for a new alliance with the English.

Although Plymouth's Major William Bradford was far from respectful of Awashonks when he arrived in the region with his military force, demanding that the squaw sachem be conducted to Plymouth as a prisoner of war, she and her son were eventually allowed to make their case. The new alliance was formalized in a treaty at the end of June; Awashonks and Church thereupon staged a joyous celebration on the shores of Buzzards Bay at Mattapoisett. First a great bonfire was piled up and set ablaze

> and all the Indians great and small gathered in a ring around it. Awashonks with the oldest of her people, men and women mixed, kneeling down, made the first ring next the fire, and all the lusty stout men standing up made the next; and then all the rabble in a confused crew surrounded on the outside. Then the chief Captain stepped in between the rings and the fire, with a spear in one hand and a hatchet in the other, danced around the fire, and began to fight with it, making mention of all the several nations and companies of Indians in the country that were enemies to the English.

These he disposed of symbolically by his dancing. One by one the other men joined him, and Church was informed that he was witnessing the swearing in of warriors who would fight for him. Ultimately Church himself was given "a very fine firelock." Now he had his own native army.

And with that adept team of warriors and scouts, he was able to wage a newly successful war across the woodlands and into the deepest swamps of southern New England. Church's methods may have been unorthodox in terms of traditional English warfare of the period, but he was as disciplined as he was inventive. In his account of the sorties carried out that summer of 1676, three tactics became recognizable: first, never to return from an area via the same route you took going in (thus he avoided the ambushes that Philip and others set for him); second, always to "march thin and scatter," that is, to proceed into a new area with each man a fair distance from the next and without gathering "in a heap together"; and, third, to trust your native allies, even those whom you have recently captured. He found, ironically, that some of his best soldiers were those who had looked most treacherous and "surly" when he first encountered them. They came to trust and "love" him just as he trusted and led them.

Church admitted, in his account of this extraordinary campaign, that one reason for his great success in capturing and killing the enemy (rounding up fifty or sixty at a coup) was that the Connecticut and Massachusetts armies were now hammering away successfully in the north. They were out of the garrisons and on the track of the fleeing natives, driving them in his direction. (Other dispersed Algonquians were fleeing in the direction of Maine.) Because of these driven refugees, the area around Bridgewater and Taunton, Massachusetts, was particularly productive for his searchings and capturings since this was a junction point for many of the native trails. One day near the first of August, in company with some volunteers from Bridgewater, Church came upon a "great tree" that had been brought down so that it would make a bridge across the Taunton River. Church

> spied an Indian sitting upon the stump of it on the other side of the river. And he clapped his gun up, and had doubtless dispatched him but that one of his own Indians called hastily to him, not to fire, for he believed it was one of his own men. Upon which, the Indian upon the stump looked about, and Captain Church's In-

dian, [seeing] his face, perceived his mistake, for he knew him to be Philip; [he then] clapped up his gun and fired, but it was too late, for Philip immediately threw himself off the stump, leapt down a bank on the side of the river, and made his escape.

Philip was indeed the prize that Church and his men sought first and foremost. Though he was now discredited in his allies' eyes, he remained to the English the essence of the war, the source of the terror they had endured. So, even when Church came upon the tracks of men fleeing westward (they proved to be those of Quinnapin and his still sizable force), he was not tempted to follow them. He was hunting not a Narragansett sachem, not the greatest possible battle, but Philip of Po-kanoket.

Soon after the exciting glimpse Church had enjoyed of Philip on the stump, he succeeded in capturing Wootonekanuska, Philip's wife, sister of the eldest of Quinnapin's wives; and with her was the son she had borne to Philip, now nine years old. Like all captives from this region, they were taken away to Plymouth for trial. Church frequently and warmly expressed his dislike of this judgment-and-slavery business. He must have been distressed to hear that, a group of clergymen having been specially brought together by the General Court to decide what might be God's verdict for these high-ranking captives, it was decided that slavery was correct and justifiable. Though the fate of Philip's wife and son is not definitely known, they were probably shipped off to the West Indies for sale to the highest bidder. Philip, on hearing of their capture, is said to have cried: "My heart breaks; now I am ready to die."

During that turned-around summer, the hunt for Philip and others went on. Hundreds and hundreds of the native peoples were rounded up and sold. One by one the most famous of the native leaders were caught. Quinnapin fell; One-eyed John, Sagamore Sam, and Muttawmp too, were taken to court, executed before the end of September. Weetamoo's body was found, drowned in a river she'd tried to cross. Once Church came so close to Philip as to find his still-warm campfire. And in a battle in the middle of August, Church and his allies (a force of not more than 50) captured or killed 173 of Philip's men.

From the pattern of his appearances, it seemed that Philip was fleeing first here, now there, finally crossing the Taunton River and running toward his home at Mount Hope on the Pokanoket Peninsula. Elusive and clever as a fox . . . but he must have been exhausted. When one of his counselors suggested peace, Philip's mood was such that he killed the man with his own hand.

It was the brother of the man Philip killed, Alderman by name, who stepped forth at the end of August and offered to take Benjamin Church directly to Philip's hideout. The quid pro quo for his treacherous act was that he himself would be spared by the court. He told Church (who had hastened across from his home in Rhode Island to the mainland upon getting the news of Alderman's offer) that Philip "was now upon a little spot of upland that was in the south end of the mirey swamp just at the foot of the mount." Church listened to Alderman— "who was a fellow of good sense and told his story handsomely"—and made his plans. He and his men would surround Philip's camp by night while expecting Philip to run to the other side, away from the expected English attack, just as Canonchet had. Church told the senior officer who had come to observe the operation: "Sir, I have so placed [my men] that 'tis scarcely possible Philip should escape them."

Although the first English soldier to fire on the sachem's

camp did so prematurely, at early dawn, the situation developed precisely as Church had planned. Philip, hearing the exchanged shots, "threw his *petunk* [pouch] and powder horn over his head, catched up his gun, and ran as fast as he could scamper, without any more clothes than his small breeches and stockings." He ran, as it happened, directly toward the spot where Alderman and the English soldier with whom he was paired were standing.

They let him come within shot, and the Englishman's

> gun missing fire, he bid the Indian fire away. And he did so to purpose, sent one musket ball through [Philip's] heart, and another not two inches from it. He fell upon his face in the mud and water, with his gun under him.

In the background, Church could hear Philip's chief officer, Annawon, yelling to the others, *"Iootash! Iootash!"* ("Stand and fight!"). But the fight was over.

"And a great, naked, dirty beast he looked like," Church commented on viewing the great sachem's body. In recognition of the leadership role Philip was supposed to have played in the grand rebellion of the native peoples, Church ordered that the head be chopped off by an Indian executioner, then the body quartered (standard operating procedure for the seventeenth century). First the appointed executioner made a speech about how this had been "a very great man"; then he chopped "his ass for him."

The head was presented to Plymouth where it was set on a spike, visible to passersby for decades. Cotton Mather relished the sight and more than once "took off the jaw from the skull of that blasphemous leviathan." Awashonks's chief captain had been right: Philip's head was collected by the English and their ancillary forces before the Indian corn was ripe.

The four quarters were hung on trees, here and there, so as not to hallow a traitor's body by burial. Alderman was allowed to cut off one of Philip's hands, for which he received a reward as well as rounds of free drinks in future tavern visits.

The evaluation of Philip personally and as a leader was left to the Puritans and to those who followed in the chroniclers' wake. A continuing challenge. Reviled, romanticized, ridiculed, and revised by successive generations of commentators, his reputation has suffered from the American culture's passion for superstars: we must have our heroes and our villains. But by no means can the war in its totality be explained by Philip's personality or personal ambitions (or those of any other individual, for that matter). Even at the war's earliest beginnings, it was the people of Pokanoket, not a superchief, who caused the first shot to be fired. If neither Alexander nor Philip had been inclined to form alliances and to take the Pokanoket braves into combat when injustices became intolerable, another leader would surely have been elevated to the task. The people were collectively in revolt, having had enough of Plymouth's lash.

And though Philip seems to have been rather ineffective, either in galvanizing the alliances he'd sought out or in conducting battlefront operations, we must remember how small was his own military force. He brought but few local chips to the table of the intercultural confrontation that grew and grew until it involved all of inhabited New England and affected international affairs as well. Yet with the English he was a fairly adept negotiator, whether for peace or for time. There is also the possibility that Philip's leadership qualities lay in different areas—as communicator, as pathfinder, as friend; we do not know. But we do know, as proved in the close escape from

Pokanoket in August of 1675, that devoted men were willing to die for him.

As for his attitudes, it was he who helped Mary Rowlandson through the swamp and to the hope of freedom. This act of mercy must be remembered even when we think of his summary hatcheting of Alderman's brother. No less fierce than his times, he seems to have been a man of moods, ranging from petulance and self-centeredness to sympathy and generosity. He was a prince, not a king, who did what he could for his people, his family, and himself. What more can one ask? Church reported that the native executioner who quartered Philip's body said of the defeated prince: "He had been a very great man, and had made many a man afraid of him."

But Annawon, Philip's war captain, remained. And his capturing lives on as one of the most fascinating parts of Benjamin Church's narrative. The aged warrior Annawon, who had served under Massasoit, had all the skills of a survivor. Now, recovering from the attack in which his sachem had been killed, he was in retreat from Mount Hope to a location near Rehoboth, about six miles west of Taunton. There, as he knew, was a hill with a rock shelf virtually unapproachable from below. The only way to it was by rope from above, one person let down at a time.

Church followed the war captain's trail, tracking and questioning as he went north. Finally, at the beginning of September, he encountered an old man and his daughter who had but recently come from Annawon's well-concealed camp. Enlisting them, Church and his small force hurried toward the camp as the day ended. Then, from the top of the hill, he could see the campfires of the enemy being lit, and Annawon and his son preparing for sleep. Church urged his guides to clamber down the rope ahead of him with their packs full of supplies, and he prepared to follow immediately, in their shadow. When he reached the ground, however, Church was spotted at once, greeted with the astonished cry of *"Howoh!"* ("Who's there?!"). But after he had identified himself and informed Annawon and his son how the situation lay, the surrender took place quite peacefully. It was an act of extraordinary courage and ability.

As the night wore on, however, even bold Benjamin Church began to have his doubts about how peaceful the scene would remain. He lay on the ground feigning sleep, keeping an eye on Annawon, his own men having secured the rest of the encampment. The aged Pokanoket war captain was also awake; the two of them staring at each other through the darkness. At length Annawon stood up and went off into the woods, perhaps to relieve himself, perhaps for a more deadly reason.

> Captain Church began to suspect some ill design and got all the guns close to him, and crowded himself close under young Annawon, that if [Annawon] should anywhere get a gun, he should not make a shot at [Church] without endangering his son. Lying very still awhile, waiting for the event, at length he heard somebody coming the way Annawon went. The moon now shining bright, he saw him at a distance coming with something in his hands, and, coming up to Captain Church, he fell upon his knees and offered him what he had brought. And, speaking in plain English, said: "Great Captain, you have killed Philip and conquered his country, for I believe that I and my company are the last that war against the English, so suppose the war is ended by your means; and therefore these things belong to you."

What he presented to Church was the regalia of the sachem, King Philip: the two enormous belts of wampum, one edged with red hair from Mohawk country, the two horns of "glazed powder," the red cloth blanket on which Philip would sit when appearing "in state" . . . they were wondrously crafted, valuable beyond measure. Annawon was quite right: Benjamin Church deserved them, if only because he respected them more than anyone else. But he gave them, according to form, to Plymouth's Governor Winslow. And he, in turn, gave them to Charles II of England—though it is doubtful that they ever reached him. So they were thrown away and lost, these unique evidences of a once rich culture.

Annawon was wrong, however, in believing that his capitulation marked the end of the war. The northward-traveling sparks had found ready tinder in Maine. There the war raged on—and there it would end in a quite different way.

6

Dawnlanders and Down Easters

The Continuation of War Along the Coast

On July 11, 1675, Henry Sawyer at York, Maine, received a letter telling him of the alarming outbreak at Swansea, on Plymouth's Narragansett Bay frontier. Sawyer concluded, in the words of William Hubbard (who wrote a separate account of the Maine phase of the war), that the Indians had formed the "Design of a general uprising." This suspicion of a grand rebellion across all New England seemed confirmed by rumors that some warriors from certain Androscoggin villages had hastened south to join King Philip and the Narragansetts. Other warriors would undoubtedly strike at targets in Maine. Hubbard, seeking to explain this terrible treachery, this perverse racial rebelliousness, could only refer to the eternal antipathy between the snake and humankind. It was like that.

Henry Sawyer immediately called together a number of his fellow settlers to consider how to make a preemptive thrust into the heart of the imagined threat. It was, indeed, only an imagined threat for, as Hubbard himself had to admit, the settlers of the Province of Maine had been "in good correspondence with the Indians" for many years before 1675; surely this crisis too could be negotiated, if anyone cared to. But no: determined to confront the enemies of English society with force, the armed settlers marched sixty miles north and east to the Sheepscot River. There they demanded that the assembled natives surrender their weapons as evidence of loyalty. Such a surrender would, of course, prevent the native hunters from bringing in enough meat for that fall and winter; starvation for families would be the price of loyalty.

Attempting to put a diplomatic face on things, Sawyer and his companions offered the few trinkets they had brought along as cordial conversation openers. But it is difficult today to see their march and their assertion of power as anything but an aggressive overreaction to news from afar. Modern scholars have deduced from local histories, however, that the settlers' intention, as well as to stifle coordinated uprisings in Maine, was to remove the need for any intervening force to be sent into Maine by meddlesome authorities in Boston. The Down Easters wanted to handle their natives their own way.

The response of various indigenous people along the north-eastern frontier to the settlers' demand on the Androscoggins was curious. They recognized apparently that, because of the trouble in the south, they now faced an altered political situation; this was more than just another twist in the long saga of dealings between them and Europeans of various nationalities. So, in some cases, demonstrations of loyalty were made, weapons surrendered, and vows exchanged. A Canabas sachem named Robinhood (Mohotiwormet) went so far as to stage an elaborate dance in honor of his people's ancient alliance with the English. Others made their own plans, contemplating flight to the north, where they could continue to hunt under the benign gaze of the Roman Catholic French. Still others decided that this was the time to stand and fight.

The explosive and climactic events of King Philip's War that then occurred in Maine and New Hampshire assumed a definite character of their own—though certain commentators tend to downplay the significance of the easterly actions. Hubbard himself at first omitted this frontier from his narrative of the war. Then he changed his mind and described much of what happened in confused detail, as if uncertain about its godly meaning. It may also be that he simply disliked Maine and its unorthodox people altogether, ". . . the whole tract of land being of little worth, unless it were for the Borders thereof upon the Sea-coast, and some Spots and Skirts of more desirable Land upon the Banks of some Rivers." Yet he knew that what happened here was somehow pertinent . . . and ultimate.

Though very much a part of the total disaster, the Maine episodes do appear as a rather strange coda at the end of the war. This is not merely because many of those events took place after Philip's death and after the unvictorious southern victory proclaimed by the exhausted Puritans. What happened in Maine stands as a recapitulation and clarification of many of the war's themes, important for the very reason of the slight remove in time and place from the main seat of the war. In the reflective light of these Maine actions we are better able to draw conclusions about the war—one of which is that it did not end with Philip's death, nor did it end as generally described. Also, how and why the war began in the discrete parts of New England is revealed with extra clarity by early events along this rocky, east-tending coast.

Well before Henry Sawyer's forceful march north, the Androscoggin people had commenced their contacts with white society, unfortunately in the person of an Englishman named Thomas Purchase. At his trading post above Pejebscot Falls (present-day Topsham) he practiced skulduggeries that would not be forgotten. First a coastal fisherman, then an upriver settler (c. 1628), Purchase profited handsomely from his tradings; like many other freewheelers at this stage in colonial development, he found there was nothing to stop him from playing by his own rules. Who would hold him to account for the way he cheated the local people?

As reported by Samuel Drake (one of the more meticulous nineteenth-century historians), Purchase used liquor as the key ingredient in his defraudings. He had the distinction of being the first to make the Androscoggins drunk or to encourage them

> to make themselves drunk with liquors and then to trade with them, when they may easily be cheated both in what they bring to trade and in the liquor itself, being of half or nothing but spring water . . . which made one of the Androscoggin Indiance [sic] once complain that he had given an hundred pound [worth of furs] for water drawn out of Mr. Purchase his well.

It was against this unscrupulous, remotely located trader that a few Androscoggins decided to take action after the exciting news from Swansea. The preventive move by Sawyer's armed force was not going to quiet or quench their hatred for Purchase.

In September 1675, the vengeful men who approached the post, pretending they were on a trading mission, found to their disappointment that Purchase and his sons were away. Or perhaps the Androscoggins knew that he had departed and planned their raid to coincide with his absence. Either way, they went about their business of plundering with zeal: they killed a calf and a sheep, they ripped up the feather beds for their ticking, they took away the weapons and powder and liquor. But they left the women at the post alone, as would decent Algonquians anywhere. When they then saw that one of the Purchase sons was riding up to the post, they attempted to capture him. But he, spotting a rifle under the blanket of the approaching Androscoggin, recognized what was up and dashed away to give warning. The raiders quickly withdrew, warning Mrs. Purchase that their next visit would be more punishing.

This small-scaled, rather predictable raid in what was then interior Maine might well have taken place anywhere in New England in 1675. But here the history and the people and the consequences were different. The Purchase family had no garrison house in the neighborhood to which they could flee, for in these locations there had been during the past few years no "collisions as to lead to the fear of war," as expressed by one regional historian. Nor were there (occasionally) helpful structures of New England biracial society: ancient treaties or fair-minded courts or thought-unifying churches. It was all fragile and new. Each location tended to have its own spirit, what might be called the individualistic spirit of the American frontier. Individual attacks like the one on the Purchase outpost, combined with many other, bloodier subsequent attacks gave this battlefront its unique shape—a shape that fits uncomfortably into the total pattern of King Philip's War.

The Province of Maine had its own biracial history. Ever since 1625, the hospitable Kennebecs (as opposed to the bilked and angry Androscoggins) had been unshakably committed to the English cause. The first Pilgrim negotiators who had come up the river then, bringing with them the baskets of their first successful corn harvest for trade in this potentially rich fur region, had established at once a harmonious relationship with the Kennebecs. In the words of the insightful French observers whose territory abutted the Kennebecs on the north and east, these Algonquians had become "the special clients of the Plymouth Colony." Even after the Pilgrims sold their trucking post (located at the site of present-day Augusta) to a team of Boston merchants in 1661 after years of profitable and trouble-free trading, the Kennebecs remained solid allies. And as time advanced they attempted to remain in the golden era of harmonious trade relations.

Along with Maine's other natives, the Kennebecs are Abnaki. This name embraces a sizable number of people of diverse locations and affections. One of the best portraits of the historic Abnaki peoples is found in Kenneth M. Morrison's intriguingly entitled *The Embattled Northeast: The Elusive Ideal of Alliance in Abenaki-European Relations.* Morrison speaks of the Abnakis as "tiny groups of related tribes," occupying villages far removed from each other across a vast territory. How strange it is that both the settlers and these natives shared the ideal of individualism and yet could not come together either ethically or politically.

The more recognizable Abnaki groups, from southwest to northeast, were the Pennacooks (living north of the Merrimack River and into New Hampshire); the Sacos or Sokokis; and Androscoggins and Kennebecs and Wawenocks and Penobscots of central Maine; and the Passamaquoddys and Maliseets of eastern Maine. Lacking any kind of political unity, the Algonquian-speaking Abnakis were also varied in their economic pursuits. Most were farmers but some were not: the Maliseets (or Micmacs) of the far east, for example, still preferred hunting and trapping to tilling the shallow soil and to hoeing and weeding the corn hills.

They were all distinctly Abnaki peoples, however, the name meaning "People of the Dawn Place," or Dawnlanders. They had their own ways of dealing with or ignoring the Europeans— which makes them, in the eyes of Morrison and other ethnohistorians—quite different from the Massachusetts, the Mohegans, and other Algonquian groups who had willingly adjusted themselves to the settlers' way of life at an early stage of red-white contact. Here one found a certain insouciance and casualness about the peoples' external relations (except, possibly, for the Kennebecs). Life was so fulfilling and abundant for these people that, in the view of a well-placed observer, Father Pierre Biard (a French Jesuit of the seventeenth century), the men did not have to work hard enough—or at least hard enough to please a work-oriented European. It was a problem to pin down the Dawnlanders.

Yet, according to another observer, training for a man's life work among the Abnakis was unusually intense. Historian Howard Russell reports from his studies that the Abnaki hunters endured many trials and much instruction to enable them to serve their villages. The fleetest of the young men "were trained to run down a deer or moose, a feat that might take more than a single day."

And despite the temptations of the traders' blankets and pots and tools, the Abnakis never surrendered their pride and became dependent servants. On the contrary, they seemed to possess sufficient skills as politicians and diplomats to play the French-English rivalry for their own ends, profiting independently from the era of international trade. Yet, for many generations, they themselves had been wracked by intergroup hostilities. John Smith found that the Micmacs were "mortal enemies" of the western Abnakis, who had to fortify their villages in self-defense. Of the bold eastern Abnakis, Smith said, "We [found] the people in these parts verrie kind but in their furie no less valiant." Presumably these natural rivalries were exacerbated by the tensions of trade with the Europeans, just as we have seen in other sections of New England.

In the far-ranging power contest between Europe's empires, it seemed from the Abnaki perspective that the English fared less and less well, the French appeared more and more admirable. Historian Neal Salisbury reminds us, however, that the successful French colonists should not be viewed as altruistic champions of the native Americans; in the decade before King Philip's War the French repeatedly battled with the Mohawks in the St. Lawrence valley. The French did seem to possess a greater tolerance, nonetheless, and they made few blunders.

As early as 1603, the English explorer Martin Pring had set dogs on the Abnaki people when he encountered them on Maine's coastal islands; in 1604 George Weymouth had kidnapped a group of Abnakis and taken them to England. In 1614 John Smith's colleague Thomas Hunt seized and made off with twenty-four Abnaki young people—an act of barbarism hard to forgive. While the English were known for these outrages (here, as in southern New England, they were called cutthroats), the French priests seemed to carry on their Maine affairs with honesty and trustworthiness. Samuel Penhallow, an early historian of King Philip's War, was as prejudiced against the French priests and the "Bloody Pagans" as any other Puritan, but he brought to mind

> a remarkable saying of one of [the Abnakis'] Chief Sachems, whom (a little before the war broke out) I asked, Wherefore it was they

were so much bigoted to the French? Considering their traffick with them was not so advantageous as with the English. He gravely replied That the *Friars Taught them to Pray, but the English never did.*

The hold of the French on North America, dating back to Champlain and other relatively well-behaved French explorers in the early part of the seventeenth century, had been greatly strengthened by the terms of the Treaty of Breda (1667). This kingly agreement between Charles II of England and Louis XIV of France gave to France the vast and rich land of "Acadia" (Maine's easternmost territories plus Canada's provinces of New Brunswick and Nova Scotia). And although New Englanders had to accept the legality of the treaty, they viewed it as a royal insult: had they not conquered Acadia by their own courage and under Cromwell's orders in the campaigns of 1654? Now, as the French established the capital of Acadia at Pentagöet (Castine) on Maine's Penobscot Bay, and as they took over the fur-trading business from there, it appeared that one of North America's most productive territories was lost to English settlers. The pope-loving French and the undependable Abnakis would become masters of the northeastern frontier without firing a shot.

This was indeed an unstable and contested frontier, along which volcanic tremors shuddered for many years. The long-lasting historical theory is that although King Philip's War engaged only the western Abnakis, the effects of that war eventually spread to include their eastern cousins. And when the French came actively to the support of the eastern Abnakis, that was the beginning of the next century's French and Indian Wars. By that time, the western Abnakis had either been demolished or had fled to the east. This gives to the entire process of settler-native relations an air of inevitability and Hegelian process. But it leaves out the individualistic and local and personal factors that were so much the making of it. It's the observation of but one regional writer—Edward E. Bourne, who produced *The History of Wells and Kennebunk*—that if the Puritans had acted as Christians, the war and its severe consequences would never have taken place here, despite the fragility of the frontier. And as for the Puritans' prayers to God that he come more vigorously to their assistance, Bourne remarked that "it requires a wonderful boldness at the throne of grace to pray to be saved from the consequences of our own iniquities."

What this regional historian had in mind was the string of crimes and corruptions practiced by Thomas Purchase and his ilk. They, not any abstract or thermal forces, caused the tensions along this frontier of six thousand settlers and twice as many natives. If another criminal example is needed, one might look next at the activities of the first permanent settler of the Portland area, Walter Bagnall. He had established a trading post on Richmond Island as early as 1628. And while saluting him for that accomplishment, a prideful and recently published profile of Portland had to admit about Bagnall that "his claim to fame was brief . . . in 1631 he was murdered by the Indians he had cheated."

An even more gruesome incident that took place just before King Philip's War should be credited, however, for having swayed many Abnakis' sentiments toward rebellion. It occurred when the wife of one of the region's most influential sachems— Squando, sachem of the Sacos or Sokokis—was traveling by canoe with a baby boy across Casco Bay. In the words of William Hubbard, she was subject to the "rude and indiscreet act of some English seamen." In fact, their behavior was more murderous than rude. The seamen, presumably drunken hands from an English trading vessel in the Portland area, were curious about a legend launched by chronicler John Josselyn that Indian children had the instinctive ability to swim. So when they spied the child in the canoe of Squando's wife, they charged the craft, upset it, and marveled to see what might happen to the baby when dropped into the water. He sank like a stone. Instantly, the anguished mother dove in after him; finally she emerged with her half-drowned son in her hands. But, not long after being brought to shore, the boy died.

Squando, though once a Christianized Indian and friend of the English, went on to become one of the Abnakis' most vengeful war leaders. Hubbard, in summarizing the episode, pointed out that the child would most surely have died eventually. He furthermore reminded his readers that "the Indians naturally delight in bloody and deceitful actions." So why shed a tear for one of theirs?

Maine, while different from the other battlefronts of King Philip's War, produced a panorama of carnage as destructive as any. At first, however, the outbreaks seemed manageable. Soon after the Androscoggins' attack on the Purchase trading post, attacks spread throughout the Casco Bay area. Or, in the words of the Puritan chroniclers, the Abnakis made their way "by blood and rapine" across the land. On September 12, the Falmouth house of John Wakely went up in flames. Spying the smoke from Casco Neck, a relief party rushed to the scene but arrived too late. In the blackened ruins they found the bodies of seven mangled men and women; two girls had been seized and taken away. After urgent warnings from still friendly Sokokis, some of the area's settlers took refuge in the fortified house of Major William Phillips farther south, on the Saco River. From there the torchings of raiders could be seen, closer and closer—and then the attackers fell upon the garrison itself.

Before nightfall they succeeded in wounding the major and in terrifying the besieged settlers with their taunting cries and bold charges. But the attackers fell short when a cart piled high with flaming combustibles, launched against the garrison, failed to reach its target.

As Hubbard narrates the tale of a subsequent attack on the nearby settlement of Newichawannock (South Berwick), the viewer has the uneasy feeling of having shared adventures with these archetypical characters before. Here a brave maiden was just able to close the door of her house before the attackers drove their arrows and axes into the door's paneling. Other inhabitants having escaped out the back door toward a nearby garrison, the brave "virago" (Hubbard's word, then of nobler meaning than now) held the door closed as long as she could. But finally it fell beneath the ax blows and she was knocked on the head as the enemy charged through the house in pursuit of the rest of the family. They succeeded in catching two little girls, one of whom was killed, the other taken captive. As for the heroine, she lived to give Hubbard and other narrators the terrifying details of her ordeal.

A few weeks later, Newichawannock was again surrounded by a large force of attackers; this time they seemed determined to besiege the town until it capitulated. The nearest fortified point to which the settlers could appeal was Dover, on the banks of the Piscataqua River, which divides Maine from New Hampshire. To Dover, five miles away, a messenger was sent on October 14 with the following plea:

> To Mr. Richard Waldron and Lieutenant Coffin: These are to inform you that the Indians are just now engaging us with at least one hundred men and have slain four of our men already—Richard Tozier, James Barren, Isaac Bottes, and Tozier's son—and have

burnt Benoni Hodsdon's house. Sirs, if you ever have any love for us and the country, now show yourselves with men to help us, or else we are all in great danger to be slain, unless our God wonderfully appears for our deliverance. They that cannot fight, let them pray. Nothing else, but rest yours to serve.

—ROGER PLAISTED
GEORGE BROUGHTON

Plaisted and his sons were killed in the action that followed. But ultimately, just before help arrived from the town of Eliot, the attackers abandoned their seige.

No part of southwestern Maine seemed immune from the harassment of these light and deadly attacks. At Saco, where the embittered Squando was familiar with the pattern of settlement, thirteen English inhabitants were killed and many houses and barns burned. The Cape Neddick area, just north of York, was subjected to a series of attacks beginning September 25. Soon thereafter, storms of natives struck Newichawannock once more, while simultaneously striking Wells. According to Maine historian Charles Banks, seven persons were killed and almost all houses in the respective towns were burned to the ground.

Something about the character of these attacks convinced historian Banks (writing in 1967) that the victims of these raids endured "a type of barbarity *not* experienced among the Abenakis"—implying that at least some of the attackers must have come from elsewhere, most probably from southern New England. There the Algonquian warriors had learned all the cruelties of contemporary European warfare and had invented some new twists themselves under the stress of the times. To show the type of unusual cruelty he had in mind, Banks turned to Williamson's famous *History of Maine*, finding this quote:

For instance, after dashing out the brains of a nursing mother, [the Indians] pinned her infant to her bosom and in this awful condition was the babe found alive with one of the paps in its mouth.

We cannot be sure, however, whether that grotesque scene is or is not a propagandistic exaggeration, repeated from the time of the chroniclers. Nor can we be sure, at this early stage, if there had been any exchange of warriors from south to north. The statistics tell a story that, while grim, seems by no means cataclysmic: in the attacks and counterattacks of August to November 1675, on the northeastern frontier, 150 English settlers were killed or captured, along with perhaps twice as many natives. Because of the exposure and isolation of the Maine communities and the lack of coordinated defense, the panic that ensued is understandable. Exaggerations were quite in keeping with the events of those dreadful months.

From the spotty settlements along Maine's mid-coast sector, farmer families fled oceanward, down to the more easily defended peninsula tips and islands. This retreat represented a turning back of the clock, for it was on these rocky islands and glacier-defined peninsulas that Maine had begun in the first decades of the century. Then fishermen's rude stagings could be seen at rugged locations like Monhegan Island and the Isles of Shoals; then fishing stations such as the commodious ones at Richmond Island and Damariscove marked the barest beginnings of New England's northern settlements.

Advancing from those settlements, Down Easters had turned to building homesteads upriver, saltwater farms from which they could both fish and farm by the season. Visitors by land (unlikely) or sea (most often) would come upon a snug, one-story house with rough-board siding and thatched roof, usually sited nearby a deep tidal river. Often that homestead was an unintegrated part of a larger community. As regional historian Edward Bourne observed: "When thirty or forty families had gathered . . . [away from the sea and] away from any ruling authority [in one of these communities], many began to think they could do as they pleased."

From Puritanical Boston, Maine's salty settlements were indeed far removed in religious philosophy, of which they proudly had little, and in political thinking. Here each man did as he would, or that was the idea. But by swift sailing vessel they were not really far removed physically from the rest of New England. As Samoset, the personable, powerfully built Abnaki sachem who had walked into Plymouth one day in 1620, explained to his astonished hosts (in good, working English, which he had learned among the fishermen), his land of Pemaquid lay but "a day's sail [away] with a great wind and five days by land."

That relative accessibility to the capital of Massachusetts Bay gave the settlers little comfort, either in peace or in wartime. They were almost as fearful of the heavy-handed nabobs and of their repressive theological controls as they were terrified by the native attacks. As early as 1637 and 1643, Bay authorities had sought to take over New Hampshire's four towns—Exeter, Dover, Hampton, and Portsmouth. And the Puritans' push in the direction of Maine, carried on with extra vigor during the Cromwell years, had been only slightly modified by the restoration of the Stuart kings and by the king's ministers' imperialistic, antisettler colonial concepts. Such Down Easters as Henry Sawyer, even now that the war had begun, wanted no helmeted and booted officers from Boston to come riding north telling the townspeople what to do.

Yet the administration in Boston responded swiftly and strongly to the news that the Abnaki warriors had joined "Philip's" rebellion. Even though the Massachusetts Bay forces were then hard-pressed in the south (the Pokanokets having escaped and joined the Nipmucks, and towns all the way to the Connecticut River coming under attack), the Puritans' council decreed in October 1675 that assaults on the inhabitants of "Piscataque" (and the neighboring section of Maine) would be relieved by a recruited army. The financial charges for this sizable task force "shall be allowed in the general Account of the colonies."

For the Bay Colony and its confederates, on the edge of bankruptcy, this seemed a bold and somewhat bizarre move. The revisionists have no difficulty understanding it, however, finding this decision by the Puritans but another symptom of their compulsion to invade and acquire coveted New England territories. No matter what it cost, the military machine would now be aimed north, taking advantage of the natives' unrest to reassert Puritan claims all the way to the Penobscot. Another interpretation is that the Bay Colony, here as in the attack on the Narragansetts, was undertaking a risky maneuver, more from weakness than from strength. That view—the concept that the Puritans were primarily motivated by a need for food and funds—finds support in the language of the orders issued to the expedition's leaders, orders that speak frankly to the expectation of slave-trade revenues. "Without doubt," the orders read, "if [the Abnakis'] squaws and papooses be at Assabee [Ossipee, the designated target for the expedition], and God be pleased to deliver them to our hands, it would be much for our interest." Things had reached such a pass in John Winthrop's "Citty on a Hill" that a campaign to capture innocent slaves from among the native populations was apparently the only way to uphold New England.

The native encampment at Lake Ossipee did indeed look like an easy and profitable objective. With civilians and supplies cooped together in one primitively fortified village, and with warriors off on the track hunting winter food, the Abnakis would surely fall without much difficulty. If that's what the Puritans intended, they had reckoned without the rigors of northern New England's winters. It was not until the beginning of December that the expedition, under the command of Major Daniel Denison (brother of the Connecticut captain who would capture Canonchet), was sufficiently organized to strike out toward Maine. Then, according to Hubbard, Denison's task force immediately found itself staggering through snowdrifts four feet high. Perhaps this was the same snowfall that had swirled across the scene of the attack on the Narragansetts' Great Swamp fortress, for the two drives occurred simultaneously. But here Denison found the going impossible. Turning his men around, the major reported to Boston that the getting of the squaw slaves would have to be postponed for the season.

The winter pause gave Puritan commanders and Maine settlers alike an opportunity to reconsider how to deal with the Abnakis. Yet it was fear and ambition that pervaded these deliberations, not reason: fear of King Philip, that figure so magnified by the propagandists, and ambition for new lands. The whole story of how the red and white cultures had evolved in Maine was twisted by writers and preachers to justify and impel the war. That distorted, self-righteous presentation (which quite ignored the activities of such hateful traders as Thomas Purchase, not to speak of various kidnappings and land thefts) lived on in the histories of some nineteenth-century historians. Take, for example, this passage from George Folsom's *History of Saco and Biddeford* (1830):

> . . . the records of 1636 show, that while the [Maine] planter was required to use his best endeavor to apprehend, or kill, any Indian

known to have murdered any English, or destroyed their property, he was also compelled to pay satisfaction to the Indian he wronged. In this manner the utmost tranquility appears to have prevailed in the Province throughout the lives of the first colonists, in their relations with the natives. The friendly intercourse of the natives with the inhabitants continued undisturbed, till the bold and restless spirit of the chief of the Wampanoags of Narragansett Bay, commonly styled King Philip, conceived the design of exterminating the whites by a general insurrection of the tribes throughout New England.

Historian Folsom's only adduced evidence for this it's-all-Philip's-fault theory was the story of the unfortunate Elizabeth Wakely, aged eleven, who was captured in the raid on her parents' house at Falmouth soon after the raid on the Purchase household. After most other members of the Wakely family had been killed by the raiders, Elizabeth "was carried away, it is said, among the Narragansetts; a circumstance that shows the connexion between the western and eastern Indians in these hostilities."

In an attempt to explain the irrational conclusions of the Maine settlers, America's most grandiloquent historian, George Bancroft, apologized that "Fear [had] magnified the plans of the tribes into an organized scheme of resistance." But other late nineteenth century writers found it necessary to admit that the notion was absurd. Even John Fiske (1889) wrote: "The Tarratines in Maine had for some time been infected with the war fever. How far they may have been comprehended in the schemes of Philip and Canonchet, it would be hard to say." But those latter-day efforts to balance the record came too late to help the propaganda-bedeviled citizens of Maine as they shivered through the terrible winter of 1675–1676: they knew that Philip and his Narragansetts were at their doors.

At the same time, there were those who continued to hope that, sufficient blood having been shed, now might be the time to bring the two societies back together. Thomas Gardiner of Sagahadoc (the coastal area to the east of the Kennebec River) expressed the heretical belief that the Abnakis constituted no real threat to the English settlements. He pointed out that there was at that moment a cessation of hostilities and that the Kennebecs and Penobscots, always ready for negotiations, had continued to stay out of the fray. Let the authorities, with their expeditions and heavy-handed tactics, not take charge in a way that would make peace talks impossible.

Though Gardiner may have had some sympathizers among the citizens, his rational message was exactly the kind of subversion that the Puritan authorities could not tolerate. The Province of Maine was at that time under the administrative rule of Massachusetts Bay, and those administrators would expect the same conformity of the Down Easters as of Bay residents. Gardiner was arrested and summarily taken to Boston for trial for treason. When pleading before the court, he tactlessly put the blame for the war on the initial English demand for the surrender of Abnaki weapons. And he maintained

> I do not find Any thing I Can discerne that the Indianes East of us ar[e] in the least our Ennimies, [they] only fly for fear from Any boats or English they se[e] & good Reason for thay well Know it may Cost them their Lives if the wild fishermen meet with them.

Fortunately, despite Gardiner's unwillingness to buy into the myth, his innocence was proved. But though he was then released, the authorities failed to heed what he was saying.

Whenever the Puritans became aware of the possibility of discussions with the Abnakis, they simply saw some trick afoot—and perhaps with justification. Yet thought was never given to the working out of mutual problems in any equal-minded way. With the Kennebecs and the Sokokis pressing for talks in the spring of 1676 and the Penobscots still peaceable, the military leaders concluded (in the words of Hubbard) that the hostile Indians were "cunningly" seeking to conceal themselves behind negotiations until "a bogus peace could be forged." Then, of course, they would fall upon the settlements again with all the greater effect.

As the year went on with its spate of battle reports from the south, the citizens of Maine and New Hampshire took heart from the news of Canonchet's execution and Philip's death. But now there was the possibility that bands of embittered Narragansetts and Nipmucks would stream north to take their vengeance on the Down Easters. And though these fears were played upon by the propagandists, the alarm-ringers were quite right to acknowledge the arrival in Maine of certain refugees and veteran warriors. Perhaps the most formidable of the warriors was Simon, "the Yankee Killer," a Narragansett who had once been a Praying Indian but who had become widely famed for his remorseless raids on Newbury, Amesbury, Haverhill, and Bradford.

In August of the peace-or-war year 1676, Simon led an attack on the farm of Anthony Bracket, located on Portland's Back Cove. After one of the Bracket family members had been killed, the rest were captured along with many others from the neighborhood, a total of thirty-four people. Some escaped, and Mrs. Bracket herself, who had been foresighted enough to bring needle and thread along, took note of an abandoned, bashed-in canoe as the captured party trudged along. Perhaps the birch bark could be mended, she thought (in much the manner of Mary Rowlandson). Slipping away from the rest of the party with her five-year-old child, she found that she could indeed make the damaged craft seaworthy. And thus, by a thread, she effected their escape.

Beyond raided Portland and desolated Falmouth (blasted the previous year), as far east as Woolwich on the Kennebec and Wiscasset on the Sheepscot, isolated families were seized and taken away as captives. The attack on the Woolwich trading post of Richard Hammond was marked by particular ferocity, as he had been a trader of the stripe of Purchase, known for cheating his native suppliers. By means of their many captives taken that summer, the Abnakis hoped to bolster their position in whatever talks might take place later that year. Perhaps they could even force the stand-fast English to come to the bargaining table.

The most significant attack of the season was directed at the thriving trading center at Arrowsic, the dramatically beautiful island of cliffs and coves that reaches seaward on the east side of the Kennebec. Here Captain Thomas Lake and Benjamin Clark from Boston had built with their parents a large, fortified community, including grist mill and store. On the fourteenth of August (just two days after Philip's death), the Abnakis staged an assault that, for its sophistication and magnitude, indicated the war in Maine had advanced to a level beyond small-scale raids and hit-and-run strikes.

The assault began innocently enough. Into the Arrowsic community the natives sent one of their women, alone, seeking shelter for the night within the stockade. Admitted, she waited until late at night to sneak forth and open the gates. In rushed the Abnakis and allied forces, slaying many of the inhabitants, taking others captive. Captain Lake and only one or two others escaped across to neighboring Georgetown Island. From there they succeeded in alerting the settlers of Sagahadoc to the heightened nature of the war. Though William Hubbard told the story of Arrowsic in his usual melodramatic prose, bemoaning the savages' cruelty and highlighting Captain Lake's escape, he could not resist adding a humorous Latin tag. Noting the velocity with which the captain had sped across land and water, he wrote: *"Timor addidit ala."* ("Fear supplied wings.")

Today, leisurely wanderers along the shores of these rocky, current-gouged island shores may, if lucky, find a flint arrowhead or two, half-buried in the sand of a cove. Tiny but dynamic, the discovered arrowhead is a fierce reminder of the failed negotiations, the terrifying cruelty of the resultant fight. That struggle between Maine's seventeenth-century peoples seems entirely encapsulated in this one, minuscule artifact, gleaming in the shoreside sunlight. It tempts the viewer to conclude that all history is determined by a weapon—not by people attempting to build civilizations or preserve traditions, but by the inhuman force of arms. Still, the crafting of this arrowhead is marvelous to behold; it was created by someone of refined skills, whether an art work was attempted or not.

The Arrowsic assault and eastward-spreading character of the hostilities convinced Massachusetts Bay authorities that more dramatic strategies and more imaginative leaders would have to be employed in the war against the Abnakis. Already Boston had caught sight of an officer whose boldness appealed to them; this was Richard Waldron of Dover (the man to whom the besieged settlers of Newichawannock had appealed so eloquently the year before). Waldron's signal accomplishment that had particularly engaged the favorable attention of the Puritans was his success in leading a large force of 120 soldiers across the Province to the Casco Bay area the previous autumn. Benjamin Church might have scoffed at this commander and his unwisdom in utilizing insufficient native scouts and ancillaries—

Waldron himself had admitted that he and his English soldiers "never could see an Indian" during the course of their march— but Boston had been impressed by his willingness to push among the Abnakis and to deal with them forcibly. He would serve well as the Puritans' new-model commander in the east.

Richard Waldron's harsh approach to the Abnakis, the approach that now took the place of peace negotiations on this frontier, was completely in character. He had come to Dover (Cocheco) many years before, in 1640, and acquired a monopoly of the fur trade in the area. Soon he added a sawmill to his trading post, and business flourished; he was then able to open another post at Concord (Pennacook) on the upper Merrimack. He also carried a reputation as a black marketeer in liquor to the natives. Briefly he was suspended from the position of magistrate for such dealings. But Waldron's faithful lieutenant Peter Coffin stated to the court that it was he, not Waldron, who was responsible. The major was restored to respectability and Lieutenant Coffin seems to have suffered very little for his loyalty.

A rather unorthodox Puritan, Waldron represented the independent, upward-striving local elite of New Hampshire and southern Maine, where there was a bit more allegiance given to Boston than in the middle portions of the Province. Here also the men of the towns were organized into standard militia units, which added up to a considerable force of nearly a thousand soldiers, fit command for an ambitious officer. The size of these militia units from Maine alone as given by local historians, was as follows: 180 men from Kittery, 100 each from Saco and Black Point (Scarborough); and 80 each from York, Wells, Cape Porpoise, Casco Bay, and Sagahadoc.

Fond of parading his well-staffed Dover militia unit here and there, Waldron obtained authorization in the spring of 1676 for another drive into Abnaki country. This one (which would be similar to Henry Sawyer's forceful march into Androscoggin territory) would press east into the lands of the Penobscots; his purpose was to demand a reassertion of their allegiance. Having arrived at the village of the distinguished Penobscot sachem Madockawando, Waldron presented his demand with customary vigor. But the sachem pointed out that many of the Abnakis in his region, deprived of their weapons and their ammunition by the preceding year's treaty, had starved to death. At the same time, the English, their supposed allies, had done nothing to help them. This argument and other legitimate complaints were laid before Waldron—who regarded them as insolent. He even had the bad grace to interrupt one of the Penobscots' senior spokesmen during the debate around the council fire; he refused to give any guarantee whatsoever that the English would pay attention to the Penobscots' needs. Hearing that, Madockawando courageously terminated the talks.

Later in the year, after the devastating attacks on Portland and Arrowsic, and after Puritan authorities had selected Major Waldron as their man, his militia force was reinforced by two companies of 130 English soldiers and 40 Natick Indians. The two companies and ancillaries, representing the Bay Colony's new order of military control over the Province, arrived on September 6, 1676. Throughout the region garrisons were strengthened and forts built, for that was still the basic exercise of the military philosophers. Ironically, one of these fort builders from the south was none other than Benjamin Church himself, who seems to have laid aside for the moment his preference for the more mobile type of warfare; he dutifully oversaw the construction of a new bastion at Portsmouth's Casco Neck, Fort Loyal.

But Waldron's activities were by no means restricted to the

bolstering of fortified towns. Under orders to round up all "manslayers," including any conspiring Algonquian warriors from the Narragansett or Nipmuck camps, he issued a set of instructions that gave carte blanche to any Englishman who wanted to dispose of a native. In the words of Rufus King Sewall, respected historian of Maine in the last century, this let loose the most "unprincipled seamen" along the coast, inviting the slaying of more innocent victims like Squando's murdered son. It was precisely this kind of English villainy against which peace seeker Thomas Gardiner had warned.

Given free rein by Waldron's directives, a skipper named Laughton soon enticed a dozen or more Micmacs aboard his sloop at Cape Sable and sailed them off into salvery, pocketing a handsome profit. That action succeeded in bringing Maine's hesitant easternmost Abnakis into the war on the side of the Androscoggins and other aroused natives. In viewing this strategic error, Edward Bourne wrote that thus "new acts of folly and wickedness on our part kindled the fire again."

The English policy of depriving the Abnakis of their weapons—to which the Kennebecs objected, as did the Penobscots —was truly murderous, resulting in the deaths of many innocent people. Unmoved by that, or by the enslavements along the coast, Richard Waldron found a way to carry the systems of annihilation one step further. Soon after his reinforcements arrived from Boston, he and Captain William Hawthorne devised a scheme that would swiftly remove many natives from the scene.

Their plan took shape when a delegation of Algonquian negotiators came to him bearing a truce flag, requesting a political agreement whereby they and their people could live undisturbed by the settlers. Waldron's worst suspicions were stirred by this innocent-seeming, independent action. So the plan went into effect: he and Hawthorne proposed to the delegates that they join the English in staging a sham military maneuver, a let's-pretend battle. But, after the Abnakis and their native allies had fired their muskets into the air, and before they had a chance to reload, the English seized all four hundred of the visitors, impounding their weapons and subjecting the captives to trial. The leaders were swiftly executed, some two hundred sold into slavery, and only a few "friendly Indians" (such as the people of Wonnalancet) released with heavy warnings.

In his account of the reprehensible affair, Hubbard is quick to point out that such escapees from the war as the Nashaways' One-eyed John and Sagamore Sam were successfully caught in Waldron's net. But he remains silent about the morality of the seizure. In John Fiske's account, the author covers his embarrassment at Waldron's admittedly "unworthy stratagem" by recounting that "a terrible retribution was in store" for the treacherous major thirteen years later: the enraged Abnakis killed him in one of the first battles of the French and Indian Wars.

Reverting to their dogged policies of forts and bastions, the Puritan commanders in Maine ignored the fact that here (as opposed to southern New England) numbers and time were not on their side—the Abnakis, though starving and poorly equipped, continued to hold the advantage of manpower. Another disadvantage of the bastion policy here was that the Down Easters could not abide the Puritan soldiers sent from Boston. At York for example, where the alarmed citizens had initially claimed that English soldiers were desperately needed for the defense of the town, those same citizens now chafed at the military restrictions and complained to the courts about the soldiers' behavior. The bastions were divided from within.

Nonetheless, such reinforced towns as York remained relatively safe and secure in 1676, while the neighboring towns of Kittery and Wells "received a number of visitations" from the Abnakis. Indeed it appeared that the Abnakis and their allies were developing strategies and field commanders that would permit them to dominate the Province by well-directed large-scale attacks.

The military leader who then arose from among the Abnakis was quite a different personality from Richard Waldron, more subtle but equally lethal. His name was Mugg Hegone, as reported in chronicles of the time, though those chronicles disagree as to whether he was an Androscoggin sachem or an embittered Kennebec. Whatever his origins, he showed again and again the typical Abnaki characteristic of individualistic behavior. Among Mugg's other personal advantages as a player on this bicultural battlefront was that he spoke the settlers' language fluently. For "from a Child [he had] been well acquainted with the English and lived some years in English families," according to Hubbard. Indeed, he himself was a product of the prosperous trader society that had for so long blessed both cultures of Maine with its cruelties and its largesse. Now this son of that mixed society would strike back in wrath.

The first time Mugg and his dangerous combination of personal strengths and native alliances broke upon the English awareness was at the Scarborough fort called Black Point in the fall of 1676. This stronghold was of special significance now that settlers had fled from the communities to the north and east; Black Point held the line below Portland, guarding the security zone to the south. Conversely, it seemed to Mugg that Black Point would be an ideal base for the Abnakis' future attacks if it could be seized. But he recognized that the fort was far too strong to be taken by the usual sort of raiders' attack; indirection was needed.

Sending a message into Henry Jocelyn, commander of Black Point, Mugg suggested that he was ready to parley. And he proposed that Jocelyn meet him at a mutually safe discussion point some miles away. Jocelyn agreed and set forth with an appropriate guard at the appointed time. Then, with the commander absent from his fort, Mugg's warriors staged a mock attack which easily frightened the members of the garrison (who had never trusted their military guests, and knew not when or whether they would return) into abandoning the position. When Jocelyn returned to his fort, he and the deserted town were swiftly taken by the triumphant Mugg.

But when he attacked Wells and demanded its surrender, Mugg was greeted with an impressive show of arms and a resounding "Never!" from the commander of its militia. This was apparently a town whose citizens had the will to fight back. So, rather than lose his warriors in what would surely be a punishing battle, he contented himself with the slaying of a few men outside the walls and the capture of their cattle. He was less interested in Wells as a position than in victory for the long haul. He was later quoted as boasting that, having taken all of Maine from the English and having swollen the ranks of his armies with men and supplies, he would advance on Boston and push the Puritans into the sea.

At this same time—the autumn of 1676, when it appeared that the Puritans, though rejoicing in Philip's defeat and death, might be facing mightier enemies in the northeast—the military minds in Boston again decided that a postseason knockout punch might be the best gamble. So once more an expedition was sent forth when the falling of the leaves made for greater visibility and when the natives were snugly in winter quarters. But for the second time good fortune was denied the Puritans: when Captain Hawthorne arrived at the site of the Ossipee fortress on November 5, he found the village totally deserted. Further attempts to find any groups of hibernating Abnakis were also futile.

Yet another timely proposal from Boston to the command in Maine was that a large number of Mohawks be brought in to assist the English soldiers and their ancillary forces against the Abnakis and their allies. This obviously dangerous plan accomplished nothing but the slaying of several friendly Indians and the further weakening of the English command's communication with those few Abnakis who had been willing to listen to diplomatic proposals.

It was at this point that Mugg determined to play another of his cards, a political card. Pleading that his desire to discuss peace was sincere—certainly more sincere than Major Waldron's intentions had been when he welcomed the delegation of natives under a flag of truce two months before—he was able to impress the English with his importance as a spokesman for all the Abnakis. The settlers believed that, because Mugg "acted in the name of Madockawando," he in fact controlled the Penobscots as well as the Kennebecs and the Androscoggins. Eager to cut short the struggle, to reclaim their loved ones who had been taken hostage, and to get the oppressive Puritan occupation off their backs, the settlers urged Bay authorities to pay attention to this well-spoken mediator.

Thus Mugg found himself in Boston in November of 1676, talking about a cessation of hostilities with such Puritan leaders as Increase Mather. That eminent divine's diary entry for November 11 states: "Discoursing with Mugg, he told me that this winter many Indians at the eastward had starved to death [as a result of their being denied hunting weapons], and particularly that there were three sachems starved to death." This notation in Mather's pages exhibits no sorrow at the starvation, of course. Nor did sorrow characterize Hubbard's report that, as early as June 1676, the natives on the northeastern frontier had begun to seem "strangely dispersed and dispirited." Their mood might be compared to that of Mary Rowlandson's captors at about the same time—a mood brought on by hunger and the deaths of both warriors and innocent civilians. The Kennebecs and the Penobscots, despite their advantage in manpower over the local settlers, were quite serious about desiring an honorable peace.

What Mugg found in Boston, however, was a mind-set that would not allow any honorable agreement. Punishment and retribution seemed to be the controlling words in the Puritans' vocabulary. Rather than being welcomed for an equal discussion of points, he was harassed and threatened, compelled to accept the following terms (in summary): that all acts of hostility against the English should cease, that captives be returned and all damages to English settlements be satisfied; that henceforth the Indians would be permitted to buy ammunition from Boston-appointed officials only; and that the slayers of the Richmond Island settlers be apprehended and turned over to the English. Furthermore, the Penobscots were asked to take up arms against their eastern neighbors should the latter not cease their warring.

Though early histories say that Mugg accepted these terms, it is likely he did so only at threat of death. Under any normal circumstances, he could not have acceded to the last point, for he had no power to commit the Penobscots to any such action (nor would they have agreed to it themselves). Mugg is quoted by the Puritan chroniclers as saying: "I pledge myself an hostage in your hands till the captives, vessels, and goods are restored." Further: "I lift my hand to Heaven in witness of my honest heart in this treaty." One can imagine the crossed fingers behind his back as he spoke (if he spoke) those words. Or perhaps his quite understandable cynicism permitted him to say anything, make any pledge, without a gesture or a thought.

It was not the cynical Mugg but the remorseless English, however, who shed the next blood on the northeastern frontier. In a confrontation between Major Waldron and the sachem Squando and other Abnakis at the icy mouth of the Kennebec in February—a parley that was supposed to lead to peace talks through the release of hostages—a large number of Abnakis were killed under duplicitous circumstances. Taking note of this deception and other betrayals by the English, all the Kennebecs and the Penobscots finally abandoned their positions of neutrality and went in on the side of the rebels. Waldron's brutalities had again succeeded in making a possible peace unworkable.

Thereafter, attacks by the Abnakis and their Algonquian allies increased both in size and coordination. The Down Easters, in their terror, realized that the Bay commanders' determination to conduct the war without scruples and to discourage any serious negotiations was laying waste to their once-promising Province. With one Puritan military blunder following another, all the towns to the east were successively destroyed or abandoned. It was now the turn of the more secure settlements to the south and west, below Black Point, to hear the onrushing cry of the enemy and to be destroyed.

Mugg was deploying his forces toward those objectives in synchronization with Simon the Yankee Killer and other Algonquian leaders. Each of their task forces numbered in the hundreds. The first town on their joint list of likely targets was the already-battered Wells, whose weary citizens became aware that something new was about to occur when an aged Abnaki woman walked down the main street. Benjamin Swett, the garrison's commander, watched her with special care: Was this another of Mugg's tricks? he must have wondered. He sent out a company of soldiers beyond the town's walls to discover if the woman had come from a larger party of natives. Who were they and could they be stopped before they could prepare a siege?

But that removal of a company of soldiers was exactly what Mugg had hoped for. His warriors, who had been waiting in ambush, swiftly disposed of the reconnoitering company, then stormed into the weakened town. Wells, which had resisted for so long, now fell before their fury.

Next, Mugg planned a far-ranging naval maneuver. That is, he concluded that a possible way to strike the Down Easters where they lived was by destroying their prime asset, their fishing fleet and the fishing communities. If those vessels fell into Abnaki hands, the settlers would have nowhere to turn economically, their farms and inland towns having already been seized. But for all its brilliance, the idea was not so easy to execute. As the Abnaki warriors here and there along the coast descended by nightfall upon the unprotected harbors, and as they attempted to bring the captured vessels together, they faced an array of technological problems. The fishing craft were too big to be controlled by native seamen used only to canoes and dugouts; the vessels could not be paddled, and the complexities of the sails were beyond understanding. By the end of July some twenty vessels had been taken in hand—and abandoned, drifting freely away from their captors onto the rocks.

Before then, Mugg and Simon the Yankee Killer had launched a large-scale attack against the Black Point redoubt at Scarborough, which the English had had the temerity to rebuild. From his post, Lieutenant Bartholemew Tippen, now in command, could follow the pattern of the assault. And he took special note of which native officers seemed to be directing the warriors. Having spotted the key figure, he aimed and shot at that boldly exposed leader—killing Simon, he hoped. But in fact it was Mugg he killed, an even worse loss for the native allies.

Yet, in terms of manpower, the English suffered an even greater loss that spring. Although the Bay's General Court had by this time learned enough about the proper tactics of King Philip's War to send two hundred battle-wise Praying Indians along with two hundred conscripted Englishmen to the assistance of the Down Easters, the officers and the English soldiers were still novices in frontier fighting. Benjamin Swett, the lieutenant who had fallen for Mugg's ruse at Wells and barely escaped from the assault, had been promoted to captain; he was sent with the augmented force to "assail and annoy [the enemy] as much as in you lieth." In the opinion of commentator Leo Bonfanti, another weakness of Swett's task force was that the men who sailed with him to Black Point in June to commence their mission were the bottom-of-the-barrel dregs of Boston's war-wasted and unemployed. As well as being untrained, they were unhealthy and unresponsive. The Puritan war machine had reached the point where it was now sustained only by these poor victims of the Bay Colony's inequitable social system.

It took the raw recruits and their amateurish officers only a few days to fall into the most punishing ambush of the war. When the surrounding Abnakis rose from their hiding places and sent the first volley into the English ranks, Swett's two companies panicked and ran. The captain tried valiantly to reform his squads, but both Praying Indians and English collapsed around him. He himself, though severely wounded, nearly made it back to the garrison but was finally brought down by a blow to the head. Of the ninety men who had set forth with him that morning, half were killed; many more were wounded so badly that they died later. It could only be called a slaughter by mismanagement, final proof that, by their old military techniques, the Puritans could not win this war.

The war in King Philip's name, which had all but destroyed southern New England and which was going even less well in northeastern New England (where ineptness was compounded by lack of manpower), revealed all too clearly the rottenness of the Puritan's theocracy. As close observers viewed the scene, it was as if a great old oak had been slashed open by a summer's lightning bolt and, inside, one discovered nothing but decay. Within the Puritan-controlled colonies at this time, four-fifths of the citizens were denied the right to vote or to hold office; the natives were being mishandled with lethal consequences for both sides. But though this revelation of the formerly proud Puritans' incapabilities must have delighted King Charles and his courtiers, they could not ignore the strategic weakness this disarray brought to their northern American colonies. With New England burned, battered, and badly in debt, what was to prevent the French from moving in?

The king's brother, the Duke of York (later James II), to whom New York's Governor Edmund Andros reported, determined to take action to secure this, his part of the New World. Acting in his name, Andros dispatched a sizable force from New York to Pemaquid in the summer of 1677, soon after the dreadful massacre at Black Point. The fortress of Pemaquid, formally called Fort Charles but nicknamed the "Jamestown of the North" for its importance to imperial planning, then became the bulwark for the future security of the region that lay behind it. Only by this strong move by the crown's legions could New England be held.

Located some fifteen miles east of the mouth of the Kennebec, and but fifty miles west of Acadia's capital of Pentagöet, Pemaquid had by the 1670s already acquired a notable history for its geopolitical importance. In the 1630s, because of its vitality as a fishing and trading location and its centrality in colonial planning, it had rivaled Quebec in size and strength, boasting a population of five hundred and a residential community of eighty-four families. As Maine grew away from those beginnings, up the rivers and into the interior, Pemaquid had diminished. But now, by Andros's orders, its former glory would be restored. He decreed that this would be Maine's single port of entry; settlement of the interior would be discouraged; all traders and dealers with the Abnakis would have to get clearance from royal officials at Pemaquid. Authority would be taken out of the clumsy hands of the Puritans in Boston, and the troublesome war would come to a halt.

With the king's flag raised at Pemaquid and the warring parties summoned for the discussions they had not been able to manage themselves, peace was imposed on the province. The Kennebecs, Sokokis, and Penobscots, never eager for the war, were among the first to accept and help work out the treaty's terms—which were far more lenient than those which the Puritan authorities had attempted to ram down Mugg's throat. The so-called Peace of Casco (finally signed on April 12, 1678) provided for the release of all captives without ransom, for the safe passage of all refugees to their own homes, and for an annual quit-rent payment by each Down Easter family of one peck of corn to the Abnakis. A curious addendum to this last provision required that Major William Phillips of Saco, being so mighty, pay a *bushel* of corn a year. The lower classes, whether red or white, must have taken special joy from the penalty levied on the haughty major. He had once been so powerful that he fined a settler for whispering to a friend that "Major Phillips's horse is as lean as an Indian dog."

In the view of most historians, the 1678 Peace of Casco marked the end of King Philip's War. Finally the paroxysm that had cost thousands of lives—the greatest loss, proportionately, that Americans would ever suffer in 350 years of colonial and national history—would be eased. Finally, with Maine calmed down, it appeared that lives and livings could be put back together. But New England's agriculture and trade lay in ruins; of the region's ninety towns, fifty were razed or destroyed. The people of both races continued to suffer as their wasted land offered neither roofs for their heads nor crops for their harvests. War debts in excess of 1000 pounds would prove an almost impossible burden to bear: not for one hundred years would New England again achieve its pre-1675 level of prosperity. Plymouth's share of that debt was so great (though the Pilgrims had declined to take part in the Maine aggressions) that it exceeded the value of the colony's private properties. Although Casco was a name strange on the ear to many New Englanders, a place way down the coast, settlers and natives throughout the region must have heard that name with special gratitude; it had brought them peace at last.

But to the Down Easters themselves, Andros's imposed treaty was only momentarily acceptable. Perhaps in the eyes of some of them—peace lovers like Thomas Gardiner—the creation of a mutual society in the Province might seem feasible, with flexibility and respect on both sides. But in the view of most, the quit-rent they had to pay was too sharp an insult to be tolerated for long, and the "arrogance" (meaning the independent landholdings) of the Abnakis could not be endured.

To the Puritans in Boston, the Peace of Casco was a total

disgrace. In his famous literary monument, *Decennium Luctuo-sum*, which portrays the difficulties of the century's final decade (between 1689 and 1699), Cotton Mather begins by referring to the King Philip's War era, when "the desolations of war had overwhelmed all the settlements to the North-East of Wells." He goes on to deplore the hated treaty that Sir Edmund Andros had put in place, blaming that document for all the troubles that were to come in the French and Indian Wars. Mather complained that only "a sort of peace had been patched up, which left a body of Indians, not only with horrible murders unavenged but also in the possession of no little part of the country, with circumstances which the English might think not very honorable."

To the Abnakis, the imposed peace seemed better than war, but still lacking in that essential ingredient, mutual under-standing; lacking, too, in any political system that would allow for continuing discussions of the issues between the societies. With that lack in mind, two Kennebec sachems sent to author-ities in Boston a remarkable analysis of the late war and of native-white relations:

> This is to let you understand how we have been abused. We love you but when we are drunk you will take away our [goods] and throw us out-of-doors. If the wolves kill any of your cattle, you take away our guns and arrows for it. And if you see an Indian dog, you will shoot him. If we should do so to you—that is, cut down your houses or kill your dogs or take away your things—we must pay a [fine of] 100 skins.
>
> Because there was a war with the Narragansetts, you came here when we were quiet and took away our guns and made prisoners of our chief sagamores. And that winter, for want of our guns there were several starved. . . . Now we hear [rumors] that you say you will not leave war.

As long as one Indian is in the country, we are owners of the country. And it is wide and full of Indians, and we can drive you out. But our desire is to be quiet.

This wonderfully eloquent communication from the Kennebec sachems seems central to anyone's understanding of the terminal period of King Philip's War. The document was published by Professor Kenneth M. Morrison, whose perceptive comments succeed in describing the ever-widening breach between the English and the Abnakis. In his view, the Down Easters, for all their war exhaustion, remained determined to deal with the Dawnlanders only by push-and-shove. And, aggressively overreacting to the slightest hints of Abnaki unrest, the colonists of Maine for their part felt unrestrained by the terms of the Peace of Casco, by no means stopped from carrying on business as usual. They would indeed shoot the above-mentioned Indian dog whenever the opportunity presented itself.

Compounding that shoot-first and discuss-never attitude at the settler level was blindness at the administrative level. After Andros left the New York governor's chair, it was occupied by the equally imperious Thomas Dongan. His officers at Pemaquid reconfirmed the policy of peace by restraint—but they too declined to discuss any troubling issues with the sachems. Furthermore, the new governor entertained the proposal from New Hampshire that the Mohawks be brought in to quell new disturbances among the eastern Abnakis. That possibility, though not executed, again terrorized the frontier.

And although the Down Easters stirred themselves to attempt an agreement with the western Abnakis in 1685 that would create some mechanisms for resolving difficulties, that attempt soon broke down in mutual recriminations. Precisely the same kind of incidents that had led to the outbreak of hostilities in 1675 now recurred: unfenced and wandering English cattle, violations of native rights, settlers' river nets blocking the passage of fish to the natives' traditional fishing sites. Confronted with a worsening situation, the western and eastern Abnaki peoples cast differences aside and formed what came to be called the Wabanaki Federation. By 1688 a new war was under way—a war that led to the native capture of the royal fort at Pemaquid and the opening of the French and Indian Wars.

It seems difficult, therefore, to agree wholly with those commentators who hail Andros's Peace of Casco as both the definitive end of King Philip's War and as the triumph of imperialist policies over less rational local forces. No lid could contain the festering hostilities and resentments and ambitions that characterized the frontier where Down Easters and Dawnlanders met. And what made the situation worse was that from the pulpits came an unvarying message: King Philip's War had been a bloody, sacrificial combat against an evil native genius. The fathers of the new generation had fought him, had killed him, had thereby saved New England. No one should forget that sacrifice: let it be remembered in literature, in monuments, in land grants to veterans. Most important, let it be remembered in the future conduct of native affairs—only by the sword can we make peace.

In New England no William Penn emerged to suggest that the English immigrants might live peaceably with the natives, on the divine theory that they, too, were children of the universal spirit. Yet in New England there were individual spirits of peace, famous and less so, such as Roger Williams and Thomas Gardiner. There were decades and decades when a respectful relationship was reinforced by economic circumstances. And there were groups of people like the Kennebecs and the Niantics and the Quakers who did everything possible for mediation. Also there were the missionaries and the Praying Indians who tried to construct, for all its difficulties, some kind of interracial society. So it is also difficult to find in New England of the seventeenth century a pattern of built-in racial murderousness, on either side. There was simply not the confidence and wisdom and political skill to make one culture of two that were not that different.

As a result, most of us lost forever in this war and in later, similar brutalizations the possibility of sharing the native American heritage. Instead, what we did inherit from King Philip's War was an ineluctable sense of guilt. Wandering the river valleys and the island shores, we ask where the people have gone, knowing all the while. Their arrow pierces our heart.

Acknowledgments

Because this book was, from its beginnings, so directly derived from the different sections of New England with their distinctive physical and cultural characters, the author must take this opportunity to thank the institution staff members and the individuals and institutions that assisted him, region by region, across New England. But before naming them (by chapter, below) he would like to recognize with continuing gratitude the guidance and encouragement given him by Professor Neal Salisbury of Smith College; it was through introductions assisted by Professor Salisbury that many of the essential conversations and interviews were made possible with both academic and native American sources.

Grateful recognition is also due to the American Indian Archaeological Institute in Washington, Connecticut, where the author first became aware of the exciting work now being conducted in the field of native American studies to supplement, or possibly correct, the work of past generations' historians. This work—carried out by a range of social scientists, ecologists, archaeologists, and anthropologists—is carefully coordinated with the research programs of the native American peoples themselves, often under the aegis of a nearby university. Perhaps the best example of this is the program led by Dr. Kevin McBride, Assistant Professor of Anthropology at the University of Connecticut, to discover the true heritage of the Pequots (whose tragic but unended story prefigured the subsequent experiences of other native American peoples in New England). For that program he receives effective support from the Mashantucket Pequot Tribe of Ledyard, Connecticut. Dr. McBride is but one of the many professionals who gave generously of their time and freely of their knowledge to the construction of this book.

Throughout New England there were also many small, seemingly less distinguished historical societies and centers whose unfailingly cooperative personnel provided the author with significant clues to the communities and regions. Typical of these imaginative and deeply probing facilitators was Moira Taylor, research librarian of the Town Library in Lancaster, Massachusetts, who helped guide the author to a totally revised comprehension of the relations between natives and white settlers in that town, scene of one of the most famous episodes in King Philip's War. A battle and a seizure, yes . . . but with what special, local motives of intercultural pay-back?

Yet the author must admit that, on some occasions, visits to libraries and historical societies across New England were managed on his part with more enthusiasm than thoroughness. If, therefore, the names of any assisting individuals or institutions have been omitted from the list that follows, pardon is requested.

To the staffs of the Oliver Wolcott Library in Litchfield, Connecticut, and of the Witherle Library in Castine, Maine, as well as to that of the Maine Maritime Academy Library in Castine, the author would like to express particular appreciation, for it was in these facilities that most of the background research was carried out. No request was regarded by these men and women as of anything less than terrific importance; no work, however drudging, was treated with anything less than fresh enthusiasm. It was a privilege to work in the company of such committed professionals. A privilege it was as well to work in the company of Miriam Anne Bourne who, while contributing vast amounts of solid research, editorial advice, and professional and personal assistance, should be held in no ways accountable for the results.

In the collection of maps and illustrations for this book the author also incurred considerable indebtedness to the staffs of museums and libraries in the respective regions. Although recognition of the granting institutions is given in the list of illustrations, special mention must be made of certain individuals who were of extraordinary help in hunting down requested documents, namely, James P. Thurber, Jr., of the U.S. Embassy in Ottawa, Canada; Henry Adams of the Thomas Hart Benton Collection at the Nelson Atkins Museum in Kansas City, Missouri; and the staffs of the National Museum of American Art and the Catalog of American Portraits at the Smithsonian Institution in Washington.

Throughout the research and writing stages described above, friendly support, literary wisdom, and practical guidance were supplied by the editors at Atheneum, particularly Thomas Stewart and Susan Leon. What follows is an attempt to highlight the specific organizations, individuals, and other-than-bibliographical sources that yielded pertinent information to respective chapters.

Chapter One

Primary thanks for assistance in researching the red and white societies of southeastern Massachusetts are owed to the archival and educational facilities at Plimouth Plantation, and particularly to Nanepashemet, curator of the Wampanoag Indian Program at Plimouth.

Initial introduction to a number of the historians and scientists who are now working to restore a balance to the portrayals of English settlers and native Americans in New England was made at the Mashantucket Pequot Historical Conference at Ledyard, Connecticut, in October 1987. To the organizers of and participants in that conference the author wishes to express his gratitude. In addition to the institutions and individuals named above in the opening of the Acknowledgments, the author would like to express personal thanks to certain counselors who encouraged him as he began to identify pertinent research sources in southern New England; these mentors include Alvin Josephy, Russell Handsman, and Karen Coody Cooper.

Chapter Two

As well as thanking once again Dr. Kevin McBride and the Mashantucket Pequot tribe for their generous assistance, the author would like to express his appreciation to others who have labored to bring forth the history of the Pequots and Mohegans of Connecticut. These include Gladys Tantaquidgeon of the Tantaquidgeon Indian Museum;

Richard Hayward, Tribal Chairman of the Mashantucket Pequots; Courtland Fowler, Tribal Chairman of the Mohegan Council; the research staff of the Pequot Library, Southport, Connecticut; and Carol Kimball of the Indian Research Center, Mystic, Connecticut.

Chapter Three

To scholars and lay visitors alike, the Haffenreffer Museum of Anthropology in Bristol, Rhode Island, has long offered an opportunity to get to know the land, the character, and the artifacts of those Algonquians (the Pokanokets) whose early reaction to cultural and economic changes of their region gave the name "King Philip's War" to the disturbances of this era. Highlighted is the man Metacom, or Philip, himself whose alleged "throne" is on the museum's grounds. Haffenreffer programs in archaeology and anthropology are opening up fresh interpretations of the daily life and cultural values of the Pokanokets and other native Americans. The author extends thanks to the many museum and library staffers at Bristol who assisted him in his researches.

And to local historical societies in towns immediately affected by the outbreak of the Pokanokets' rebellion (namely, Warren and Barrington, Rhode Island, and Swansea and Rehoboth, Massachusetts), the author would also like to express his thanks for their courteous assistance. In the area of Dartmouth, Massachusetts, he is particularly indebted to the staff of the Old Dartmouth Historical Society of New Bedford, to the Southworth Library of South Dartmouth, and to Dr. Frederick V. Gifun of Southeastern Massachusetts University (whose "Land Use in Dartmouth" stands as a model of integrating historical research with present-day community planning).

Chapter Four

Epitomizing the spirited cooperation of local historical resources, the staff of the Henry N. Flynt Library at Historic Deerfield, Massachusetts, devoted much creative thought to the challenge of how to bring forth from the collections of the Pocumtuck Valley Memorial Association the best possible presentation of Connecticut River Valley culture and economy in the seventeenth century. The author wishes to give special thanks to librarian Charlene Proudy for her cordial assistance.

Into the land of the Narragansetts, the author's way was illuminated by the scholarship and the kind generosity of Dr. Paul Robinson of the Rhode Island Preservation Commission. The pertinent research that he brought to the author's attention plus the recollection of conversations with native American sources were invaluable to the author's understanding of how this three-centuries-old business between white and red societies is both long-buried and much alive.

Chapter Five

As previously mentioned, the Town Library of Lancaster, Massachusetts, was of tremendous assistance to the author in researching the bilateral story of north-central Massachusetts as a climactic meeting place of English and native societies. The town's Historical Society is also to be congratulated for bringing forth a guide to the remembered spots around Lancaster that make the drama of the encounters of 1675 and 1676 come so vividly to life. On a personal note, the author would like to honor the memory of the late Frederick L. Weis, longtime pastor of the Unitarian Church on the Green, for introducing him many years ago to the resonant saga of Mary Rowlandson.

Because Benjamin Church remains everyone's best guide to this period of southern New England history, the author must express special thanks to the Historical Society of Little Compton, Rhode Island, which keeps actively in view not only those sites relevant to Colonel Church but also those sites important to his cross-cultural friend Awashonks and her related peoples. In the words of that society's editors Alan and Mary Simpson: "We [in our editing of Church's diary of King Philip's War] were also under the spell of the long-gone race that had left stone bridges across our brooks, arrowheads in our soil, graves beneath our pavements, and names on our streets."

Chapter Six

The regional history of northern New England is divided into even more segments than Maine State weather maps. The author is grateful to kind advisers in many of those sectors. Three typically diverse sources stand out as deserving special mention: Harald E. L. Prins of Bowdoin College's Department of Sociology and Anthropology; Debra Allen Cunningham of the Old York Historical Society's library; Elizabeth Maule of the Maine Historical Society at Portland.

Dr. Prins (who has assisted Maine's Micmac group of Abnakis in establishing their historic identity and their present-day case for survival) demonstrated to the author that the formerly accepted, static manner of looking at the territories of all Algonquians—and particularly the Abnakis—was so erroneous that it warped the judgment of many historians of New England in the period of King Philip's War. Mrs. Cunningham was tireless in her efforts to locate nineteenth-century histories of the Maine towns in which the Abnakis and the English settlers came most interestingly together. Ms. Maule located original documents that were helpful for understanding not only the settler-native tensions in Maine but also the tugs-of-war between the Down East colonists and their governing authorities in Boston and London. To these individuals, their institutions, and to many other wise counselors encountered on the coast of Maine the author is profoundly thankful.

\

Bibliography

To facilitate the reader's search for references within certain subject areas, the Bibliography has been broken down into four parts, as follows: King Philip's War, Native Americans and Indian History, American History, and Regional History.

I. King Philip's War

Abbot, John S. *The History of King Philip*. New York: Harper & Bros., 1857.

Axtel, James. *The Invasion Within: The Contest of Cultures in Colonial North America*. New York: Oxford University Press, 1985.

Bodge, George M. *Soldiers in King Philip's War*. Boston: 1906.

Bonfanti, Leo. *Biographies and Legends of the New England Indians*. Wakefield, MA: Pride Publications, 1971–1976.

Broadstreet, Howard. *The Story of the War with the Pequots, Re-told*. New Haven: Tercentenary Commission of the State of Connecticut, 1933.

Church, Colonel Benjamin. *Diary of King Philip's War, 1675–1676*. Alan and Mary Simpson (eds.). Tiverton, RI: Lockwood Publications, 1975.

Ellis, George W., and Morris, John E. *King Philip's War*. Grafton: 1906.

Fiske, John R. *The Beginnings of New England, or The Puritan Theoc-*

racy in Its Relation to Civil and Religious Liberty. Boston: Houghton Mifflin, 1900.

Horowitz, David. The First Frontier: The Indian Wars and America's Origins. New York: Simon & Schuster, 1978.

Hosmer, James Kendall (ed.). Winthrop's Journal, "History of New England, 1630–1649. New York: Barnes & Noble, 1908.

Hubbard, William. The History of the Indian Wars in New England from the First Settlement to the Termination of the War with King Philip. Samuel G. Drake (ed.). New York: Lenox Hill, 1971 (reprint).

Jennings, Francis. The Invasion of America: Indians, Colonialism, and the Cant of Conquest. Chapel Hill: University of North Carolina Press, 1975.

Leach, Douglas Edward. Flintlocks and Tomahawks: New England in King Philip's War. New York: Norton, 1953.

Leach, Douglas Edward (ed.). A Rhode Islander Reports on King Philip's War. Providence: Rhode Island Historical Society, 1963.

Lincoln, Charles A. (ed.). Narratives of the Indian Wars, 1675–1699. New York: Scribners, 1913.

Mather, Increase. A Brief History of the War with the Indians in New England. Boston: 1682.

Raulet, Philip. "Another Look at the Causes of King Philip's War." New England Quarterly, March 1988.

Rodman, Thomas R. "King Philip's War in Dartmouth." Old Dartmouth Historical Sketches, 1903.

Sears, Clara Endicott. The Great Powwow: The Story of the Nashaway Valley in King Philip's War. Boston: Houghton Mifflin, 1934.

Segal, Charles M., and Stineback, David C. Puritans, Indians, and Manifest Destiny. New York: Putnam's, 1977.

Stock, Daniel, Jr. Pictorial History of King Philip's War. Boston: Houghton Mifflin, 1851.

Vaughn, Alden T. New England Frontier: Puritans and Indians, 1620–1675. Boston: Little, Brown, 1965.

Webb, Steven Saunders. 1675: The Death of American Independence. New York: Knopf, 1987.

II. Native Americans and Indian History

Barrat, Joseph. The Indians of New England and the Northeastern Provinces. Middletown, Connecticut: 1851.

Brodeur, Paul. "The Mashpees." *The New Yorker*, November 6, 1978.

Cronon, William. *Changes in the Land: Indians, Colonists, and the Ecology of New England.* New York: Hill and Wang, 1983.

DeForest, John W. *Indians of Connecticut.* Hamden, CT: Shoe String Press (reprint).

Drake, Samuel G. *The Old Indian Chronicle, or Chronicles of the Indians from the Discovery of America to the Present Time.* Boston: 1836.

Gibson, Susan G. *Burr's Hill: A Seventeenth Century Wampanoag Burial Ground in Warren, Rhode Island.* Bristol, Rhode Island: Haffenreffer Museum of Anthropology, 1980.

Josephy, Alvin M. J. *Now That the Buffalo's Gone.* New York: Knopf, 1982.

———. *The Patriot Chiefs.* New York: Viking, 1961.

Kupperman, Karen Ordahl. *Settling with the Indians: The Meeting of English and Indian Cultures in America, 1580–1640.* Totowa, NJ: Rowman and Littlefield, 1980.

Miller, W. J. *Notes Concerning the Wampanoag Tribe of Indians.* Providence: 1880.

Morrison, Kenneth M. *The Embattled Northeast: The Elusive Ideal of Alliance in Abenaki-European Relations.* Berkeley: University of California Press, 1984.

Penhallow, Samuel. *History of the Indian Wars.* Williamstown, MA: Lerner House, 1963 (reprint).

Russell, Howard S. *Indian New England Before the Mayflower.* Hanover, NH: University Press of New England, 1980.

Salisbury, Neal. *Manitow and Providence: Indians, Europeans, and the Making of New England, 1500–1643.* New York: Oxford University Press, 1982.

Simmons, William S. *Cantantowwit's House: An Indian Burial Ground on the Island of Conanicut in Narragansett Bay.* Providence: Rhode Island University Press, 1970.

———. *Spirit of the New England Tribes: Indian History and Folklore, 1620–1984.* Hanover, NH: University Press of New England, 1986.

Washburn, Wilcomb E. *The American in America.* New York: Harper & Row, 1975.

Whipple, Chandler. *First Encounter: The Indian and the White Man in New England.* Stockbridge, MA: Berkshire Traveler Press, 1972.

Williams, Roger. *What Cheer, Netop! Selections from "A Key into the Language of North America."* Hadassah Davis (ed.). Bristol, RI: Haffenreffer Museum of Anthropology, 1986.

III. American History

Bancroft, George. *History of the United States: from the Discovery of the American Continent* (2 vols.). Boston: Little, Brown, 1837.

Boston Museum of Fine Arts. *New England Begins* (3 vols.). Boston: Museum of Fine Arts, 1982.

Bradford, William. *History of Plymouth Plantation.* Boston: 1879.

Carol, Peter N. *Puritanism and the Wilderness: The Intellectual Significance of the New England Frontier, 1629–1700.* New York: Columbia University Press, 1969.

Champlain, Samuel de. *Voyages of Samuel de Champlain, 1604–1618.* New York: 1907.

Covey, Cyclone. *The Gentle Radical: A Biography of Roger Williams.* New York: Macmillan, 1966.

Craven, Wesley F. *The Colonies in Transition, 1660–1713.* New York: Harper, 1968.

Fitzhugh, William W. *Cultures in Contact: The Impact of European Contacts on Native American Cultures, AD 1000–1800.* Washington, D.C.: Smithsonian Institution Press, 1985.

Gura, Philip F. *A Glimpse of Zion's Glory: Puritan Radicalism in New England, 1620–1660.* Middletown, Connecticut: Wesleyan University Press, 1984.

Leach, Douglas Edward. *The Northern Colonial Frontier, 1607–1763.* New York: Holt, 1966.

Morgan, Edmund S. *Roger Williams: The Church and State.* New York: Harcourt, Brace & World, 1967.

Morison, Samuel Eliot. *Builders of the Bay Colony.* Boston: Houghton Mifflin, 1962.

———. *The Oxford History of the American People.* New York: Oxford University Press, 1965.

Orr, Charles (ed.). *History of the Pequot War: The Contemporary Accounts of Mason, Underhill, Vincent, and Gardiner.* Cleveland: Helman-Taylor, 1897.

Slotkin, Richard. *Regeneration Through Violence: The Mythology of the American Frontier, 1600–1860.* Middletown, Connecticut: Wesleyan University Press, 1973.

Stilgoe, John E. *Common Landscape of America, 1580–1845.* New Haven, Connecticut: Yale University Press, 1985.

Van Dusen, Albert E. *Puritans Against the Wilderness.* Chester, Connecticut: Pequot Press, 1975.

Wertenbaker, Thomas Jefferson. *The Puritan Oligarchy.* New York: Scribners, 1947.

Williams, Selma R. *Kings, Commoners, and Colonists: Puritan Politics in Old New England, 1603–1660.* New York: Atheneum, 1974.

Willison, George F. *Saints and Strangers.* New York: Reynal & Hitchcock, 1945.

Woloch, Nancy. *Women and the American Experience.* New York: Knopf, 1984.

Ziner, Feenie. *The Pilgrims and Plymouth Colony,* New York: American Heritage, 1961.

IV. Regional History

Allen, Zacharia. "Defense of Rhode Island's Treatment of the Indians." *Bicentenary of the Burning of Providence.* Providence: Rhode Island Historical Society, 1876.

Baker, William Avery. *A Maritime History of Bath, Maine, and the Kennebec River Region.* Bath, Maine: 1873.

Banks, Charles Edward. *History of York, Maine.* (2 vols.). Baltimore: Regional Publishing Company, 1896.

Bicknell, Thomas W. *Sowams.* New Haven, Connecticut: 1908.

Bourne, Edward E. *The History of Wells and Kennebunk.* Portland, Maine: 1875.

Clark, Charles E. *Maine: A Bicentennial History.* New York: Knopf, 1970.

Delany, Edmund. *The Connecticut River, New England's Historic Waterway.* Chester, Connecticut: Globe Pequot, 1983.

Ellis, Leonard B. *History of New Bedford and Vicinity.* Syracuse, New York: 1892.

Everts, Louis H. *History of the Connecticut Valley in Massachusetts* (2 vols.). Philadelphia: Lippincott & Co., 1879.

Faulkner, Alaric, and Faulkner, Gretchen F. *The French at Pentagoët: An Archaeological Portrait of the Acadian Frontier.* Augusta: Maine Historic Preservation Commission, 1987.

Folsom, George. *A History of Saco and Biddeford.* Saco, Maine: Putnam, 1830.

Hatch, Louis C. *Maine, A History.* Somersworth: New Hampshire Publishing Company, 1974.

Judd, Sylvester. *The History of Hadley.* Somersworth, New Hampshire: 1863.

Kimball, Gertrude Selwyn. *Providence in Colonial Times.* Boston: Houghton Mifflin, 1912.

La Fantasie, Glenn W. "A Day in the Life of Roger Williams." *Rhode Island Historical Society Journal,* 1986.

MacLeod, Maryanne. "The Great Sachem of the Nashaways." Unpublished manuscript from the Lancaster Collection of the Lancaster, Massachusetts, Public Library.

Marvin, Abijah Perkins. *History of the Town of Lancaster.* Lancaster, Massachusetts: 1879.

McBride, Kevin A. *History of the Pequot War.* Storrs: University of Connecticut, 1988.

McCrillis, Herbert O. "Pemaquid: The Jamestown of the North." *Pinetree,* 1907.

Morgan, Forrest. *Connecticut as a Colony and as a State.* Hartford: Publishing Society of Connecticut, 1904.

Ricketson, Daniel. *The History of New Bedford.* New Bedford: Massachusetts, 1858.

Roberts, Kenneth. *Trending into Maine.* Boston: Little, Brown, 1858.

Sheldon, George A. *History of Deerfield* (2 vols.). Deerfield, Massachusetts: 1895.

Smith, Marion J. *A History of Maine from Wilderness to Statehood.* Portland, Maine: Falmouth, 1949.

Taylor, Robert J. *Colonial Connecticut: A History.* Milwood, New Jersey: KTO Press, 1979.

Van Dusen, Albert E. *Connecticut.* New York: Random House, 1961.

Wheeler, George A., M.D. *History of Brunswick, Topsham, and Harpswell, Maine.* Boston: 1878.

Williamson, William D. *History of Maine.* Hallowell, Maine: 1832.

Willis, William. *The History of Portland from 1632 to 1864.* Portland, Maine: 1865.

Wing, William A. "John Russell." *Old Dartmouth Historical Sketches,* 1935.

Woodward, Carl R. *Plantation in Yankeeland.* Chester, Connecticut: Pequot Press, 1971.

Worth, Henry. "The First Settlers of Dartmouth and Where They Located." *Old Dartmouth Historical Sketches,* 1897.

Index

261

Russell Bourne, former editor-publisher of American Heritage Books and senior editor of Smithsonian Books, is the recent author of *The View from Front Street: Travels through New England's Historic Fishing Communities.* Having begun his writing/publishing career at *Life* magazine and Time Inc., he specialized in books on American history and technology in various positions at *American Heritage, U.S. News & World Report,* the *National Geographic,* and the *Smithsonian.* A special agent in U.S. counter-intelligence, Berlin, during the Korean War, he now lives in Litchfield, Connecticut, and Castine, Maine.